Annie Armstrong: Dreamer in Action

Annie Armstrong
Dreamer in Action

Bobbie Sorrill

BROADMAN PRESS
Nashville, Tennessee

Library of Congress Cataloging in Publication Data

Sorrill, Bobbie, 1935-
    Annie Armstrong, dreamer in action.

    Bibliography: p.
    Includes index.
    1. Armstrong, Annie.   2. Baptists—United States—Biography.   3. South-
ern Baptist Convention—Biography. I. Title.
    BX6495.A67S67   1984   286'.132'0924 [B]   83-70842
    ISBN 0-8054-6333-X

4263-33

ISBN: 0-8054-6333-X

Dewey Decimal Classification: B

Subject Headings: ARMSTRONG, ANNIE WALKER//WOMAN'S MISSIONARY
                  UNION—HISTORY

Library of Congress Catalog Card Number: 83-70842

Printed in the United States of America

Contents

Prologue

Who was the real Annie Armstrong? As I began the assignment of writing her biography, I often asked myself this question. I knew only two things about Annie Armstrong. (1) She was the first corresponding secretary of Woman's Missionary Union; (2) she had a lot to do with home missions, so much, in fact, that the annual offering for home missions was named in her honor.

As the research unfolded, and this great woman became a real person to me, I determined to do four things through the pages of this biography:

● To show Annie Armstrong not only as a saint but also as a real human being who lived what she believed and taught;

● To reveal her extraordinary gifts as an organizational genius and a stateswoman par excellence who had a vision of the worldwide possibilities for women in missions and organized this dream into action;

● To portray the tremendous legacy Annie Armstrong left Southern Baptists in missions and missions education, for it was she who set in motion many of the wise policies and programs we take for granted today;

● To motivate you, the reader, to find your role in missions and get involved, as Annie Armstrong did, especially as you increase your giving through the Annie Armstrong Easter Offering for the support of home missions.

It was extremely difficult for me to separate the life of Annie Armstrong from the early history of Woman's Missionary Union and the Southern Baptist Convention, for in a very real sense the support of missions work was her life.

As I learned more and more about Annie Armstrong, I had several reactions to her. Most often, I was overwhelmed and amazed at her energy, the unbelievable amount of work she did, the ever-increasing new ideas she carried out, her amazing ability to keep in mind so many different things, and her unswerving loyalty to the Southern Baptist Convention. At other times, I wondered whether I really liked the woman, for I was sure I would not have wanted to be on her staff. But when my research was completed, I not only liked Annie Armstrong but had utmost respect and admiration for this remarkable and gifted woman. I would have followed this missions pioneer anywhere. She was uniquely suited for the role she played in a voluntary, struggling, expanding organization. It took a person of her strength and stability.

For the sake of brevity, I chose to call her "Annie" throughout the biography. However, when I have the opportunity of meeting her in heaven, I am sure I will call her "Miss Annie" or "Miss Armstrong" out of respect. I hope, too, with all my heart, that I have done justice to her story and furthered the cause of missions.

When I read the sermon Dr. W. Clyde Atkins, Annie's pastor, preached at her memorial service, I was struck by the way he captured the essence of her life in the phrase: "a dreamer in action." I chose to include this phrase in the title. It epitomized for me the real Annie Armstrong. She had dreams beyond belief and the practical ability to carry them out.

BOBBIE SORRILL

Key Persons
in the Biography

Family in Baltimore
Annie W. Armstrong
Alice Armstrong—Annie's sister
James J. Armstrong—Annie's brother
James Dunn Armstrong—Annie's father
Mary Elizabeth Walker Armstrong—Annie's mother
William D. Armstrong—Annie's brother
Ann Sater Levering—Annie's aunt
Eugene Levering, Jr.—Annie's brother-in-law (and cousin)
Eugene Levering, Sr.—Annie's uncle
Harriett Ellis Levering—Eugene Levering's second wife
Joshua Levering—Annie's cousin
Mamie Armstrong Levering—Annie's sister

Pastors and Woman's Missionary Union Leaders in Baltimore
W. Clyde Atkins—Annie's assistant pastor and pastor, Eutaw
  Place Baptist Church, 1930-38
Mrs. John Eager—WMU executive committee member
  (Maryland vice-president)
F. M. Ellis—Annie's pastor, Eutaw Place Baptist Church,
  1884-94
Richard Fuller—Annie's pastor, Seventh and Eutaw Place
  Baptist Churches, 1850-76
O. F. Gregory—pastor, Fourth Baptist Church and secretary,
  Maryland Baptist Union Association (convention), 1888-
  1902

Elridge B. Hatcher—secretary, Maryland Baptist Union Association (convention), 1903-14

J. W. Millard—Annie's pastor, Eutaw Place Baptist Church, 1895-1904

Mrs. James Pollard—WMU executive committee member

H. M. Wharton—publisher of *The Baltimore Baptist* and pastor, Brantly Baptist Church

Dr. and Mrs. J. W. M. Williams—First Baptist Church pastor and wife

Woman's Missionary Union, Southern Baptist Convention, Leaders

Mrs. John A. Barker—WMU president, 1903-06

Mrs. W. J. Cox—WMU president, 1925-33

Edith Campbell Crane—WMU corresponding secretary, 1907-12

Mrs. Abby Manly Gwathmey—WMU president, 1894-95

Fannie E. S. Heck—WMU president, 1892-94, 1895-99, 1906-15

Mrs. W. C. James—WMU president, 1916-25

Kathleen Mallory—WMU corresponding secretary, 1912-48

Juliette Mather—Young People's secretary, 1927-48

Martha E. McIntosh (later Mrs. T. P. Bell)—WMU president, 1888-92

Mrs. Charles A. Stakely—WMU president, 1899-1903

Southern Baptist Convention Leaders and Missionaries

Anne Luther and William Buck Bagby—missionaries to Brazil

A. J. Barton—assistant corresponding secretary, Foreign Mission Board; field secretary of work with blacks, Home Mission Board

T. P. Bell—assistant corresponding secretary, Foreign Mission Board, 1886-93; corresponding secretary, Sunday School Board, 1893-96; editor, *The Christian Index*, 1896-1915

E. E. Bomar—assistant corresponding secretary, Foreign Mission Board

Samuel Boykin—editor, *Kind Words*

Albert E. Brown—superintendent, Mountain Mission Department, Home Mission Board

Marie Buhlmaier—home missionary, Baltimore

Lansing Burrows—recording secretary, Southern Baptist Convention

Dr. and Mrs. Philip S. Evans—missionaries to China

James M. Frost—corresponding secretary, Sunday School Board, 1891-93, 1896-1916

Dr. and Mrs. R. H. Graves—missionaries to China

B. D. Gray—corresponding secretary, Home Mission Board, 1903-28

Jonathan Haralson, president, Southern Baptist Convention, 1889-98

Dr. and Mrs. J. B. Hartwell—missionaries to China

F. H. Kerfoot—Annie's pastor, Eutaw Place Baptist Church, 1877-82; corresponding secretary, Home Mission Board, 1899-1901

F. C. McConnell—corresponding secretary, Home Mission Board, 1901-03

Lottie Moon—missionary to China

E. Y. Mullins—assistant corresponding secretary, Foreign Mission Board; president, The Southern Baptist Theological Seminary, 1899-1928

W. J. Northen—chairman, SBC Committee on Training School, 1903-04

E. Z. Simmons—missionary to China

Lura Stump—home missionary in Indian Territory

I. T. Tichenor—corresponding secretary, Home Mission Board, 1882-1899

H. A. Tupper—corresponding secretary, Foreign Mission Board, 1872-93

I. J. Van Ness—editorial secretary, Sunday School Board, 1900-17

R. J. Willingham—corresponding secretary, Foreign Mission Board, 1893-1914

State Baptist and Woman's Missionary Union Leaders
Eliza Broadus—Kentucky WMU leader
Mrs. J. L. Burnham—Missouri WMU leader
Mrs. W. D. Chipley—Florida WMU leader
A. E. Dickinson—editor, *The Religious Herald*
Mrs. J. D. Easterlin—Georgia WMU leader
T. T. Eaton—editor, *Western Recorder*
Jennie L. Spaulding—Florida WMU leader
Mrs. Stainback Wilson—Georgia WMU leader
Mary Emily Wright—Georgia WMU leader

Other Significant Persons
R. H. Boyd—National Baptist Convention home missions leader
Mary G. Burdette—corresponding secretary, Northern Baptist Woman's Home Mission Society
Nannie Helen Burroughs—corresponding secretary, Woman's Convention, National Baptist Convention
L. G. Jordan—National Baptist Convention foreign missions leader
Mrs. Shirley Layten—president, Woman's Convention, National Baptist Convention
A. J. Rowland—American Baptist Publication Society leader
Anna Schimp—Baltimore woman, Annie's traveling companion

Annie's Key Southern Baptist Convention Relationships

Period	WMU President	Foreign Mission Board	Home Mission Board	Sunday School Board	The Southern Baptist Theological Seminary
1888-92	Martha E. McIntosh	H. A. Tupper (1872-93)	I. T. Tichenor (1882-99)	J. M. Frost (1891-93)	
1892-95	Fannie E.S. Heck (1892-94) Abby M. Gwathmey (1894-95)	R . J. Willingham (1893-1914)		T. P. Bell (1893-96)	
1895-99	Fannie E.S. Heck			J. M. Frost (1896-1916)	W. H. Whitsitt (1895-99)
1899-1903	Mrs. Charles A. Stakely		F. H. Kerfoot (1899-1901) F. C. McConnell (1901-03)		E. Y. Mullins (1899-1928)
1903-06	Mrs. John A. Barker		B. D. Gray (1903-28)		

KEY TO ILLUSTRATIONS

Annie Armstrong

Family of Annie Armstrong

Friends and Colleagues of Annie Armstrong

Places in Annie Armstrong's Life

Map

Other

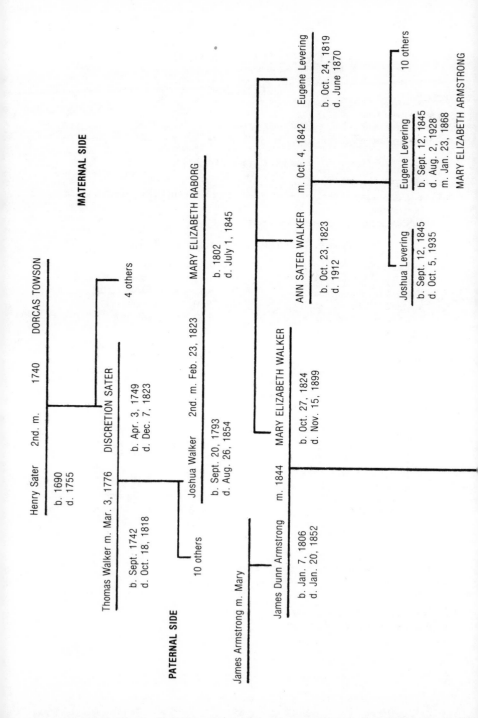

MATERNAL SIDE

Henry Sater   2nd. m.   1740   DORCAS TOWSON
b. 1690
d. 1755

DISCRETION SATER
b. Apr. 3, 1749
d. Dec. 7, 1823

4 others

Thomas Walker m. Mar. 3, 1776

b. Sept. 1742
d. Oct. 18, 1818

MARY ELIZABETH RABORG
b. 1802
d. July 1, 1845

Joshua Walker   2nd. m. Feb. 23, 1823
b. Sept. 20, 1793
d. Aug. 26, 1854

10 others

ANN SATER WALKER   m. Oct. 4, 1842   Eugene Levering
b. Oct. 23, 1823   b. Oct. 24, 1819
d. 1912   d. June 1870

Eugene Levering
b. Sept. 12, 1845
d. Aug. 2, 1928
m. Jan. 23, 1868

10 others

Joshua Levering
b. Sept. 12, 1845
d. Oct. 5, 1935

MARY ELIZABETH ARMSTRONG

PATERNAL SIDE

James Armstrong m. Mary

James Dunn Armstrong   m. 1844   MARY ELIZABETH WALKER
b. Jan. 7, 1806   b. Oct. 27, 1824
d. Jan. 20, 1852   d. Nov. 15, 1899

Mary Elizabeth
Armstrong

b. Sept. 4, 1845
d. Dec. 21, 1915
m. Jan. 23, 1868

Alice
Armstrong

b. Nov. 13, 1846
d. Dec. 15, 1928

James John
Armstrong

b. Apr. 10, 1849
d. May 6, 1885

Annie Walker
Armstrong

b. July 11, 1850
d. Dec. 20, 1938

William D.
Armstrong

b. Apr. 2, 1852
d. May 14, 1858

EUGENE LEVERING

CHILDREN

EUGENE
b. July 13, 1869
d. 1924
m. ADELAIDE L. GARY, Nov. 14, 1896

MARY ARMSTRONG
b. Feb. 9, 1875
d. Apr. 26, 1952
m. JOSEPH HASWELL ROBINSON, 1905
CHILDREN: MARIEL L. and FRANCIS W.

ETHEL
b. June 10, 1878
d. May 10, 1966
m. JAMES MARVIN MOTLEY

View of Baltimore Street at Marketplace, 1850s (PEALE MUSEUM, BALTIMORE, MARYLAND)

1
Who Was
Annie Walker Armstrong?

Baltimore, Maryland. The year was 1850. July 11 dawned just about like any other day during the hot summer. But before it ended, according to the *Baltimore Sun*, there was a great happening—a big fire in Philadelphia. Also, the death of President Zachary Taylor had occurred two days earlier. But another great happening which the paper did not take note of was the birth of a baby daughter. The proud parents were James Dunn and Mary Elizabeth Walker Armstrong, and the baby was their third daughter and fourth child. Mr. Armstrong's cigar, tobacco, and snuff store ran a larger than usual advertisement on that day.

The baby was Annie Walker Armstrong, destined to become Southern Baptists' "dreamer in action." Who was Annie Walker Armstrong? Her roots and the era into which she was born shaped her for the role she was later to play. She had a mother who was strong in the Christian faith and involved actively in her church. Annie's Baptist heritage included not only her mother but also a great-great-grandfather who began Baptist work in Maryland. Another pivotal person in her life was a pastor who helped to build Annie's deep convictions and life-style of ministry. The stirrings of missions deep in the lives of Mrs. Armstrong and other women important to Annie created a missions environment in her home and church. This environment ultimately turned Annie toward missions and a life of total commitment to the Lord and his work.

The city in which Annie lived had an excellent harbor and rail system which linked it with a broader world and helped plant the seed for Annie's later concern for all kinds of people and needs. Living in a border state, with both Northern and Southern influences, Annie grew up in an area where a woman could emerge as a leader in Southern Baptist life. By the time of Annie's birth, Baltimore was a large, prosperous, and active port city. Located on the north side of the Patapsco River, which flowed into Chesapeake Bay and on into the Atlantic Ocean, this key Eastern Seaboard city's population was somewhere between one and two hundred thousand. Annie's uncle owned clipper ships which sailed in bringing coffee, sugar, and copper and taking out wheat and flour. The coffee trade gave the Baltimore waterfront the smell of roasting coffee. Textile manufacturing and other steam-powered industries abounded. Little did Annie realize as a child, as more and more railroads such as the Baltimore and Ohio came into being, that she would later spend days on trains as she crossed the South and Midwest on behalf of missions.

Probably early in life Annie developed an interest in immigrants and blacks. She saw them daily as they lived and worked, meeting the increased demand for laborers in Baltimore. By 1860, just ten years after Annie's birth, over 35 percent of the city's population were natives of Germany or Ireland or were Afro-Americans.[1]

The prevailing work ethic—doing and working rather than leisure—had an impact on the later life-style of Annie Armstrong. Current events in the United States also were potential influences on Annie's life. Although by 1850 there were two national political parties dedicated to preserving the Union, the North and the South were pulling apart. The South had adjusted itself to a slave and cotton economy. The North was being transformed by the industrial revolution, inexpensive transportation, and educational and humanitarian movements. These influences particularly touched the border states such as Maryland.[2]

1859 View of Baltimore (MARYLAND HISTORICAL SOCIETY, BALTIMORE)

Annie Armstrong's parents, James Dunn and Mary Elizabeth Walker Armstrong

The Southern Baptist Convention—Annie's denomination—was still in its infancy. In 1845 Southern Baptists had separated from their Northern counterparts and formed a strong, centralized denominational body to oversee multiple benevolences. With the purpose of "eliciting, combining and directing the energies of the whole denomination in one sacred effort for the propagation of the gospel," Southern Baptists immediately set up a Foreign Mission Board and a Board of Domestic Missions (later Home Mission Board).[3] By 1860 there were more than 645,000 Southern Baptists (4,143 in Maryland) and 7,760 churches.[4] The fledgling denomination was beginning to make progress in difficult times.

Annie's father was a merchant. The firm of J. D. Armstrong & Thornton dealt in wholesale tobacco and ran a cigar and tobacco store. Located in Baltimore's business district, the firm offered for sale seventeen-pound boxes of tobacco, smoking pipes, Garrett's snuff, fifty different brands of imported cigars, and 1,500,000 other good, medium, and low-priced cigars. J. D. Armstrong & Thornton also had a warehouse located on Cheapside Street.[5]

From all indications James Dunn Armstrong was a wealthy man. The 1850 census noted for him a real estate value of $37,000, equal to or higher than many other business and professional people in his area.[6]

Annie's father was possibly of Scotch-Irish descent and was born in Maryland on January 7, 1806, to James and Mary Armstrong. James Dunn Armstrong and Mary Elizabeth Walker, who was eighteen years younger than he, were married in 1844. They lived at 41 North Calvert Street, not far from the port or business district. The Joshua Walkers, Mrs. Armstrong's parents, owned several pieces of property on Calvert Street.

The Armstrongs had three daughters: Mary Elizabeth (called Mamie), born September 4, 1845; Alice, born November 13, 1846; and Annie, born July 11, 1850. Their two sons were James John, born April 10, 1849, and William D., born April 2, 1852.[7]

Shortly after Annie's birth, Armstrong suffered severe financial reverses. After a brief illness, he died at the age of forty-eight on January 20, 1852, three months before his youngest son was born. At the time of his death, Armstrong held one-fourth interest in a First Presbyterian Church pew, so he is presumed to have been a Presbyterian.[8]

The causes of Armstrong's financial losses are unknown. However, the 1850 Maryland tobacco crop was not a good one. Increasingly, new tobacco stores were opening up in Baltimore in the area near Armstrong's firm. Perhaps competition was keen or the tobacco trade glutted. In 1851 a number of fires occurred in Baltimore, destroying many businesses.[9] These or other factors could have caused Armstrong's financial downfall.

Armstrong left no will, but there are indications that his widow received some property. When he died his estate was only a little over $10,000, well below the valuation in the 1850 census. He had a number of debts, and a large amount of money had to be paid out of the estate.[10]

Although Annie's father died when she was a toddler, Annie's mother, Mary Elizabeth Walker Armstrong, was to live with and influence her for forty-nine years. Annie's Baptist roots came through the Walkers, whose lineage went back to Henry Sater, the founder of the first Baptist church in Maryland.

Born in 1690, Sater, Annie's great-great-grandfather, came to Maryland from England in 1709 and settled in Chestnut Ridge, a few miles north of Baltimore. Sater became a wealthy planter, raising tobacco and acquiring much land and many slaves.

Sater was an active and zealous Baptist. There were no Baptist churches in Maryland, but Baptist ministers traveled and preached wherever they were invited. Often Sater would invite them to preach in his home. Encouraged by the number of persons who attended these services, Sater, at his own expense, erected a meetinghouse on his land. In 1742 he and his wife gave to the General Baptist congregation the lot on which the building stood. Persons of all denominations were invited to worship there. And so the Chestnut Ridge (now called Sater's) Baptist Church became the first Baptist congregation in Maryland.[11]

When he was a childless widower of fifty, Sater married Dorcas Towson. Their fourth child, a daughter named Discretion, born in 1749, was Annie Armstrong's great-grandmother. Supposedly, Discretion eloped and married Thomas Walker of Baltimore. Walker was a captain in the Maryland Navy, which existed before there was a U.S. Navy. Shortly after their marriage Walker became a farmer, and the Walkers moved to a farm south of Westminster in Carroll County. In 1796, they moved to Baltimore, where he acquired a great deal of property.[12]

Joshua, the youngest son of the Walkers, was Annie's grandfather. Born in 1793, Joshua Walker became a prominent merchant in Baltimore and owned much property in Maryland and New York. At one time he owned not only the Carleton House in New York City but also a large plantation on the James River near Richmond, Virginia. Joshua Walker married Mary Elizabeth Raborg in 1823, and they had eight sons and nine daughters.

Two of these daughters played prominent roles in Annie Armstrong's life. The oldest daughter, Ann Sater, was born in 1823 and married Eugene Levering of Baltimore in 1842. Supposedly Annie was named for Ann Sater Levering. The second daughter, Mary Elizabeth, born in 1824, was Annie's mother. Mary Elizabeth Walker married James Dunn Armstrong in 1844. Annie's maternal grandmother, Mary Walker, died in 1845, before Annie was born. Joshua Walker, her grandfather, died in 1854, when she was four years old. Walker may have left a sizable inheritance to his children.[13]

One can only raise questions and make suppositions about Annie Armstrong's childhood. Little is known about that period of her life. How did the family live after James Dunn Armstrong's

death? Mrs. Armstrong, left with five small children, never was
employed. Perhaps there was inherited wealth from the Walker
side of the family. Or Mrs. Armstrong might have had financial
advice or assistance from her wealthy brother-in-law, Eugene
Levering. Apparently the family had adequate means, for the
1860 census indicated Mary Elizabeth Armstrong's real estate
value as five thousand dollars and personal estate as four
thousand dollars. Also, two female servants lived with the family,
and the Armstrong children went to private schools.[14]

When Annie was six years old, the Armstrongs moved to 53
McCulloh Street. They might have moved because the downtown section was becoming an undesirable area in which to live.
Industry was bringing pollution, and the downtown slums were
growing. McCulloh Street, running northwest of the center of
town, had block after block of brick row houses typical of
Baltimore. The Armstrongs' new neighborhood was cultured and
made up primarily of Presbyterian and Baptist families.[15]

About the same time a tragedy occurred in the family. An
older playmate pushed Annie's youngest brother, William, while
playing, resulting in fatal injuries. Mrs. Armstrong called the
children around her and charged them never to mention who
was responsible for the accident. She never again mentioned it.
William was buried in Westminster Burial Grounds next to his
father's grave.[16]

One wonders whether Annie ever thought about her father.
She had been too young at the time of his death to remember
him, and in later letters she did not refer to him at all. However,
there were reminders in the home. Annie could look at a beautiful oil portrait of her father and a photograph (daguerreotype)
of her parents, showing the clean-shaven, tall-looking man. Mrs.
Armstrong displayed the certificates of life membership in
charitable organizations to which he subscribed for her and their
two older daughters, Mamie and Alice. Perhaps Mrs. Armstrong reminded Annie and the other children that their Presbyterian father had been a principal donor to the building fund of
Seventh Baptist Church.[17]

Druid Hill Park entrance placed in 1871—the famous place for family outings and rides in Annie Armstrong's day

Sundial in Druid Hill Park where time anywhere in the world can be determined

Park house and lake in background—Druid Hill Park

As a child, Annie found much that captured her attention. Baltimore had a number of famous squares surrounded by brick block houses. On summer evenings families would bring out flat straw mats and sit on the front marble steps. The children played on the streets and in the squares. Perhaps Annie and her family went to the new Druid Hill Park which opened in 1860. Druid Hill had numerous attractions—beautiful views, wooded pathways, formal promenades, lakes for swans and boats, and an elegant and formal entrance.

Ships in the harbor and horsedrawn trolleys were possibilities for a child's vivid imagination. Baltimore was noted for education, culture, and entertainment. These opportunities and books were readily available to Annie. She probably developed a love of music as a child, for she later liked to memorize hymns and often led the singing. By going to the market with her mother or watching Mrs. Armstrong handle business matters in their home,[18] Annie may have developed her interest in business.

Another question relates to where Annie received her education. There was no question that she went to school, for the 1860 census showed the ten-year-old Annie as having attended school during the year, as did Mamie, Alice, and James. Later in life, in a letter to Robert Josiah Willingham, corresponding secretary of the Foreign Mission Board, Annie referred to receiving a five-dollar gold piece for the Christmas Offering from "an old lady of nearly 90 years, to whom, when a little tot, I went to school."[19]

Mamie and Alice attended the Southern Home School at 233 North Eutaw Street, the fashionable day school for young ladies run by Virginians Mr. and Mrs. Wilson M. Cary. The two Cary daughters were notable and notorious during the Civil War for their ardor for the South. In direct disobedience to a Federal order forbidding the display of the secession colors, red and white, the Cary daughters and other Monument Street girls delighted in annoying the Federal authorities by wearing rosettes of red and white in their hair and white aprons trimmed in red.[20] No doubt Annie attended another private school in

1423 McCulloh Street, Baltimore, where the Armstrong family lived for many years

Baltimore. Her later literary, speech, and business skills testify that she was well educated.

When Annie was thirteen, the family moved again. This time they moved further north, into a row house at 1423 McCulloh Street. This big, three-story brick house was to be Annie Armstrong's home over the next sixty years.

Typical of many Baltimore homes, the house adjoined another row house on either side and was only about fifteen feet wide. Its front steps were right at the sidewalk, with no yard. Upon entering the front door, one immediately stepped into a hall with a long, winding stairway going upstairs. The first floor contained a formal parlor behind the stairway, a formal dining room on the front of the house, and a huge kitchen. Used only on special occasions, the parlor was kept closed. A big front room with a high ceiling, the center of most family activities, and bedrooms were on the second floor. There were also bedrooms on the third floor. Food could be transported from the kitchen to the second floor via the long, winding stairway or a dumb waiter. In the back was a small yard with outside steps to the basement. Used for storage, the basement also served as a summer kitchen.[21]

The new McCulloh Street house was only a few blocks from Eutaw Place, where the Leverings lived. Perhaps Mrs. Armstrong was interested in getting closer to her sister and her family. In 1868 Mamie Armstrong, Annie's oldest sister, married Eugene Levering, Jr., her first cousin. They, too, lived nearby. At some point during these years brother James ran away to sea.[22] Only Annie and Alice now remained at home with their mother.

Annie's family and the Leverings were close. Mrs. Armstrong's older sister, Ann Sater, had married Eugene Levering, Sr. Levering, first in the grocery business, then a wealthy coffee merchant, was active in First Baptist Church and later in Seventh Baptist Church. The twelve Levering children must have created a lively household and many playmates for the Armstrong brood. Annie was especially close to the twins,

Eugene and Joshua, only five years older than she. Perhaps she was envious when the twins were taken into their father's business, for she had a keen interest in business.[23]

Although it is not known whether the Walkers continued the Baptist tradition established by Henry Sater, Mrs. Armstrong and her children attended Seventh Baptist Church. Mrs. Armstrong's sister, Ann Levering, and her family attended Seventh Baptist, too. In 1846 the church had been organized from the First Baptist Church with ninety-two members and located in the northwestern suburban area of Baltimore at Paca and Saratoga Streets. The church separated from First Church over church government and such advanced ideas as the right of women members to vote on church business. Seventh Baptist set up a highly-centralized government with authority vested in a small advisory board. Women were excluded from committee membership and from voting, which was common practice for this period except for First Church. At First Church, the membership was almost entirely women.[24] The Armstrongs' move to Seventh Church may have shaped Annie's later views about women's role in the church and denomination.

Tall, Harvard-educated Richard Fuller was pastor of Seventh Baptist Church. Born in South Carolina, Fuller practiced law after graduation from Harvard, married, and allied with the Episcopal Church. After conversion in a revival and ordination to the Baptist ministry, Fuller pastored in his native Beaufort, South Carolina, for thirteen years. He ministered to a small white membership and hundreds of slave members and developed a keen interest in work with blacks. Fuller was an outstanding and skilled preacher, often invited to speak at revivals and conventions. He went to the new and untried Seventh Baptist Church in Baltimore because of the potential for unusual service he saw in the members and to consider the slavery problem in a climate of opinion different from the deep South.[25]

Fuller led Seventh Baptist Church in a spirit of love and harmony through the troubled days of the Civil War. Once a slaveholder, Fuller supported the African Colonization Society and advocated freeing the blacks and colonizing them in Africa. Although he had been on the committee which introduced resolutions of sympathy with the Confederacy to the Southern Baptist Convention in Savannah in 1861, Fuller maintained allegiance to the Union during the war. Suffering losses himself as well as family misfortunes in South Carolina, Fuller disagreed with some Union policies and pleaded for peace. Perhaps young Annie and the Armstrongs attended the daily prayer services Fuller held in Seventh Baptist Church in May, 1861. On the day of fasting and prayer after President Abraham Lincoln's assassination in 1865, Fuller preached a sermon which was said to have helped pull alienated citizens back together, concluding with the words of Ephesians 4:31-32. [26]

The Civil War and Baptist response to it, especially Fuller's attitude, had an impact on Baltimore and no doubt on the Armstrong household. Baltimore was divided in sentiment. The city's heritage included abolitionism and slavery, old Southern families and recent immigrants, industries, and remnants of a landed aristocracy. The culture was predominantly Southern, but Baltimore's business was mainly with the North. One writer compared the city to the narrow neck of an hourglass, with the factories of the North and the plantations of the South funneling into the passage of Baltimore. The city bought cotton, wheat, and tobacco from the South, and sold Northern manufactured goods to the South. Opinion was divided. Some Baltimoreans supported Lincoln, some secession. Some fought for the North, some for the South. [27]

On April 19, 1861, blood was shed in Baltimore as a Massachusetts regiment was transferred between railroad stations. Hostile crowds lined the streets, cheering for the South and denouncing the Yankees. The turmoil flared into a full-scale riot, and the troops were blocked by the angry crowd. When shots were fired,

Seventh Baptist Church, Baltimore, in which Annie Armstrong was baptized

Dr. Richard Fuller, Annie Armstrong's pastor when she became a Christian and was baptized

twelve persons were killed and many injured.[28]

Three days later, the Baltimore Young Men's Christian Association sent a group to President Lincoln. They urged him to allow no more troops to pass through Baltimore. As spokesman for the group, Dr. Richard Fuller, the Armstrongs' pastor, begged the President to prevent war at all costs, even if it meant letting the South leave the Union.[29]

Trouble broke out again in Baltimore, for the city was full of secessionist sympathizers. On his way to Washington after his election, President Lincoln was warned of an assassination plot in Baltimore and had to alter his plans. In 1861, hearing that treason was rife, Union General Benjamin F. Butler seized and fortified Federal Hill overlooking the harbor and business district. Because he had taken this action without authorization, Butler was moved in May. During the war the military ruled the city. Often, they arrested people simply on suspicion. The display of Confederate colors was prohibited. Newspapers were suppressed. Ministers were in danger for disloyal sermons or prayers. Constitutional liberties were curtailed.[30]

In later years, Annie expressed a strong aversion to war, although there is no indication of where the Armstrongs stood on the bitter sectional controversy. However, their pastor's leanings toward the Union and peace influenced the Armstrongs. One of the twin cousins, Eugene Levering, Jr., was a strong Unionist, but Joshua sympathized with the Southern cause. Perhaps the Southern sympathies of the Carys caused Mrs. Armstrong to send young Annie to a school other than the Southern Home School.

Maryland Baptists for the most part agreed on the preservation of the Union. The Maryland Baptist Union Association (convention), however, remained neutral and endorsed the policies and actions of neither the North nor South. The association played a major role in seeing that Southern Baptist missionaries in China and Africa were supported when the sea blockade made communications between the Foreign Mission

Board and the missionaries impossible. Missionaries could not count on receiving their salaries. Primarily at Richard Fuller's suggestion, Maryland Baptists formed a Provisional Foreign Mission Board to transmit funds to missionaries and to keep correspondence flowing. As president of the Southern Baptist Convention, Fuller got permission from the secretary of state for funds of the Board in Richmond to be sent by flag of truce to Baltimore. During the war years, the provisional board collected a sizable amount of money to relieve missionaries abroad and in Maryland.[31]

Events that transpired during these childhood years laid the foundation for Annie's yet-to-be-developed spiritual strength. In the late 1860s, Dr. Fuller and a number of Seventh Baptist laymen realized that the church's community was changing. The church was being transformed from a suburban church in a wealthy residential area to a downtown church in a highly-developed commercial area. This led to the establishment of Eutaw Place Baptist Church, a new church in the suburban section of Baltimore. Deacon Hiram Woods gave a valuable piece of property in the northwestern section of the city and $5,000 to erect a building. Within six months, the group subscribed almost the amount needed for a building, and construction was begun. The building was completed two years later at a cost of $102,000.[32]

Mrs. Armstrong and her children attended regularly Seventh Baptist Church. In times of need in later years, Annie often called to mind a Bible verse or the stanza of a hymn she had learned as a child in Sunday School. Richard Fuller no doubt had an influence on the Armstrong family and on young Annie's later beliefs and practices. He was noted not only for his strong evangelistic and doctrinal preaching but for knowing his members and visiting in their homes. Perhaps Annie looked forward to talking with Fuller about his interest in helping blacks, beginning new churches in Baltimore, and caring for the sick and neglected, for she, too, later had these interests. Annie may even have read some of the numerous books written by her pastor.[33]

Though small physically, Mrs. Armstrong attained great spiritual strength. She was faithful to her church and known as a woman of prayer and action. With a strong, farseeing mind, she instilled a love of ideas in her daughters. She modeled for her daughters that a cultured woman could choose a life of service rather than a life of society and civic involvement.

The Holy Spirit worked in Annie's life. Annie was fascinated by life, and her heart was not at peace. One Sunday morning, Dr. Fuller said in his sermon: "The religion of Jesus Christ gives peace in the midst of trouble." Annie claimed this promise, wanting to be victorious over sorrows and troubles, as was her mother. That morning she surrendered her life to Jesus Christ as her Lord and Savior. In December, 1870, when Annie was twenty, Dr. Fuller baptized her into Seventh Baptist Church membership. She had often said earlier that she could be a Presbyterian or an Episcopalian but never a Baptist. After conversion, Annie claimed she could not be anything but a Baptist. The Armstrong girls were all church members now, for Annie's sisters had been baptized six years earlier.[34]

Although Mrs. Armstrong and her two daughters, Alice and Annie, had deep ties to Seventh Baptist Church, they must have watched with interest the construction of Eutaw Place Baptist Church near their home. They, along with 130 others, including Dr. Richard Fuller and the Leverings, in February, 1871, became charter members of Eutaw Place Baptist Church. Annie Armstrong would be an active member of Eutaw Place for sixty-seven years, until her death in 1938.[35]

Well-informed about Baptist matters, Mrs. Armstrong subscribed to *The True Union*, an early Maryland Baptist paper. Interested in missions and active in charitable endeavors, her attention was captured when in 1867, in Baltimore, Mrs. Ann Graves, a Methodist, held a woman's missionary prayer meeting. The women prayed for Mrs. Graves's son, Baptist missionary doctor Rosewell Hobart Graves. They also prayed for the support of native Bible women in Canton, China. Dr. Graves had been training these women to make contact with the Chinese women. Mrs. Graves further aroused interest in missions when she invited to a meeting in 1869 a missionary to India who was visiting in the United States.[36]

It is possible that Annie, Alice, and Mrs. Armstrong attended the Southern Baptist Convention when it met in Baltimore in 1868. Although women could not be messengers from their churches, they could attend Convention sessions. Mrs. Graves invited the women visitors to join with her and other Baltimore women in a separate meeting. During that meeting she told of the work of her son in China and the need for native Bible women to reach the Chinese women. Mrs. Graves urged the women to organize missionary societies to raise funds for the work.[37]

In 1870 a number of women from various Baltimore churches organized an interdenominational mission society with Mrs. Graves and Mrs. J. W. M. Williams, wife of the pastor of the First Baptist Church, as leaders. The society was so successful that Mrs. Williams and Mrs. William W. Lawrason, sister of Eugene Levering, Sr., decided to organize a similar group of members exclusively from Baptist churches in the city. Woman's Mission to Woman was organized in 1871 with Mrs. Franklin Wilson, the wife of a pastor and secretary of the Maryland Baptist Union Association (convention), as president. There were several vice-presidents, including Mrs. James Armstrong from Eutaw Place Baptist Church. Mrs. Armstrong remained active in this society for many years, often leading the prayer and presiding when the president was absent. Mamie Levering also was later to play a prominent part in the society as treasurer.[38]

Most of the society's leaders were established, older women, so Annie would not have joined. Formed "to give light to women in darkness by taking the gospel into their homes through Bible women," the society collected money at first to support the work in China. Later, the money was sent to the Southern Baptist Foreign Mission Board to be used as the society designated. The society later supported mothers' meetings in Italy, girls' schools in Mexico, and work for women and girls in Africa and Brazil.

Money was raised by family contributions. Each family member was expected to give at least two cents a week to the mite box. A mite box probably was prominent in the Armstrong home, and Annie dropped in her coins. She developed early in life the habit of regular and systematic giving. The society's method of raising money must have been effective, for contributions from the Baltimore women increased from $141.29 in 1868 to $1,041.63 in 1880. In addition to mite boxes, the society later used other methods for collecting money for missions—yearly subscriptions, weekly envelopes, and offerings at meetings.

Woman's Mission to Woman met monthly for information and prayer, with representatives from each church attending.[39] Mrs. Armstrong probably shared the missions information and her concern with her daughters, and they prayed about these needs at home. On one occasion, when requested to lead the singing for the society, Annie was impressed with the circle of kneeling women. So few in number, they were mighty in prayer and faith.

Seeds had been sown in young Annie's life. She had become a Christian as a young adult and was beginning to exercise her newfound faith. She was a charter member of Eutaw Place Baptist Church and would develop over the years an intense loyalty to and active involvement in her church and denomination. Mrs. Armstrong's faith and prayer life had set an example for Annie. Her mother's interest in foreign missions bore fruit as Annie developed into a strong advocate for missions—both foreign and home—and became the pioneer leader in developing a national women's missionary organization for Southern Baptist women. Growing up in Maryland where women seemed to have more freedom to organize and express themselves in missions allowed Annie to develop into a leader of national stature.

Eutaw Place Baptist Church, Baltimore, where Annie Armstrong was a charter member

Notes (See pages 295-310 for Key to Sources.)

1. *Baltimore Sun*, July 11, 1850; Suzanne Ellery Greene, *Baltimore, an Illustrated History*, pp. 73-125; Hamilton Owens, *Baltimore on the Chesapeake*, pp. 250-251.

2. Samuel Eliot Morison, *The Oxford History of the American People*, 2:214-217.

3. Robert A. Baker, *The Southern Baptist Convention and Its People, 1607-1972*, p. 169.

4. Ibid., pp. 183, 219.

5. Inscription on tombstone in Green Mount Cemetery, Baltimore, Maryland; 1850 Census Schedules of Maryland, Ward 10; Charles E. Hoye, "Garrett County History of the Armstrong Family," Armstrong File, Maryland Room, Enoch Pratt Library, Baltimore, Maryland; Baltimore City Administration Accounts NH63, pp. 624-625, James D. Armstrong, 11 June 1856.

6. 1850 Census Schedules of Maryland, Ward 10.

7. Inscriptions on tombstones in Green Mount Cemetery, Baltimore, Maryland; *Matchett's Baltimore Directory*, 1849-1851. In 1877, 41 North Calvert Street became 221 North Calvert Street. On the southwest corner of Calvert and Saratoga Streets is now the Maryland National Bank Building. *Baltimore City Directory*, 1877; Barbara Elder to the author, January 28, February 10, 1983; Land Records, ED #66, Folio 390, August 30, 1854, ED #30, Folio 458, February 28, 1853, Superior Court, Baltimore, Maryland.

8. Matchett, R. J., *Matchett's Baltimore Directory*, 1849-1853; *Baltimore Sun*, December, 1849, July, 1850; *True Union*, 1849-1850. Before 1850, J. D. Armstrong & Thornton was located at 241 Baltimore Street between Charles and Hanover Streets; this address became 13 Baltimore Street in 1877. After 1850 the firm's address was 259 Market Street at the corner of Hanover. The warehouse was at 37 South Cheapside Street, which became 129 South Cheapside Street in 1877. *Baltimore City Directory*, 1877; Barbara Elder to the author, January 28, February 10, 1983.

9. Baltimore City Administration Accounts NH60, pp. 247-250, James D. Armstrong, 13 July 1853; Elizabeth Marshall Evans, *Annie Armstrong*, p. 1; *Baltimore Sun*, July 13, 1850, January 7, 1852. The information on Annie Armstrong's childhood is scanty. The author learned from interviewing Elizabeth Marshall Evans in 1982 that, prior to release of her 1963 biography, Mrs. Evans had visited Ethel Motley, Annie Armstrong's niece. Many facts about these years were supplied to Mrs. Evans by Ethel Motley.

10. Baltimore City Administration Dockets, 14:1-2, James Dunn Armstrong, 31 January 1852; Administration Accounts NH60, pp. 247-250, James Dunn Armstrong, 13 July 1853; NH63, pp. 248-249, 29 December 1855; NH63, pp. 624-625, 11 June 1856; Inventories NH66, pp. 320-328, James Dunn Armstrong, 13 March 1852; Land Records ED #86, Folio 222, July 3, 1855, Superior Court, Baltimore, Maryland.

11. Scharf, *History of Baltimore City and County*, pp. 552-554; "Maryland Heraldry," *Baltimore Sun*, January 14, 1906.

12. *Baltimore Sun*, January 14, 1906; Isaac Walker Maclay, *Henry Sater 1690-1754*, pp. iv-xvi; "Henry Sater, The Recital of the Life and Character, Sater's Baptist Church, Maryland, 1742-1917, Sater Genealogy."

13. Ibid.; article in *The Jeffersonian*, September 23, 1949, on file in Maryland Room, Enoch Pratt Library, Baltimore, Maryland.

14. Interview with Rosalind Robinson Levering, 1978; 1860 Census Schedules of Maryland, Ward 20; 1870 Census Schedules of Maryland, Ward 12. It is interesting to note that by 1870 the real estate value had increased to ten thousand dollars and the personal estate to five thousand dollars.

15. *Matchett's Baltimore Directory*, 1836-1857; Greene, *Baltimore, an Illustrated History*; Evans, *Annie Armstrong*, p. 2. In 1877, 53 McCulloh Street became 1020 McCulloh Street. This site between Biddle and Preston Streets now holds apartment houses. *Baltimore City Directory*, 1877; Barbara Elder to the author, January 28, February 10, 1983.

16. Evans, *Annie Armstrong*, p. 1; inscriptions on tombstones in Green Mount Cemetery, Baltimore, Maryland; Mrs. W. H. Wharton, "One Woman's Vision," WMU. James D. Armstrong and son were buried in Westminster Burial Grounds; they were removed from Westminster to Green Mount Cemetery on June 3, 1880. Carolyn Kirschbaum to the author, February 15, 1983.

17. J. F. Weishampel, *History of Baptist Churches in Maryland*; Evans, *Annie Armstrong*, p. 2; Interview with Elizabeth Marshall Evans, 1982.

18. Greene, *Baltimore, an Illustrated History*, pp. 98-99; Rosalind Robinson Levering, *Baltimore Baptists*, p. 49.

19. 1860 Census Schedules of Maryland, Ward 20; Annie Armstrong to R. J. Willingham, December 12, 1899, FMB.

20. *Baltimore Sun*, September 2, 1860; Evans, *Annie Armstrong*, pp. 4-6; Francis F. Beirne, *The Amiable Baltimoreans*, pp. 84-85; Greene, *Baltimore, an Illustrated History*, pp. 140-142. The General Assembly did not authorize statewide public schools until 1865.

21. Interviews with H. O. Walters and Elizabeth Marshall Evans, 1982; Land Records, GES #240 Folio 260, November 23, 1863, Superior Court, Baltimore, Maryland.

22. Evans, *Annie Armstrong*, pp. 6, 9. In the 1870 census James was still listed as "at home." He died in 1885 and is buried in Green Mount Cemetery in Baltimore, Maryland.

23. John Levering, *Levering Family History and Genealogy*.

24. Robert Warren Hays, *A History of the Seventh Baptist Church*, pp. 4-5; Levering, *Baltimore Baptists*, pp. 40-41.

25. Levering, *Baltimore Baptists*, pp. 33-35.

26. Ibid., pp. 44-46; J. H. Cuthbert, *Life of Richard Fuller*, pp. 259-276.

27. Greene, *Baltimore, an Illustrated History*, p. 114; Levering, *Baltimore Baptists*, pp. 44-46; Bruce Catton, *The Coming Fury*, pp. 222-225, 354-356.

28. Catton, *The Coming Fury*, pp. 340-343; *Baltimore Sun*, April 19-20, 1861.

29. Levering, *Baltimore Baptists*, pp. 45-46.

30. Catton, *The Coming Fury*, pp. 222-225, 354-356.

31. *Baltimore Sun*, August 3, 1928; Norman H. Maring, *A Denominational History of Maryland Baptists, 1742-1888*; Levering, *Baltimore Baptists*, pp. 44-47.

32. Hays, *A History of Seventh Baptist Church*; *Maryland Baptist*, March, 1902.

33. Annie Armstrong to J. M. Frost, July 13, 1896, SSB; Wharton, "One Woman's Vision," WMU; *Encyclopedia of Southern Baptists*, 1:514-515.

34. Records from Seventh Baptist Church, WMU; Hays, *A History of Seventh Baptist Church*; Evans, *Annie Armstrong*, p. 10; interview with Elizabeth Marshall Evans, 1982; Wharton, "One Woman's Vision," WMU; Memorial Tribute, Mrs. Eugene Levering, January 29, 1939, WMU. The actual date of Annie Armstrong's baptism cannot be verified.

35. Minutes, Eutaw Place Baptist Church, 1871.

36. *The True Union*, 1853-1857; Levering, *Baltimore Baptists*, pp. 35-43; FMJ, February, 1882. The August, 1868, issue of *The Baptist Visitor* notes that Mrs. Graves, a Methodist since childhood, had been baptized several weeks earlier by Dr. J. W. M. Williams, pastor of First Baptist Church, Baltimore.

37. Blanche Sydnor White, *Our Heritage*, p. 39; Alma Hunt and Catherine B. Allen, *History of Woman's Missionary Union*, pp. 11-12. White says the meeting was held in the lecture room of Seventh Baptist Church, where the Convention was meeting; Hunt says First Baptist Church. The author could not locate the precise meeting place in a primary source.

38. FMJ, February, 1882; Levering, *Baltimore Baptists*, pp. 53-54; Minutes, Baltimore Branch of the Woman's Mission to Woman, 1872-1897 (hereafter referred to as WFMS); Secretary's reports, Woman's Mission to Woman, 1880-1889; *The Christian Index*, September 27, 1900. In 1885 the name of the organization became Maryland Society of Woman's Mission to Woman in Foreign Lands. In 1892, it became the Woman's Baptist Foreign Mission Society of Maryland.

39. Ibid.

2
What Got Her Interested in Missions?

Perhaps one reason Annie enjoyed Eutaw Place Baptist Church so much was that women were involved in the work and ministry of the church from its beginning in 1871. The women had already contributed money for the building. Before the church even began regular worship, the female members were called in to help put the finishing touches to the building. Mrs. Armstrong presided over the group of thirty-five who responded, which no doubt included her daughters, Annie and Alice. Many gifts and purchases—carpets, furniture, tack hammers, and glue—were recorded and put to use.

In April, 1871, the "Working Society" was organized with Mrs. Armstrong as president. The society was designed to care for the female members of the church and to provide an organization through which they could work. The organization met quarterly to discuss reports from three societies—the Dorcas Society, mothers' meeting, and a sewing school. There was a ladies' prayer meeting led by Jane Norris, who along with her sister Charlotte was a friend of Annie's; membership averaged forty in the early days. Six committees visited the poor and new members, took care of the church building, assisted candidates for baptism and took care of gowns, and prepared for the Lord's Supper services. Annie's specific involvement was not indicated, but it is possible she worked with the mothers' meeting or the poor, for she later did much with these groups.[1]

Interest in missions was not prevalent at the church in those early days but was to emerge later. However, Mrs. Armstrong and Jane Norris were officers in Woman's Mission to Woman, the new general foreign mission society in Baltimore. They were learning and, no doubt, sharing information about veteran missionary Dr. Rosewell Graves's work in China. They were giving money and prayer support to the work of native Bible women in China. Jane Norris became the second Mrs. Graves in 1872 and went with Graves to China.[2] This gave Annie and Eutaw Place a personal touch with missions.

On April 17, 1872, the church held a special service of dedication and prayer for eight missionaries on their way to China. Along with the Graveses, the group included Dr. and Mrs. Jesse Boardman Hartwell, Mr. and Mrs. Nicholas Butt Williams, Lula Whilden, and Edmonia Moon (sister of Lottie Moon).[3] No doubt Annie Armstrong was in that service which included two single women missionaries, the first appointed by the Foreign Mission Board in years.

While the work of the women's societies and committees was necessary and commendable, it did not fulfill the church's missions responsibility. In 1876 collections for foreign missions were sought through mite boxes. The church later took annual collections at set times to finance missionary and benevolent work. During the church's first decade, a women's society was organized to meet monthly to study the fields under the Foreign Mission Board, especially China, for which the church had special ties through Dr. and Mrs. Rosewell Graves. When the church appointed a home and foreign missions committee in 1878 to arrange a missionary meeting once a month on Wednesday evenings to foster a missions spirit in the church, Alice Armstrong was one of the seven appointed to this committee.[4] It was most unusual during this period for men and women to serve on committees together. This practice in Eutaw Place Church provided a climate in which a woman could emerge as a leader. Perhaps Annie saw her older sister Alice in this role and had the desire to get involved in leadership herself. Possibly Annie commented to Alice on the committee's plans and gave suggestions.

Eutaw Place again had opportunity to bid farewell to mission-

Interior of Eutaw Place Baptist Church; pointer shows fifth row where tradition says Annie Armstrong usually sat

aries in 1881, this time to William Buck Bagby and Anne Luther Bagby, the first Southern Baptist missionaries appointed to Brazil. Leaving Texas in late 1880, the Bagbys stopped briefly for a visit with the Foreign Mission Board's corresponding secretary, Dr. Henry Allen Tupper, and his wife in Richmond. The Bagbys reached Baltimore for departure in early January, 1881. They were to sail to Brazil at a reduced rate on the E. Levering and Company ship, the *Yamoyden*, a 483-ton sailing vessel used to export flour and import coffee.

Probably at this time Annie began her lifelong friendship with Anne Bagby. The Bagbys attended a night service at Eutaw Place. Dr. Rosewell Graves delivered a lecture on Asian missions, and Bagby spoke briefly on Brazil. The church members welcomed the Bagbys warmly and sent them forth to Brazil with Godspeed. It is likely that some of the members accompanied the Bagbys to the ship.[5]

The Eutaw Place Foreign Mission Society now had a personal interest in both China and Brazil. At times the society sent boxes of clothing to South America and China. Also, the church saw missions needs at its doorstep and started a Chinese Sunday School at the church for Chinese people living in Baltimore.[6]

Church committee assignments during the 1880s reflected Annie's interests. At various times she served as a member of the committee on the poor, the young converts' committee, and the missions committee.[7]

From all indications, Mrs. Armstrong, Alice, and Annie customarily attended every service at Eutaw Place. When the church was organized, it adopted the pew system as one method of financing. The Armstrongs rented a pew and occupied it regularly. Harriett Levering, daughter of pastor Frank M. Ellis, remembered seeing the "two, tall, stately sisters walking the length of the aisle and seating themselves in a pew (near the front), with a frail, little lady wearing a white ruche in her bonnet and soft lace at her throat."[8]

Eutaw Place was rather ornate inside and out. The floor-level marble baptistry was in a prominent place near the front of the auditorium. Well-built, sturdy, dark pulpit furniture was on the platform. Many of the members were rich and influential, and services were formal. The pastor wore morning clothes for preaching, and there were a paid choir and soloists. Many events took place in the lecture hall downstairs, and the church had educational space in two adjoining row-house-type buildings known as the Church House.[9]

Nothing is revealed in Annie's later voluminous correspondence about romances or a proposal of marriage. However, legend has it that a widowed North China missionary with several children asked Annie to marry him and go to China. Though this story cannot be verified, it is possible that Dr. Jesse B. Hartwell made the proposal.

The Hartwells had been in Eutaw Place in 1872, along with the group of missionaries being commissioned for China. Hartwell was returning to China where he had served since 1858. Because of the second Mrs. Hartwell's illness, they returned home in 1875, and she received medical treatment in Baltimore the next year. Perhaps Annie again had contact with the Hartwells. In 1879 the Home Mission Board appointed Hartwell to work with the Chinese in California. Mrs. Hartwell contracted a severe cold on the way and died at the end of the year.[10]

In the summer of 1881, Hartwell was in Baltimore visiting friends. The Home Mission Board had granted him a leave of absence to come East for the length of time needed "to accomplish the object of his visit," and authorized travel expenses for Hartwell and his wife to return to California. No doubt he had come to Baltimore to find his third wife, a mother for his children, and a companion to accompany him on his return to China.

We will never know whether Hartwell, fifteen years older, proposed marriage to Annie, but it is certain that Annie was interested in the progress of the Lord's work and loved children. Perhaps she had not yet developed a deep missions interest nor felt called to foreign missions. In August, 1881, Hartwell married

Charlotte Norris, a member of Eutaw Place, sister of Jane Norris Graves, and a friend of Annie's. Over the years Annie showed a genuine concern for and kept up with the Hartwells through letters. She was especially interested in the Hartwell children.[11]

Although she had been exposed to missions in the 1870s in her church and under her mother's influence, Annie's attention had not yet been captured in a dramatic way. Perhaps the foreign mission society, led by the older women, just did not interest Annie, though she was impressed by the faith and prayers of the women. Or, she was too much of a doer and activist to be intrigued by missions support as she saw it practiced. She directed her energies instead to the chautauqua movement, the children in her church, the orphans at the Home of the Friendless, and the city's sick and poor. These were all appropriate endeavors for a young woman in the Victorian era.

Annie and Alice completed various chautauqua reading courses and attended the summer assemblies in Chautauqua by the Lake in western New York. The chautauqua, which was started to train Sunday School teachers, became a popular lyceum and amusement enterprise of the late nineteenth and early twentieth centuries. There were lectures, classes, musical performances, and correspondence courses.[12]

In 1871, when she was twenty-one years old, Annie was put in charge of the Infant Class (later called Primary Department), which included children from the time they started coming to Sunday School to about age twelve. With the exception of a few years, she taught this age group for at least the next fifty years. Annie referred often to her love of children and how she enjoyed teaching the "little ones," or "little people" as she called them. When she had to give up teaching in the early 1900s because of heavy responsibilities, she was in tears.

Nothing deterred Annie from carrying out her responsibility for the Infant Class. She refused to let anything get in the way of arriving at Sunday School early or leading the children through their exercises on Sunday School Anniversary afternoons. Sunday School and the little people were dear to her heart, and she claimed to have taught thousands over the years. Annie invited the children, class by class, for afternoon tea in her home to get to know them better and to entertain them "with cups and saucers."[13]

When Eutaw Place Baptist Church celebrated its twenty-fifth anniversary in 1896, the church took note that Mrs. Armstrong had been secretary of the Sunday School from 1871 to about 1893, and the Primary Department had "long enjoyed the skillful supervision of one possessed of exceptional qualifications to the task, Miss Annie Armstrong, assisted by efficient lady teachers."[14] Through the years former pupils paid tribute to their teacher, "Miss Annie."[15]

Annie also began to fill her time with the Home of the Friendless, a shelter for destitute children from ages one to fifteen. Founded in 1854, the home was located at Druid Hill Avenue and Townsend Street, not far from Annie's home or Eutaw Place Church. The home, which could hold one hundred children and was usually crowded, housed, educated, and sent the children to Sunday Schools of various denominations in the vicinity. Some of these children came to Eutaw Place Sunday School each Sunday and were in Annie's Infant Class.

In 1873 Annie donated five dollars to the home and became a manager. She served on the board of managers, made up of twenty-five ladies, for over twenty years. The Leverings often donated to the home, and Annie's Aunt Ann (Mrs. Eugene Levering, Sr.) and sister Mamie (Mrs. Eugene Levering, Jr.) also served as managers.[16]

Sunday School and chapel services were also held at the home. Annie went each Sunday afternoon and taught a Bible lesson. Armed with hard candy, she often took young people from the church with her. Annie must have been an apt Bible student herself. She frequently quoted Scripture and made numerous references to specific Bible verses in her letters. Minutes of the various executive committees over which Annie presided or in which she participated made note frequently of her devotionals and explanations of Bible passages.[17]

Home of the Friendless, Baltimore, as Annie Armstrong knew it

One Christmas Annie planned a stereopticon (a projector for transparent slides) exhibit as a special entertainment for the children. She asked a gentleman friend who often helped her at the home to assist with the exhibit. It was to be a big event, and one thousand invitations had been sent to children throughout Baltimore asking them to come and bring a Christmas offering for the children in the institution. Much to Annie's astonishment, her own picture appeared on the canvas during the showing. She had had a photograph taken a few days earlier, but the photographer had not yet furnished her with copies. She was disgusted and highly indignant that her friend had used her picture.

Annie's gentleman friend, later to become an officer of the American Baptist Publication Society in Philadelphia (probably A. J. Rowland), had a stereopticon slide made of the photograph and slipped it into the showing. Annie wrote years later: "There were some circumstances connected with this that made some of my friends consider it a peculiarly amusing experience. I did not see it in the same light, and the effect it had was to lead me to assure my family that this was the last picture I should *ever* have taken, and I have strictly adhered to that determination." Annie did not identify the so-called amusing experience.[18]

The children at the Home of the Friendless meant much to Annie. Many years later, she was touched when a young man who had grown up at the home visited her and brought some money to use in making persons happy that Christmas. He claimed that no one knew better how to do this than Annie. The young man had been fond of her and remembered the Christmas occasions she had arranged for the home. Annie used his gift immediately for a Christmas dinner for poor women she gave each year at her church.[19]

Both Mrs. Armstrong and Annie's sister Mamie were on the board of managers of the Union Protestant Infirmary, and Annie visited the patients. The infirmary had been founded in 1854 by several ladies representing Protestant churches, and it came under the care of these churches. Until that time all hospitals in

Annie Armstrong

Baltimore were under Catholic jurisdiction. Dr. Richard Fuller, the Armstrongs' pastor, participated in the opening ceremonies. As a girl, Annie went occasionally to the infirmary, then located in her neighborhood at Division Street near Mosher Street. She told her family that when she had the "blues" she paid a visit to the infirmary. When she saw so many people genuinely sick and in trouble, she quickly recovered.[20]

Annie's concern for the poor was genuine. She started the Ladies' Bay View Mission, which she considered "the largest opportunity, I expect, in the city of Baltimore that one can have to reach the unsaved in one day, outside of the jail or penitentiary." The Bay View Asylum, erected in 1866, was the poor house for the city's sick and indigent. The awesome three-story edifice was named Bay View because of its view of Chesapeake Bay. About twenty-five hundred persons—white, black, foreign-born, and Baltimoreans—were admitted annually. Many were diseased and addicted to alcohol. Some were insane. Most were between the ages of twenty and fifty.[21]

Through the years, Annie, as president of Bay View Mission, relentlessly sought and got financial and other kinds of help from many sources, such as the Women's Christian Temperance Union, nondenominational organizations, Enoch Pratt Library, and Baptist women. Her purpose was to bring "religious influences to bear upon the poor unfortunates." In the summer, missionaries were employed to do the work.[22]

Weekly travel to Bay View involved taking the horse-drawn cars (later electric) as far as they went and then riding in a phaeton, a light, four-wheeled, horse-drawn vehicle. Often Annie felt "used up" and unable to do much else after a day at Bay View. After becoming corresponding secretary of Woman's Missionary Union, Annie sometimes used the travel time to Bay View to read her mail. She would have an office clerk meet her with the mail as she changed cars. On one such ride in January, Annie suffered a neuralgia attack, a problem which plagued her regularly. On another occasion the phaeton driver misunderstood a flagman's signal and was caught on the double tracks with a train coming. The horse stumbled, but neither Annie nor any of the five ladies accompanying her were injured, though one had recently suffered a stroke and another had heart trouble. Annie attributed their safety to God's keeping.[23]

Annie's missions horizons expanded dramatically as a result of events of the early 1880s. She began to join in the wider movements which led ultimately to a Convention-wide Southern Baptist women's missionary organization. It is not certain when Annie joined Woman's Mission to Woman or the foreign mission society in her church, but at some point she did. She is first mentioned in the minutes of Woman's Mission to Woman in 1884 and was frequently in meetings during 1887 and 1888. Later, during her years as corresponding secretary of Woman's Missionary Union, in letters to Dr. R. J. Willingham, Foreign Mission Board secretary, she referred to attending monthly meetings of the foreign mission society. She later served for years as president of the foreign mission circle in her church. In those meetings, she, along with her sister Alice, often gave fresh reports from missionary letters. She invited missionaries and other guests to speak at meetings when they were in town.[24]

November, 1880, marked a turning point in Annie's life. That month, Mrs. J. W. M. Williams invited to Baltimore Mrs. A. S. Quinton of Philadelphia, secretary of the National Indian Association. Mrs. Quinton spoke on home missions to the annual Woman's Baptist Foreign Mission Society meeting and urged the women to organize. Some feared this emphasis on home missions would dissipate the society's efforts toward foreign missions and create conflicting interests.

Annie was deeply moved as Mrs. Quinton spoke of conditions and needs of the Indians who had been driven from their ancient homes onto reservations and lived in wretchedness and destitution. She and other women responded. Led primarily by Annie and Mrs. Williams, Eutaw Place and First Baptist Churches each organized home missions societies. The Eutaw

Place society clothed twenty Indian boys and girls of the
Levering Manual Labor School in Wetumka, Creek Nation,
Indian Territory (now Oklahoma). The school, made possible by
a twenty-five-hundred-dollar legacy left to the Home Mission
Board by Eugene Levering, Sr., opened in September, 1881.
Mrs. Williams wrote Dr. William Hilary McIntosh, the Home
Mission Board secretary, to see if he would accept these societies
as auxiliary to the Board, and he agreed to do so.[25]

In the spring of 1882 the school was in a precarious position.
The Indian government failed to pay to the school the money
promised. The superintendent wrote to the Baltimore societies,
appealing for help. There was no way that the Eutaw Place and
First Church societies could provide the 240 summer suits
needed, so the women formed a committee to seek help from all
the Baltimore churches. It is likely that Annie was on the
committee and visited churches to enlist women. Eight white
and six black churches responded, giving money and sending
suits. Annie and the other women must have made an interesting picture as they gathered in church lecture halls to carefully
fold and pack the suits in barrels for shipment to Indian
Territory. This project generated great excitement, and more
home mission societies formed as a result. Annie must have been
thrilled as she saw Baltimore women captivated by their newfound interest in missions. It was time to think about a permanent general organization to band together the local home
missions societies for more concerted work.

Annie and the others carefully laid the groundwork and on
May 6, 1882, a general meeting of representatives from the
churches was held at Eutaw Place Baptist Church. The representatives formed a central committee, called the Woman's
Baptist Home Mission Society of Maryland. Recognizing her
leadership abilities and role in the societies, they elected Annie
as their first president. The society's objective was "cooperating
with the Home Mission Board and inducing a spirit of united
work among the women of all the churches." The society sought
to have an auxiliary in every church. The president of each

church society would serve as a vice-president of the general society to which contributions from the churches would be sent.[26]

Annie took seriously her responsibility as president of the Woman's Baptist Home Mission Society of Maryland. She not only encouraged the women to give money in support of the Home Mission Board's work, but she led them into practical ministries in their communities. The society's first priority was the Indian School, a project which continued to excite interest. At the close of the first year, eleven churches (white, black, city, country) gave $529.87 in clothing or money.[27]

In 1882 Isaac Taylor Tichenor became the new corresponding secretary of the Home Mission Board. Annie corresponded with Tichenor, for whom she developed much affection and respect, about expanding the work of the Home Mission Society of Maryland. In society meetings Annie made stirring appeals for women to give their money to support Minnie Alfred, missionary to New Orleans, to rebuild a missionary school in Cuba, and to help the Levering Manual Labor School. She was instrumental, too, in getting the women to do missions work in Baltimore. In addition to the work with the Chinese at Eutaw Place Church, Annie led the women to minister to blacks and immigrants. She petitioned the Home Mission Board to appoint missionaries to Baltimore. Lula Whilden, one of the foreign missionaries commissioned earlier by Eutaw Place Church to China, in 1887 was appointed by the Home Mission Board to work with the Chinese in Baltimore. Later, Marie Buhlmaier was appointed to work with German immigrants at the Baltimore pier.

The Home Mission Society not only raised contributions from the churches in the traditional ways used by the Foreign Mission Society but also adopted innovative methods. In order to meet the additional demand for money when state missions was added as a society project, Annie and the executive committee planned a moonlight excursion by boat to Annapolis. This excursion became an annual event. The excursion was both a social occa-

Isaac Taylor Tichenor, Corresponding Secretary, Home Mission Board, 1882-99

sion and one raising money for missions. To secure money for expenses, the society asked each woman to place a nickel into the Nickel Fund each year. Annie was firm in her conviction that all money raised be channeled through the Home Mission Board. Contributions from the churches increased from the $529.87 the first year to over $4,000 by 1892; thereafter annual contributions amounted usually to between $4,000 and $5,000. By 1886 there were forty-five Maryland societies. After reading one of the annual reports, Dr. Tichenor expressed his delight with the Home Mission Society. He wrote: "The progress you have made from year to year, and your good work, is most gratifying." He thanked the society especially for helping the Far West and New Orleans.[28]

It is easy to understand from her role in the Home Mission Society that a zeal for home missions had been deeply implanted in Annie Armstrong's life. She also had developed the desire to organize and involve women in all types of churches. For the next twenty-four years, from 1882-1906, she would lead the Woman's Baptist Home Mission Society of Maryland.[29] However, Annie's leadership was destined to extend far beyond Maryland's borders.

Women again gathered at a Convention-wide meeting in Waco, Texas, in 1883, as they had for the first time in Baltimore in 1868. There is no evidence, however, that Annie Armstrong attended this meeting. Waco is a long way from Baltimore.[30]

The following spring, 1884, the Southern Baptist Convention met in Baltimore. A large number of women gathered at the Westminster Presbyterian Church on May 8. The Maryland Foreign Mission Society had planned the meeting and invited women from each missionary society in the South. At Mrs. Armstrong's suggestion, the Home Mission Society helped to host the meeting. Therefore, Annie must have been much in evidence around the meeting. It gave her a chance to meet other state leaders. As usual for that day, and adhering to the current interpretation of 1 Corinthians 14:34-35, only women were allowed in the meeting. The women heard Adele Fielde, a returned Baptist Missionary Union missionary to China. They also were urged to subscribe to *The Heathen Helper,* a missionary paper put out by the Kentucky women. The women agreed to meet each year at the Convention under the direction of the women in the state where the meeting would be held.[31]

Joshua Levering, Annie's cousin, caused quite a stir at the Southern Baptist Convention that year when he earnestly and forcibly offered and spoke to a resolution that the Home Mission Board appoint a competent woman to be the superintendent of women's work for home missions. Under the direction of the Board, her duties would be to visit the cities to organize mission societies, give and collect information, and stimulate and strengthen in any way possible the work of women for home missions. The women were deeply interested in the resolution. No doubt this had been a major topic of conversation between Annie and Joshua. Perhaps Annie even primed the pump for Joshua. It is possible Annie heard the debate, because women could sit in on Convention sessions as visitors. There was much debate and opposition to the resolution, centering around a fear of the women's rights issue, women speaking in public, and the possibility of a separate women's organization. The resolution was referred to the Home Mission Board and on to a Board committee, but no action was taken.[32]

During those days there was a dearth of missionary literature. Maryland Baptist leaders saw a way to meet this need. At its October, 1886, annual meeting, the Maryland Baptist Union Association (convention) voted to establish a missionary library and reading room in Baltimore. The association named Baltimore pastors A. C. Dixon, F. M. Ellis (Annie's pastor at Eutaw Place since 1884), and A. J. Rowland to carry out the recommendation. It was highly significant that the two women's societies (foreign and home) were also asked to add one woman each to the committee. Women did not usually serve on state committees. The women sent a committee of two to Philadelphia to study the work of the Baptist Women's Missionary Bureau started in 1886 and the Presbyterian Mission Rooms, which had been operating longer. It is likely that Annie was on the committee which visited Philadelphia. The committee got much useful information but decided on a larger endeavor than either of these mission rooms.

The following January, a committee of women from the two societies, including Annie, met to lay plans for the library and reading rooms. Their plan was for the men to raise money for expenses and act as an advisory committee and the women to furnish the rooms and do the work. A new committee was appointed, with Annie as corresponding secretary, to operate the Maryland Mission Rooms, sell leaflets, and have on hand missions periodicals and books from all denominations.[33]

The first problem facing Annie and the committee was finding a place. Dr. Henry Marvin Wharton, a Baltimore pastor and publisher of *The Baltimore Baptist*, gave an upper room at the Wharton and Barron Publishing Company, 10 East Fayette Street, rent free. This building served as Baptist headquarters for Baltimore and often hosted meetings of Baltimore ministers and others. Since there was inadequate access to the upper room, Wharton, who was famed as an orator, offered to deliver a lecture, if the women would sell tickets, to raise money for the stairway. Soon a stairway was provided.

Much of the responsibility for setting up and managing the Maryland Mission Rooms fell on Annie. There was much work to be done before opening—furnishing the room, collecting the missions periodicals and books, securing leaflets and tracts to sell, printing a catalog, and gathering curios for display. Within two months the women were ready, and the rooms opened for daily use in March, 1887. Volunteers staffed the library for local use and filled mail orders from the catalog.

Annie held quarterly executive committee meetings, and the work grew rapidly. During the summer when most of the committee members left home, Annie carried on the work. She simply took the necessary equipment with her when the family vacationed in Virginia. By the first report to the Maryland Baptist Union Association in October, 1887, the Mission Rooms

Committee had the nucleus of a good library. It also had published a prayer card, two editions of quarterly programs, and two leaflets; advertised in *The Baltimore Baptist*; and filled orders from Canada and thirty-one states and territories.

The first prayer card was a major step, for it was the stackpole around which publication of literature centered. The four-page card presented a mission field each month with statistics and a Scripture passage. Later, the committee supplemented the prayer card with a yearly series of leaflets based on the card outline and quarterly programs; these materials were available on an annual subscription basis. Annie and the committee sought key Southern Baptist leaders as writers and advocates.[34]

Annie served as corresponding secretary of the Maryland Mission Rooms for nineteen years, from 1887-1906, and eventually got the rooms under the management of the Sunday School Board and Home Mission Board. The rooms were the only real source of missions literature for Southern Baptists other than state Baptist papers and mission board journals. Annie was acknowledged as the key to the success of the room. Oliver Fuller Gregory, secretary of the state board of Maryland and a Baltimore pastor, said of her leadership: "Miss Annie Armstrong was the corresponding secretary, and the success of the maintenance and steadily enlarging usefulness and work of the Rooms was due to her untiring and voluntary sacrifice of time, strength, thought, and energy."[35]

In 1886 the two Maryland women's societies undertook a second joint project. If the societies would try to get subscriptions to *The Baltimore Baptist,* the editors would offer a regular column in the paper. The women readily took advantage of this offer and had columns in alternating issues. Alice Armstrong edited the column for the Home Mission Society, of which Annie was president. This was a golden opportunity to give missions information and to report on what the women were doing. The columns continued until 1894 when space became too tight; the women then used the Foreign and Home Mission Board journals.[36]

By 1886 Annie Armstrong's destiny was launched. Her lifelong interest would be missions. She never lost her faithfulness and unswerving loyalty to her church and denomination. She gave herself unstintingly to the charitable institutions in Baltimore. She maintained a demanding pace for years to rally Maryland Baptist women into missions involvement and support. She pioneered in the provision of missions literature. At this point in her life, people began to describe her repeatedly as indefatigable, and somewhere along the path she began to be called "Miss Annie."

Notes (See pages 295-310 for Key to Sources.)

1. Alice Armstrong, "Woman's Work in This Church," a paper read by Deacon James Pollard at the twenty-fifth anniversary of Eutaw Place Baptist Church, April 26-29, 1896.

2. *Encyclopedia of Southern Baptists*, 1:485.

3. Catherine B. Allen, *The New Lottie Moon Story*, pp. 67-68.

4. Alice Armstrong, "Woman's Work in This Church"; Minutes, Eutaw Place Baptist Church, October 14, 1878; Twenty-fifth anniversary of Eutaw Place Baptist Church, April 26-29, 1896.

5. FMJ, February, May, 1881; letters in Bagby Letter File, FMB: E. Levering to H. A. Tupper, January 3, 1881; W. B. Bagby to H. A. Tupper, January 7, 1881; H. A. Tupper to E. Levering Co., January 7, 1881; A. L. Bagby to H. A. Tupper, January 14, 1881; Helen Bagby Harrison, *The Bagbys of Brazil*, pp. 30-32.

6. Alice Armstrong, "Woman's Work in This Church."

7. Minutes, Eutaw Place Baptist Church, 1871-1892.

8. Twenty-fifth anniversary of Eutaw Place Baptist Church, April 26, 27, 28 and 29, 1896; Annie Armstrong to R. J. Willingham, February 12, 1903, FMB; Interview with H. O. Walters, 1982; Harriett S. Levering, "A Sketch of 'Miss Annie,'" *The Window of YWA*, March, 1935.

9. Interview with H. O. Walters, 1982; Interview with Marjorie Allen, 1981.

10. SBC Annuals, 1872-1880.

11. *The Baltimore Baptist*, June 18, 1885; HMB Minutes, July 25, 1881; *Encyclopedia of Southern Baptists*, 1:484. The Register of Hartwell Family Papers, Yale Divinity School, gives Hartwell's birth year as 1835. In a letter in the WMU Archives to Mrs. C. D. Creasman, Mrs. F. W. Armstrong, and Kathleen Mallory (WMU leaders), April 3, 1944, Una Roberts Lawrence surmised that the "love story" could have been either Dr. Rosewell H. Graves or Dr. Jesse B. Hartwell, for it was purportedly a missionary to China. If

the story occurred in 1881, it could not have been Graves, for he married Jane Norris in 1872 and she lived until 1888. Perhaps the proposal was from Graves in 1872. Kathleen Mallory wrote Mrs. F. W. Armstrong on April 21, 1944, "that since Miss Armstrong did not make such love affairs known to her own niece or to Mrs. Eugene Levering (second wife) or to close friends there in Baltimore, it would appear that Miss Armstrong did not want future generations to know. Surely I think that all such matters are the property of the individual and I cannot imagine Miss Armstrong being pleased to have any such discussion concerning her." When the author interviewed Elizabeth Marshall Evans in 1982, Mrs. Evans said she knew who made the offer of marriage but was not divulging it. She thought it better not to as the family, particularly Annie's niece, Ethel Motley, had not wanted such things aired.

12. *The Story of America,* p. 137.

13. Annie Armstrong to T. P. Bell, December 13, 1893, FMB; Annie Armstrong to R. J. Willingham, April 23 and 25, 1894, January 28, 1895, March 25, 1895, February 5, 1897, August 16, 1897, May 18, 1898, April 14, 1900, October 31, 1903, May 5, 1904, FMB; Annie Armstrong to A. J. Barton, October 22, 1898, December 28, 1899, FMB; Annie Armstrong to J. M. Frost, July 13, 1896, August 14, 1897, SSB; Interview with Marjorie Allen, 1981; Interview with H. O. Walters, 1982.

14. Twenty-fifth anniversary of Eutaw Place Baptist Church, April 26, 27, 28 and 29, 1896.

15. Interview with H. O. Walters, 1982.

16. *Annual Reports,* Home of the Friendless, 1854-1889; *Directory of the Charitable and Beneficent Organizations of Baltimore and of Maryland,* p. 43; Annie Armstrong to R. J. Willingham, Christmas Eve, 1901, FMB; Recollections of Marjorie Allen, 1978.

17. Interviews with Marjorie Allen and Virginia Atkinson, 1982; Correspondence, 1888-1906; WMU minutes, 1888-1906; Minutes, Woman's Baptist Home Mission Society of Maryland, 1886-1906 (hereafter referred to as WHMS).

18. Annie Armstrong to T. P. Bell, June 22, 1895, SSB; Annie Armstrong to R. J. Willingham, May 22, 1897, FMB.

19. Annie Armstrong to R. J. Willingham, Christmas Eve, 1901, FMB.

20. Annie Armstrong to A. J. Barton, September 8, 1898, FMB; Lillian H. Hofmeister, *The Union Memorial Hospital, Its Story . . . Its People,* pp. 6-14, 212.

21. Bay View is now Baltimore City Hospitals. Annie Armstrong to R. J. Willingham, December 6, 1904, FMB; *The Strangers Guide to the City of Baltimore,* pp. 75-77; *Directory of the Charitable and Beneficent Organizations of Baltimore and Maryland;* Sherry H. Olson, *Baltimore, the Building of an American City.*

22. Annie Armstrong to H. H. Harris, June 19, 1893, FMB; Annie Armstrong to R. J. Willingham, November 15, 1893, March 20, 1895, April 15, 1896, June 6, 1896, January 27, 1897, June 28, 1897, January 19, 1898, May 18, 1898, November 17, 1898, January 16, 1899, September 27, 1899, October 4,

1899, October 17, 1901, December 6, 1904, January 4, 1905, FMB.

23. Annie Armstrong to R. J. Willingham, December 22, 1894, January 27, 1897, November 17, 1898, FMB.

24. Minutes, WFMS, 1880-1889; Annie Armstrong to R. J. Willingham, April 3, 1895, October 13, 1897, February 7, 1899, January 3, 1903, June 16, 1905, FMB; Minutes, Woman's Mission Circle and Ladies Foreign Mission Circle, Eutaw Place Baptist Church, 1890-1898; Annie Armstrong to J. M. Frost, December 2, 1897, SSB.

25. *Report,* WHMS, 1886; SBC Annuals, 1875-1877; Minutes, MBUA Executive Board, 1881-1882; Morison, *The Oxford History of the American People,* 3:60-61. Eugene Levering left twenty-five hundred dollars each to the Home Mission Board and the Foreign Mission Board. No correspondence from the period of Annie Armstrong's leadership in the Home Mission Society of Maryland or Woman's Missionary Union, SBC, is available at the Home Mission Board.

26. *Report,* WHMS, 1886; *The Baltimore Baptist,* May 8, 1884.

27. *Report,* WHMS, 1882; *The Baltimore Baptist,* May 8, 1884.

28. *Reports,* WHMS, 1882-1906; *The Baltimore Baptist,* February 10, July 28, 1887, March 28, April 25, 1889, June 5, July 3, 1890; Minutes, MBUA Executive Board, 1886; *The Heathen Helper,* June, 1886; HMB minutes, November 11, 1887.

29. The Woman's Home and Foreign Mission Societies of Maryland merged to form Maryland Woman's Missionary Union in 1913. White, *Our Heritage,* p. 57.

30. *The Heathen Helper,* June, 1883; *Texas Baptist and Herald,* May 12, 1883.

31. Minutes, WFMS, 1884; *The Religious Herald,* May 22, 1884; *FMJ,* April, May, 1884.

32. SBC Annual, 1884; *The Religious Herald,* May 15, 1884; *The Baltimore Baptist,* May 15, 1884; *The Baltimore Sun,* May 20, 1884; HMB minutes, May 19, 1884.

33. Minutes, Missions Rooms Committee, 1886-1887; Secretary's book, Mission Rooms, 1886-1888; Minutes, MBUA Executive Board, 1886-1888; Minutes, WFMS, 1887; Minutes, Eutaw Place Baptist Church, 1884.

34. Ibid.; *The Evangel,* June 26, 1895; Mrs. H. M. Wharton, "Ready Pens Proclaiming Missions 1886-1936," p. 11; *FMJ,* June, 1887, January, 1891; Alice Armstrong to John A. Broadus, August 9, 1887, SBTS; Levering, *Baltimore Baptists,* pp. 85-86.

35. *The Religious Herald,* July 21, 1887, November 21, 1901; Wharton, "Ready Pens Proclaiming Missions 1886-1936," p. 11.

36. Minutes, WFMS, 1885-1887; *The Baltimore Baptist,* October 14, 1886; *Reports,* WHMS, 1887, 1894.

3
How Did Annie Get in Charge?

As events moved more and more toward a Convention-wide woman's missions organization, Baltimore pastors and women's leaders played a major role. Apparently Annie was not in the women's meetings held in connection with the Southern Baptist Conventions in Augusta, Georgia, in 1885 or Montgomery, Alabama, in 1886. However, Baltimore pastors Dr. F. M. Ellis (Annie's pastor since 1884) and Dr. J. W. M. Williams not only were there but continued to support and encourage the women. Annie probably asked Ellis and Williams for a full report about these meetings when the pastors got home. No doubt they told her about the decision the women made in Augusta. In 1885 the women assured the Southern Baptist Convention that they did not desire separate and independent organizations to do missions work but wanted to work directly in the churches and to be represented in state conventions and the Southern Baptist Convention.[1]

Annie began to emerge as a national leader in the Louisville meeting in 1887. To see the significance of the 1887 meeting, it is necessary to understand how the Convention viewed women's work since Woman's Mission to Woman organized in Maryland in 1871. The Foreign Mission Board and Dr. H. A. Tupper, its newly-elected corresponding secretary, immediately got behind the women's work movement. Since women's societies were collecting and sending funds to the Board, the Board urged the women to organize. Soon, the Southern Baptist Convention established a Foreign Mission Board committee on women's

Henry Allen Tupper, Corresponding Secretary, Foreign Mission Board, 1872-93

work, the members of which were appointed each year. The committee was related to the Foreign Mission Board and reported to the Convention. Led by advocates such as Baltimorean J. W. M. Williams, the committees commended and encouraged the women. The Foreign Mission Board began to organize women's central committees in each state.[2]

Women were encouraged to cooperate with home missions work, but it was not until 1878 that the Convention encouraged formation of two central committees in each state, one for foreign and one for home missions, and two societies in every church. In 1881 the Committee on Woman's Work recommended that the Foreign Mission Board appoint a woman as superintendent of the work, but the Board did not consider this wise. Joshua Levering proposed a similar idea for the Home Mission Board three years later in 1884.[3]

When the Home Mission Board, reorganized in 1882, moved from Marion, Alabama, to Atlanta, and elected I. T. Tichenor as corresponding secretary, the women's state central committees and societies became more interested in home missions. With only thirty-one out of a total of no less than five hundred church women's societies contributing to the Home Mission Board, the Board noted with great interest the movement of Baltimore's Eutaw Place and First Baptist Churches to support the Levering Manual Labor School for Indians.[4]

Women's work grew steadily in the 1880s. Annie and other leaders helped develop state central committees such as the Woman's Baptist Home Mission Society of Maryland. More and more local societies were organized, and contributions to the mission boards increased. Though women could not serve as messengers to the Southern Baptist Convention, mission board leaders and key pastors constantly encouraged their work. After 1883 the women continued to meet separately each year in connection with Convention sessions.[5]

By 1887 the times were ripe for general organization. About three hundred women from many Southern states, with Annie

Armstrong and Mrs. James Pollard representing the Maryland societies, gathered in the Broadway Methodist Church in Louisville on May 6. Sallie Rochester Ford of Missouri presided, as she had done in three previous Convention-wide meetings. The program consisted of reports of women's work in the states and a message by Anne Bagby, missionary to Brazil. Annie reported for the Woman's Home Mission Society of Maryland, noting that the society had collected $2,415.48.

The women discussed thoroughly the merits of better organization, more efficient ways of getting out missions information, and more systematic giving. Mrs. G. A. Gammage of St. Louis read a paper suggesting the appointment of an advisory board to be in charge of the annual meetings and to correspond with the state central committees about their wants. The group recessed for a day to give the women time to think over this idea.

When the meeting reconvened, representative women from each state were asked to give their opinions. Annie favored organization, having led the Maryland Home Mission Society in the spring to draw up resolutions about the need for a general organization. She saw three reasons to organize: to bring before the Southern women the importance of the work; to secure accurate statistics; and to enable those who needed help to get it. All agreed that better organization was needed, but opinion was sharply divided as to timing. Some wanted immediate action; but others, who did not consider themselves delegates from their states, preferred postponement until a future meeting.

The women adopted unanimously a resolution to appoint a committee of three from each state to meet at the next Southern Baptist Convention and to decide on the advisability of organizing a general committee. They also appointed a committee of the secretaries of the state central committees to confer with the central committee of the state where the meeting would be held to select a presiding officer and arrange a program. Not considering this a separate and distinct organization, the women made it clear that they did not want to interfere with the management of the mission boards in appointing missionaries or directing work. They wanted only to be more efficient in collecting money and disseminating missionary information. Martha E. McIntosh, for a number of years a South Carolina woman's missions leader, was named chairman of the committee to arrange the next meeting.[6]

In her twenty-fifth anniversary history of Woman's Missionary Union, Fannie Exile Scudder Heck, who was president three times during the early years, said this about the roles of Martha McIntosh and Annie Armstrong in the Louisville meeting:

> Representing thus, in a marked way, the interests of both Home and Foreign Missions, knowing the practical needs and possibilities of woman's societies, wise, conservative, influential and tactful, they brought to the new endeavor a force which could but be felt.[7]

When they arrived home, Annie and Mrs. Pollard reported to the Foreign and Home Mission Societies the first chance they had. Mrs. Pollard gave the highlights of Anne Bagby's address, and Annie talked about organization. On May 9 Martha McIntosh had sent a circular and the resolutions adopted in Louisville to the state central committees and asked each to send three delegates empowered to decide the question to the next Convention. The Maryland women had not consolidated efforts into one state central committee or organization as many states did in the 1880s or early 1890s but retained two separate state organizations—the Woman's Foreign Mission Society of Maryland and the Woman's Home Mission Society of Maryland. Therefore, Miss McIntosh's request had to be considered by each state society.

In October, 1887, both Maryland societies discussed at length the subject of general organization and prayed for guidance about this important movement. Annie stated clearly to the Home Mission Society the value of a general organization as "a help to wider knowledge and better plans." She considered women's work "to be a force fore-ordained of God." The society elected her to represent them and commended Mrs. James Pollard to the Foreign Mission Society as a joint delegate from both Maryland societies.[8]

After much discussion, the Foreign Mission Society also approved of general organization. After conferring with the Home Mission Society, the society named Mrs. A. J. Rowland as delegate, with Mrs. O. F. Gregory and Mrs. James Pollard as alternates. This society instructed the delegates to vote for South Carolina as the location for the general committee.[9]

Several forces were in motion urging organization. The August, 1887, issue of the *Foreign Mission Journal*, the Foreign Mission Board journal, carried a report of the women's meeting in Louisville and a letter written in May from Lottie Moon, missionary to China. Miss Moon pointed to the intense and successful role Southern Methodist women were having in giving and sending missionary reinforcements and noted their enthusiasm, organizing power, and executive ability. Why, she questioned, were Baptists giving so little?[10]

The December, 1887, *Journal* carried another letter from Lottie Moon. She again wrote about what the Southern Methodist women were doing. She said: "I am convinced that one of the chief reasons our Southern Baptist women do so little is the lack of organization." She also noted the recent action of the Methodist Woman's Board of Missions to set aside a week of prayer and self-denial the week before Christmas, and to pray each evening for six months for the work at home and overseas.[11]

At least one state paper, *The Religious Herald* of Virginia, urged organization, noting what a power the Baptist women of the South could be. In an editorial in *The Religious Herald* in June, 1887, editor Alfred Elijah Dickinson reported on what Northern women were doing for missions and education. "They have their own Societies," he said, "and hold their own meetings, and when they speak in public, with rare exceptions, it is to their sex, and in a way in which our most fastidious Southern women could take no exception." The Northern Baptist women appointed missionaries and were soon to operate a training school.[12]

At Dickinson's request, Annie's sister, Alice Armstrong, wrote a series of articles under the pen name "Ruth Alleyn" in 1887 for *The Religious Herald*. The articles were about general organization for women's missionary societies. "Ruth Alleyn" gave the history of women's missionary organizations of various denominations since 1800, the phenomenal growth in the 1870s, and noted the strength in union. For example, since organization in 1878 Southern Methodist women had increased their contributions in nine years from $4,014 to $48,092. In comparison, Southern Baptist women who began to work for foreign missions in 1870 but without general organization gave only $11,333 in 1887, down from $16,895 in 1884. Because of these reasons, "Ruth Alleyn" noted, the Southern Baptist women had in Louisville passed resolutions to consider a general organization at their next meeting during the Southern Baptist Convention.[13]

"Ruth Alleyn" gave a number of reasons why general organization would help. A key reason was that the mission boards needed more money, and organization secured money. She wrote again about what a general organization would not do—appoint missionaries, expend its collections—and would do—disseminate missionary information, collect money. As expected, reactions to the articles were mixed, some pro and some con.[14]

With great anticipation, the women approached the Convention in Richmond, Virginia, in 1888. The times were ripe for organization. As "Ruth Alleyn" wrote in an article advocating general organization, the "Women's Century" and woman's enlarged usefulness and responsibilities in organized charities and women's organizations showed "that there is strength in union, help in council, power in knowledge, and inspiration in numbers."[15]

The nineteenth century was a century of struggle for women. The women's rights movement grew out of the abolitionist movement preceding the Civil War. During the century, women gained rights to higher education and to control their own property. After the Civil War, the priority was woman's suffrage. This early women's movement was highly religious, with church women as leaders. Church women from most major denominations began to form their own organizations, primarily on behalf of foreign missions. These groups gave women leadership roles. Southern Baptist women were about twenty years later than most denominations in forming a national organization. They were probably more conservative, preferring to work with the established mission boards. The press and the church were basically antifeminist, the church using the argument that the Bible ordained the subjugation of women. As women began to organize, there was a new wave of opposition from men to women's leadership or speaking in church. Some men viewed missionary societies as simply a version of the suffrage movement.[16]

Southern Baptist women continued to channel their energies toward missions. On May 14, 1888, in Richmond, Woman's Missionary Union was born as a national organization. On that day Annie Armstrong too began a new chapter in her life, for she emerged as a key leader in the movement. The women gathered for their now traditional yearly meeting on Friday, May 11, at the Broad Street Methodist Church. Thirty-two delegates were there from twelve states to decide on the advisability of a general organization. The thirty-eight-year-old Annie, one of Maryland's delegates, favored organization and was prepared for action.

There must have been an air of expectancy as the meeting started. Anne Whitfield, wife of Richmond pastor Theodore Whitfield, presided, though reluctant to do so. The planning committee had asked Dr. F. M. Ellis, Annie's pastor, to conduct the opening religious exercises. Feeling that the time had come for action and that wise and careful plans and proper channels would stifle criticism, Ellis commended the women and urged them to organize. He, of course, then left the meeting, according to custom.

Mrs. John Stout of South Carolina read a paper on organization. Annie immediately offered a resolution that the question be considered, with an informal and free interchange of views. After some misunderstanding, it was agreed to call the roll of states, with each state acting according to instructions. It is not surprising that Annie spoke first, stating, probably emphatically: "Maryland heartily approves of an organization." She backed this up with statistics and the success of other women's groups. In 1887 Southern Baptist women gave $11,333 to foreign missions and $5,000 to home missions, not even three cents each. Yet, Annie pointed out, thousands died daily without any hope or knowledge of the Savior.[17]

The other states followed one by one. In addition to Maryland, nine other states—South Carolina, Tennessee, Texas, Florida, Georgia, Louisiana, Missouri, Kentucky, and Arkansas—favored organization. Mississippi was not ready to make a decision, and Virginia wanted to refer the matter to the Southern Baptist Convention. Both of these needed further instructions from their states. Though North Carolina was not represented, Fannie Heck indicated the state was not yet ready to commit. Alabama had no appointed delegates.

Annie must have been extremely impatient. Opposing delay or waiting on Convention action, she urged the women to move on at once, for there was work to do. She reminded the delegates that prominent men in the Southern Baptist Convention had already spoken in favor of organization and the states had given instructions. It was moved to set aside the program and work on organization. Mrs. William E. Hatcher of Virginia was still reluctant and wanted to delay. After Annie suggested calling an extra meeting to ask and answer important questions, Mrs. James Pollard, another Maryland delegate, noted wisely that the matter had been under consideration for a year. The women voted to go on with the program and appointed a committee of one from each state to draft a constitution over the weekend and to report on Monday.

Martha McIntosh chaired the constitution committee, and

Annie represented Maryland. No doubt the committee labored long hours over the weekend and consulted with many people. It was important that the constitution meet with the approval of the men. Actually Annie and Mrs. Pollard had brought a constitution with them to Richmond. The two Maryland societies had studied organization. James Pollard, a lawyer, gave his clear mind and expert legal knowledge to the project, and Alice Armstrong was available with her great writing ability. No doubt Annie also consulted with Dr. Ellis and Joshua Levering. The Maryland Home Mission Society had adopted this constitution in April and empowered Annie and Mrs. Pollard to take it with them to Richmond. One must wonder whether the final constitution was largely a Baltimore product.[18]

On Monday morning, May 14, after missionary John Eager conducted the opening exercises, Alice Armstrong read a paper, "Special Obligations of Woman to Spread the Gospel." Her message was powerful. Alice pointed out that the delegates were in the position "where tiresome halting or painful wavering is alike needless. God's word comes to us in plain command and instructive example." The question was not whether they were obliged to spread the gospel but what the obligation was. Alice gave examples from the Bible where "earnest, godly women with willing hearts, ready hands and fire-crowned tongues, gave of their substance, their labor and their consecrated words for the cause of God and the good of their fellows." A Christian woman of America could begin to understand her obligation and debt when she compared her privileges with her degraded, hopeless sisters across the seas and nearby. Though "the gospel of Jesus Christ . . . was put into the hands of man and woman alike," Alice thought women were specially fitted to share the gospel. She believed a woman had "a tenderer heart and keener sensibilities than man," and "God-given endowments . . . and other latent abilities." There was work for women to do among women which only women could do, and Alice stated that Southern Baptist women could be a power for good, but not alone; each woman needed others to kindle her zeal.

Alice's conclusion pointed toward organization: *"Just at this point* comes in the aid of a general organization, a representative body which has delegated powers to stimulate and to sustain every such beginning of zealous work and to crystalize it into permanent form." This organization, she stated, worked through and by the church. She felt it was common sense that Southern Baptist women could be benefited by organization as others had been and that "religious work must be largely constructed on principles of common sense."[19]

Before the constitution committee reported, Martha McIntosh asked for special prayer for guidance. She stated that the committee had taken into consideration present state organizations and the work of the societies. The plan was to read the report as a whole, followed by a roll call of states. The Virginia delegates withdrew briefly for consultation. Ten states favored organization, and two did not vote. At that point, Mrs. Whitfield declined to preside any longer, and Annie was asked to take the chair. She led the delegates through an article-by-article vote on the constitution. Noted for efficiency and organizational ability, Annie, no doubt, presided most capably. She was used to doing so in the Maryland Home Mission Society. During the two Monday sessions, several changes in the constitution were approved.[20]

The new organization, to be known as the Executive Committee of the Woman's Mission Societies (later Woman's Missionary Union), had a twofold purpose. The first purpose was to distribute missionary information and stimulate missions effort, and the second was to collect and raise funds for missions. Several key initial decisions were made. The organization would work alongside and in support of the Southern Baptist Convention and the mission boards. It would not appoint missionaries or disburse funds, as many of the other denominational women's organizations were doing. The Foreign and Home Mission Boards would be asked to pay expenses, with all funds collected for missions sent to the Boards. The executive committee would also work through the state central committees.[21]

The women selected Baltimore as the location of the executive committee and elected Martha McIntosh as president. A committee, chaired by Miss McIntosh, selected the other officers— a vice-president from each state, a corresponding secretary, a recording secretary, and a treasurer. Annie Armstrong was selected as the corresponding secretary. Her duties were to secure annual reports from the states, conduct the correspondence of the executive committee, organize societies, and conduct any necessary business. There would be a local committee of managers with nine members. Alice Armstrong became one of the nine local managers.

With the exception of Martha McIntosh and vice-presidents from nine states, all of the officers were Maryland women. These included Mrs. A. J. Rowland, vice-president; Annie Armstrong, corresponding secretary; Mrs. James Pollard, recording secretary; and Mrs. John Pullen, treasurer. Nine Maryland women were selected for the local board: Mrs. J. H. Brittain, Mrs. James Tyler, Mrs. F. M. Ellis, Mrs. O. F. Gregory, Mrs. J. J. G. Riley, Miss Addie Wilson, Miss Lily Graves, Miss Alice Armstrong, and Mrs. W. J. Brown. The local committee was most significant, for this group of women conducted the business of the new organization between annual meetings.[22]

Little did Annie realize when she left Richmond in May, 1888, that this new role would, in essence, be her life for the next eighteen years. She would give it her body, heart, and soul. She truly was in charge.

Notes (See pages 295-310 for Key to Sources.)

1. *The Religious Herald,* May 14, 1885; *The Baltimore Baptist,* June 25, 1885, May 6, 1886; *The Heathen Helper,* June, 1886.

2. SBC Annuals, 1872-1876; FMB minutes, April 30, July 1, October 7, 1872, June 10, July 1, 1878; H. A. Tupper to Lily Graves, December 2, 1878,

FMB; Hunt and Allen, *History of Woman's Missionary Union,* pp. 13-16.

3. SBC Annuals, 1877-1884; Hunt and Allen, *History of Woman's Missionary Union,* pp. 16-18.

4. SBC Annuals, 1881-1882; Arthur B. Rutledge, *Mission to America,* p. 40; Mary Emily Wright, *The Missionary Work of the Southern Baptist Convention,* p. 15.

5. SBC Annuals, 1885-1886.

6. *The Baltimore Baptist,* May 12, October 27, 1887; *The Courier-Journal,* May 7-8, 1887; *FMJ,* August, 1887; "Sketch and Constitution of the Woman's Missionary Societies, Auxiliary to Southern Baptist Convention," WMU; *The Religious Herald,* July 28, 1887; Minutes, WHMS, October 18, 1887.

7. Fannie E. S. Heck, *In Royal Service,* pp. 113-114.

8. *The Baltimore Baptist,* June 23, October 27, 1887; Secretary's Report, WFMS, 1887; "Sketch and Constitution of the Woman's Missionary Societies, Auxiliary to Southern Baptist Convention," WMU; Circular letter, May 9, 1887, WMU; Annie W. Armstrong, "Women as Helpers in God's Kingdom," p. 4, WMU; *Encyclopedia of Southern Baptists,* 2:1527-1541.

9. Secretary's report, WFMS, 1887.

10. *FMJ,* August, 1887.

11. Ibid., December, 1887.

12. *The Religious Herald,* June 9, 1887.

13. Armstrong, "Women as Helpers in God's Kingdom," p. 7; *The Seminary Magazine,* February, 1900, p. 252; *The Religious Herald,* July 28, November 10, December 1, December 8, December 29, 1887.

14. *The Religious Herald,* December 29, 1887, January 19, January 26, February 2, March 22, April 19, 1888.

15. Ibid., November 10, 1887.

16. Barbara Sinclair Decker, *The Women's Movement,* pp. 246-268; Judith Hole and Ellen Levine, *Rebirth of Feminism,* pp. 2-12; Leon McBeth, *Women in Baptist Life,* pp. 51-52, 62-63, 93.

17. Minutes, the Woman's Meeting in Richmond, Virginia, May 11, 1888, WMU.

18. Ibid.; *The Baltimore Sun,* May 12, 1888; Mrs. H. M. Wharton, "As My Mother Knew Them," *Report,* WMU, 1938, p. 154; Minutes, WHMS, April 19, 1888.

19. Alice Armstrong, "Special Obligations of Woman to Spread the Gospel," WMU.

20. Minutes, the Woman's Meeting in Richmond, Virginia, May 14, 1888, WMU.

21. Ibid.; Constitution and By-Laws, 1888, WMU.

22. Ibid.

4
Organizational Genius

Annie Armstrong lost no time in assuming her role as an officer of the new organization. During the women's meeting in Richmond on May 14, 1888, she reported that the Executive Committee of Woman's Mission Societies and the work of the Maryland Baptist Mission Rooms were not connected. However, the executive committee could hold its meetings at the rooms and would of course benefit from the Mission Room's publications.[1]

Even at this early meeting, Annie was able to distinguish between the multiple leadership roles she held in various organizations. For the next eighteen years, she would effectively juggle three leadership balls simultaneously. Until 1906 Annie served as the unsalaried corresponding secretary of Woman's Missionary Union, SBC,[2] unsalaried corresponding secretary of the Maryland Baptist Mission Rooms, and president of the Baptist Woman's Home Mission Society of Maryland. She always insisted that the proper organization be given credit when credit was due.[3]

In Richmond the women took three actions which determined immediate priorities for Annie and the infant organization. The first related to finances. They agreed that all missions funds collected would be sent to the mission boards. Feeling the need to form a close, inseparable bond with the boards, the women decided to ask the Foreign and Home Mission Boards to pay the expenses of the executive committee. Annie and Martha McIntosh were appointed to confer with the Boards.

The second action approved support of a project requested by the Home Mission Board to aid in building a
church and enlarging a cemetery in Havana, Cuba. The third
action related to communications. The WMU executive committee was instructed to ask for a column in the *Foreign
Mission Journal* and to send information to *The Heathen Helper*
and *The Baptist Basket*, the two papers prepared by Kentucky
women.[4]

By constitution and bylaws, the new organization was set up to
do its work. The WMU executive committee, composed of the
officers and the local Baltimore committee of nine managers,
conducted the business of the organization between annual
sessions. Annie was in a key position as corresponding secretary.
Though the state vice-presidents were entitled to sit with the
committee, they were actually an advisory board. With the
exception of the Maryland vice-president, they did not attend
WMU executive committee meetings in Baltimore. The president presided over executive committee meetings and at annual
sessions. When she was absent, the vice-president from the state
where the committee was located presided.[5] Since the committee was located in Baltimore, this meant the Maryland vice-
president presided.

Because of this arrangement, the Maryland women were
influential in establishing precedents and directing the work of
WMU, SBC. Even in those early days, Annie's spiritual strength
and organizational genius began to be felt. There is no doubt that
she, in essence, controlled the organization by the respect she
gained and her influence over the executive committee and the
Maryland officers. She had worked with these women for several
years as they managed the Maryland Mission Rooms and in the
Maryland Home and Foreign Mission Societies.

What kind of person was the newly elected corresponding
secretary of Woman's Missionary Union? Annie was a command-
ing personality, physically and mentally. She was stately and
erect and six feet tall. It is said that Mrs. Armstrong trained her

daughters in posture as children and that they practiced with broomsticks to be ramrod straight. As was customary in her day, Annie wore long, black, blue, or gray skirts or dresses, high-necked blouses with jabots or brooches, high-topped shoes, hats, and gloves. No doubt she bowed to Victorian decorum and worked wearing a hat. She was an Eastern lady. Annie was not especially attractive, but her appearance was pleasant. Some considered her rather austere, set in her ways, and hard to get acquainted with. She had of course learned the social graces and applied them appropriately. Most people thought her sister Alice was much more outgoing and approachable.[6]

What kind of leader was Annie? Many persons in her day used the word *indefatigable* to describe her. She had seemingly unlimited energy and a deep inspiration to work. She was untiring, resourceful, persevering, always busy. Her spirit seemed indomitable. She had a strong personality, was exacting, and never at a loss for words. Though she let her opinion be known in no uncertain terms, she allowed a person to disagree with her. Annie was an organizational genius—highly skilled, able to manage large affairs, and with executive and business ability. She could stick to ceaseless, toilsome, little details, and numberless duties in a day when she had to depend on volunteer workers, little equipment, and a lack of WMU field workers in the states. She was faithful and gave all she had to the task—her time, thoughts, strengths, and influence. No task was too hard, no day too long for her.[7]

Key leaders of her day acknowledged Annie's abilities. Fannie E. S. Heck, who as president of Woman's Missionary Union, SBC, worked closely with Annie in the 1890s, labeled her as a born leader. Dr. W. O. Carver, longtime missions professor at The Southern Baptist Theological Seminary, described Annie's executive ability as "rare generalship." Franklin Howard Kerfoot, one of her pastors whom she especially respected and who later became secretary of the Home Mission Board, said she had "a will as imperious as Julius Caesar's." Ethlene Boone Cox, a

national WMU president and author of the fiftieth anniversary
history of Woman's Missionary Union, said of Annie: "She
stamped her life upon her generation and upon generations to
come."

Annie's rally cry throughout her service was taken from
Exodus 14:15, "Go forward." Believing that "not to advance was
to retrograde," she gave this challenge often. "Go forward" was
adopted as the first motto of the organization, along with the
Scripture verse, Hebrews 10:24. Because of her strong faith and
belief that the Lord directed a Christian's life, Annie was highly
motivated to serve the Lord. She saw service or work as being
"for God's glory and man's highest good." As long as there was
one person not yet reached with the gospel, or one left not at
work, there was something for her to do. Since Annie believed
firmly that God was a help in time of need and directed the
"untried future," she was able to persist and face the future with
optimism. She wrote: "But the future lies all before us . . . Shall
it only be a slight advance upon what we usually do? Ought it not
to be a bound, a leap forward to altitudes of endeavor and
success undreamed of before?"[8]

For the first four years of holding office, Annie worked closely
with Martha E. McIntosh, the WMU, SBC, president. Known
for her gentleness, quiet dignity, and patient efficiency, the
forty-year-old Miss McIntosh seemed eminently qualified to
lead the organization and to match the equally qualified, strong-
willed, thirty-eight-year-old Annie Armstrong. Martha McIntosh was known and loved by the women. She was well educated
and had served as chairman of the South Carolina Central
Committee, as well as leading her church's missionary society.
Thus, these two single young women were destined to shape the
new organization.[9]

Apparently Annie and Martha respected each other's abilities.
They worked together well from 1888 to 1891, Miss McIntosh's
years of service. There is evidence that later there were some
areas of disagreement between the two. This especially came to

Martha E. McIntosh, President, WMU, SBC, 1888-92

light after the turn of the century when Martha McIntosh was Mrs. T. P. Bell. Martha was a strong proponent of states' rights and believed in states doing their own work. Annie was busy strengthening societies and the general organization, though she fully recognized state officers.[10]

With these two leaders at the helm, the Executive Committee of WMU, SBC, held its first meeting in Baltimore on June 9, 1888. Martha McIntosh presided. Though she had to travel to Baltimore from Society Hill, South Carolina, for the meetings, Martha took this responsibility seriously. During her four years of office, she presided over at least one-third of the committee meetings. Meetings usually were held monthly in the Maryland Mission Rooms except for July and August. When Miss McIntosh was absent, Mrs. A. J. Rowland, Maryland vice-president, presided, or in her absence, Annie Armstrong.[11]

The WMU executive committee early established a pattern for the WMU Annual Meetings which were held for the election of officers and transaction of business. The committee decided to hold the annual meeting in connection with the Southern Baptist Convention, on the morning of the first day of the Convention, with other meetings to be determined as needed. The annual meetings usually included missionary messages, reports, recommendations from the mission boards and executive committee, response to organization questions, the election of officers, and transaction of business. The committee secured input from state leaders in planning the meetings. Often there was a Sunday afternoon missions rally, featuring missionaries and the corresponding secretaries of the mission boards. Annie was always a key participant in these rallies. In 1891 she led a special Sunday afternoon mission service for young people.[12] The WMU Annual Meetings were held in Memphis in May, 1889, Fort Worth in 1890, and Birmingham in 1891.[13]

The first question the WMU executive committee faced in June, 1888, was expenses. Annie and Martha McIntosh asked the two Boards to meet expenses of the committee so all money collected could be sent to the Boards. Dr. I. T. Tichenor indicated the Home Mission Board's willingness to pay half the expenses. Tichenor had already expressed his gratitude for the work of home mission societies. Dr. H. A. Tupper said the Foreign Mission Board would do even more than requested— pay expenses in proportion to receipts from the societies. This would amount to more than one-half.

The mission boards continued to assure WMU of their support and that they would meet the executive committee's expenses. Total expenses for the first year's operation, May, 1888 to April, 1889, amounted to only $353.04.[14]

Annie was extremely frugal and conscious of expenses. For example, she sent packages to the states by freight rather than by express, to keep expenses down. In her letters to the mission boards, she often expressed her concern over expenses. She refused ever to accept a salary. Her first desire was to raise more money for missions.[15]

The organization's first missions project was in response to a Home Mission Board request. Tichenor wrote a letter to the Convention-wide women's meeting in Richmond in 1888 about the critical need for a church building in Cuba and asked the women to help raise funds for the church and lot during the next year.[16]

This project must have excited Annie. In 1887 the Maryland Woman's Home Mission Society, of which she was president, had adopted Cuba as a new department of work. Also, the Maryland Mission Rooms Committee had discussed distributing the brick cards already printed by the Home Mission Board if the women did not organize in Richmond. The brick cards were novel, the outside of the double card picturing Alberto J. Diaz, pastor of the First Baptist Church in Havana, and giving some facts about Cuba and the need for a church building. The two inner sides were covered with twenty oblong red blocks resembling bricks. The plan was for the holder to solicit ten-cent subscriptions, and, when paid, write the donor's name in the red space. The card would be worth two dollars when filled.[17]

In her two Maryland leadership positions, Annie no doubt had correspondence with Tichenor before May, 1888, about Cuba and the brick cards. She had utmost respect and affection for I. T. Tichenor. The sixty-three-year-old, full-bearded, balding gentleman became leader of the depressed Home Mission Board in 1882, the same year the Maryland Baptist Woman's Home Mission Society was organized. Tichenor had rich experience as a pastor, in the Southern Baptist Convention, and as a college president. Noted for his statesmanship, Tichenor helped the Board make an amazing recovery, saved the Southern Baptist Convention during troubled years, and stemmed the tide that was turning Southern Baptists toward the North. Tichenor led in beginning missions work in Cuba.[18] As a loyal supporter of missions and the Southern Baptist Convention, Annie must have applauded Tichenor's efforts.

The WMU executive committee undertook immediately the work for the church in Cuba. This work was ratified by the Maryland Woman's Home Mission Society. The plan was to raise the money by using brick cards. Annie distributed over eleven thousand brick cards through states to societies, and funds flowed back in through state central committees to the Home Mission Board. At the WMU Annual Meeting in Memphis in 1889, Diaz addressed the meeting, and a letter of thanks was read from Tichenor. The women continued the effort through 1890.[19]

Annie helped institute another significant area of work for the Home Mission Board in 1890—sending boxes to frontier missionaries. Ebenezer Lee Compere, superintendent of missions work in Arkansas, wrote about the plight of the destitute ministers on the frontier home missions fields. The WMU executive committee discussed sending boxes of clothing and other necessities to these missionaries and instructed Annie to confer with the Home Mission Board about this idea.

On occasion, the mission board leaders met with the WMU

executive committee to confer about the work and to discuss recommendations for the next year. It was a bedrock principle of WMU, SBC, because of its auxiliary status, not to direct policies of the mission boards but to carry out suggestions from the Boards. Tichenor met with the committee in Baltimore in January, 1890. He affirmed the idea of frontier boxes. To avoid showing favoritism, however, he indicated that the Board would not determine who should be aided but would endorse the WMU executive committee's work.[20]

Dr. Tichenor wrote an impassioned letter to the WMU Annual Meeting in Fort Worth in 1890 about the need for frontier boxes. He urged the women to do something for these frontier missionaries and their families. He wrote:

> It is a fact that many of our missionaries labor on the frontier and elsewhere, are very inadequately paid for their services, undergoing many privations. They are exposed to all of the changes of weather, winter and summer, in our changeful climate. To meet their appointments, they ofttimes face cold, storm and darkness, swim swollen rivers, sleep in houses through which whistle the wintry blasts; preach in winter without fires, and in summer without shelters; and are thus dying daily for the Master and the souls of men. The families of these hearty pioneers undergo equal privations. In the long absence of husband and father, they are often left without protection and without adequate supplies of food or clothing. Their children are growing up without social advantages, and without books or opportunities for mental improvement. These men are laying the foundations of our denominational prosperity, are the burden bearers, the real heros of our missionary force. In these frontier fields are to be found the real hardships of missionary life, at home or abroad.[21]

The women approved the recommendation. Annie went to work for a cause which she pursued relentlessly during her years as WMU, SBC, corresponding secretary. The frontier and its missionaries were dear to her heart. Over the years, she wrote literally hundreds of letters to them. She had on hand for societies requesting a name a list of missionaries needing help. Annie developed a concise plan related to frontier boxes which gave each society responsibility to find out about specific needs for its assigned missionary.[22]

The idea immediately caught fire. As Annie was returning home on the train from Fort Worth, she was approached by Annie Grace Tartt of Livingston, Alabama. Having been impressed by the need and wanting to respond, Miss Tartt asked Annie for the name of a frontier missionary. This box was probably the first to be sent. Annie was especially pleased with Alabama's response. By November, this newly organized state indicated it expected to send thirty boxes.[23] When more societies wanted to send boxes than Annie had names of missionaries, Tichenor agreed to send additional names. The first year societies sent seventy-one boxes at a cash value of $4,419.80 to missionaries in North Carolina, Florida, Louisiana, Texas, Arkansas, Missouri, Indian Territory, and Idaho.[24]

The WMU executive committee backed other home missions projects, and Annie handled the numerous details. These projects included supporting a school for girls in Cuba and building chapels on the frontier and other home missions fields. This latter effort became part of the 1892 centennial celebration of the beginning of the modern missions movement.[25]

Tichenor met again with the WMU executive committee in October, 1890. The women discussed with him a number of items—the school in Cuba; frontier boxes; his support of the prayer card in *Our Home Field,* the Board's journal; WMU columns in state papers; and missionary work in West Arkansas. They also talked with him about a WMU column in *Kind Words,* the weekly Sunday School paper for children published by the Home Mission Board.[26]

Eager to inspire zeal for foreign missions as well as home missions, Annie, not long after the 1888 Richmond meeting, started searching for an exciting project related to foreign missions. She approached H. A. Tupper, who had been corresponding secretary of the Foreign Mission Board since 1872, about some special area of work to present to the women.[27]

Tupper, now seventy, had early given impetus to women's work. Slender and medium-sized, Tupper in some ways resembled the great South Carolina senator, John C. Calhoun, with his clean-shaven face and fine, long, gray hair combed straight back. Annie did not seem to personally enjoy working with Tupper. She considered that his actions indicated not much regard for "the work done by those in charge of the Woman's Missionary Union and the Mission Rooms." She later wrote: "While Dr. Tupper was Secretary of the Foreign Board, we were perfectly aware of the fact that we could hope for very little sympathy from him or cooperation in our work. This we regarded as due largely to his peculiar turn of mind, and went forward as well as we could laboring under the circumstances." Though maybe he did so unintentionally, Tupper threw obstacles in the way, Annie thought. She seemed to have a hard time getting to consult with Tupper about the work he wanted WMU to do. This was frustrating to Annie since she believed WMU was auxiliary to the Board and should seek the Board's advice about most matters. Annie felt "that it was the greatest relief when Dr. Tupper resigned in 1893." Annie's feelings about Tupper were not shared by everyone. Since the 1870s Tupper had been considered a friend of women's work and noted as guiding the women's efforts and encouraging organization. In 1888 he agreed readily for the Foreign Mission Board to support Woman's Missionary Union, SBC.[28]

In 1888 Tupper had just the project idea for Annie. For a couple of years, missionary Lottie Moon had been begging Tupper for reinforcements for the interior of China. She wrote that the doors were wide open for reaching women and children in Pingtu and other villages. So much more needed to be done than the present inadequate missionary force could do. Lottie Moon herself was near the breaking point and desperately needed a furlough. She did not understand the lack of Southern Baptist response to such a critical need and appealed in every way possible. In addition to urging the women to organize, Miss

Moon suggested setting aside the week before Christmas as a week of prayer and offering for missions.[29]

Tupper wisely saw a way to merge the China need with Annie's desire for a project. In July, 1888, he wrote Annie, sending Lottie Moon's May 24 letter requesting women workers for Pingtu. Feeling that "the only hope of China is through the women," Tupper considered this project a clear work for the women and urged the Woman's Missionary Union to undertake it. Lottie Moon was much encouraged by the action Tupper took.[30]

Annie presented the possibility in October at the next WMU executive committee meeting. She read the letter from Lottie Moon telling about the hunger for the gospel in Pingtu and the immediate need for at least two more women missionaries. Miss Moon also requested prayer. Tupper had indicated that it would take two thousand dollars to equip and pay the salaries of two missionaries. The committee agreed to ask Southern Baptist women to make a special effort to raise two thousand dollars to send two women to help Lottie Moon.[31]

The plan was for women to collect offerings during Christmas, when most Christians were especially in prayer. Women would bring their offerings to a meeting on January 9 during the World's Week of Prayer.[32] As instructed, Annie prepared and distributed materials at once. These materials included three thousand circular letters from Martha McIntosh to societies; three thousand programs for the January 9 meeting; thirty thousand offering envelopes (one kind for the women, two for Sunday Schools); and one thousand notices about ordering envelopes. Using volunteers, Annie got the materials out quickly.[33]

On January 9, 1889, women throughout the South met to pray and brought their offerings. On that same day, Lottie Moon wrote Annie, thanking the WMU executive committee for its response to her appeal. She was "holding on" until the reinforcements arrived.[34] The project was successful. A total of $3,315.26

was collected, and three, not two, missionaries were sent to North China. The expense to the Foreign Mission Board was only $72.82.[35]

The Week of Prayer and Christmas offering continued annually thereafter, and Annie prepared many materials for use in the observances. For the next three years, the money continued to go toward paying the salaries of the reinforcements sent out in 1889 and sending additional missionaries to China. The WMU also took on other foreign missions projects suggested by the Board. These included raising enough money to support all women missionaries, giving information about the new field of Japan, aiding in collecting funds for a chapel in Rio de Janeiro, Brazil, and involving children and young people in making gifts for the chapel building.[36]

Often Annie wrote Theodore Percy Bell, assistant corresponding secretary of the Foreign Mission Board and editor of *The Foreign Mission Journal,* rather than Tupper. She was used to dealing with Bell, who was closer to her age. They consulted frequently about numerous editorial and printing details. Annie said that "if it had not been for the help Dr. T. P. Bell gave, I think it would have been utterly impossible for us to have persevered in our work."[37]

Bell, noted for his strong missionary convictions and zeal, met with the WMU executive committee in February, 1890, and again in 1891.[38] Sometimes Annie tested an idea out on Bell or asked for his personal opinion. She respected his judgment and advice. Often these ideas related to fresh and novel ways of presenting the Christmas offering or some other foreign missions object. She urged more than once that Sunday Schools be asked to make a Christmas offering. On one occasion, Annie suggested that if Bell liked her plan that he present it to Tupper and the Board as his plan and not hers. She felt that men were not receptive to plans coming from women.[39]

Friction persisted between Annie and Tupper. In 1890 their misunderstanding centered around a chapel for Rio de Janeiro.

In July, 1890, the Missouri Central Committee reported on its collection for this memorial chapel and asked the national WMU to cooperate with the Missouri ladies by observing a special day when collections would be taken for the building fund. As was her custom, Annie immediately wrote Tupper for instructions. He thought WMU should stick to its stated plan of work for the year, writing: "The best thing, in the matter of foreign missions, the men and women of the country can do in my judgment is to raise money for the Board and let the Board appropriate it."

Annie and Martha McIntosh conferred carefully and asked Tupper to reconsider since the request came from Missouri. Missouri was a divided state, and Annie wanted to interest these women in the "general work." Tupper responded: "Unable to communicate with the Board in time, the corresponding secretary will assume the responsibility of endorsing the judgment of the Executive Committee about acceding to the request of the Missouri ladies, provided you do not prefer to wait more formal action on my return." Annie thought from his letter that Tupper had personally authorized action. After no response from another letter to Tupper, WMU moved ahead, agreed to cooperate with Missouri, and designated a memorial day in March. Annie visited Tupper in Richmond in November for further instructions about the plan. She was floored when he told her the Board had never approved the chapel. She wrote: "It was a little strange for Dr. Tupper, when we wrote so repeatedly asking for instruction, that he did not tell us at once that the Board had not decided to build a chapel in Rio. Dr. Tupper, when I expressed my surprise, said, that the Board did not tell its plans until it was decided what was to be done." Annie felt the rug had been pulled out from under WMU, which was allowed to go public and ask for money before the object was approved by the Board. She wrote an explicit letter to H. H. Harris, president of the Board, stating: "Pardon me if I seem to be calling in question Dr. Tupper's judgment in this matter, but I do believe very thoroughly if our work is to amount to anything, we must not be placed in a position where it would be very clearly seen that we do not know what we are about."

In December, Tupper secured Board approval for the Rio chapel building. Again Annie asked him for instructions, this time about the amount of money the WMU could spend for literature for the appeal. She wrote Bell for advice, and the WMU executive committee conferred with Bell in February. Three years later in a letter to Willingham, Annie wrote that the "little misunderstanding" over the chapel "caused some feeling and the erection of the chapel in Rio was delayed."[40]

Annie was upset in 1891 over the laconic way she felt Tupper dealt with the annual Foreign Mission Board recommendations to the WMU, SBC. He did not give definite instructions as requested. Annie thought he could do so, since the WMU planned to raise forty thousand dollars for the Foreign Mission Board. Since the WMU was an auxiliary and not independent, Annie felt she needed explicit instructions about what the Board desired and to know that proposed lines of work were backed by the Board. Because of the Rio experience with Tupper, Annie wanted an official signature on the recommendations. When she learned that the Board had a committee on women's work, she conferred with the chairman, Dr. John Pollard of Richmond. The WMU executive committee empowered the WMU president and corresponding secretary to confer in the future with the chairman of the Foreign Mission Board's committee on women's work. This was Annie's way around Tupper.[41]

As soon as the WMU, SBC, organized, Annie directed her energies toward the state WMU central committees and built strong relationships with state leaders. Another WMU bedrock principle was the supremacy of the state central committees in state affairs. The states besieged Annie constantly with pleas for help in creating interest and doing the work. She kept up a running correspondence with the state WMU secretaries. She sent them information from other states, data about mission fields for their women's papers or the state Baptist papers, and instructions about the literature and distribution. She sent a sample copy of everything issued by the WMU executive committee to them for examination; states would then order what they needed and distribute the literature to societies. Annie reported to the WMU executive committee almost monthly about work in the states.[42]

Annie did not consider literature distribution drudgery. She saw potential and possibilities as the literature reached and was used by the societies. Literature provided knowledge, and Annie thought this about knowledge: "Knowledge is power, interest and inspiration." She was especially pleased with Mississippi's efforts, having sent that state thirty pounds of literature in the first six months.[43] Mississippi had become a member of the WMU in 1888, Alabama in 1889, and North Carolina in 1890. Western Arkansas and Indian Territory soon formed a central committee.[44]

One of Annie's first tasks in the summer of 1888 centered around developing literature and getting out missionary information. The Foreign Mission Board granted space in the *Foreign Mission Journal* for the WMU; Alice Armstrong was responsible for sending in copy monthly. With her first column in the July, 1888 issue, Alice began a long and successful pilgrimage in writing and editorial work, which she did for eighteen years on a voluntary basis. The *Journal* carried organization data, the prayer card, and, later, more information each month about the prayer card's topic for the month. Later *Our Home Field*, the Home Mission Board journal, also included a WMU column. A WMU executive committee member was designated responsibility for sending regular communications to *The Heathen Helper* and *The Baptist Basket*, the two Kentucky women's papers.[45]

In the early years, the WMU printed the messages delivered at the founding, a historical sketch about the origin and purpose of the WMU executive committee, and several other leaflets. Soon leaflets were being prepared for young people's and children's work. Annie saw to the editorial and publishing

Alice Armstrong

details. Through purchasing and using the prayer cards prepared
by the Maryland Mission Rooms, the WMU, SBC, established
its study and prayer plan. The four-page card which contained
information for daily prayer and study for use by individuals or in
missionary meetings was distributed by state WMU central
committees. In addition to the twelve topics on the prayer card,
Baptist journals and state papers carried supplemental information about each missions topic. Annie gathered this material,
much of which was available in the Maryland Mission Rooms, for
the papers.[46]

Dr. Samuel Boykin, editor of *Kind Words,* in 1890 offered the
WMU space in the Sunday School series for children. Though
the WMU executive committee was reluctant to enter any new
lines of effort or to take on more work for Annie, it accepted the
offer. This series was a way of giving missionary information to
children in Sunday School.[47]

In May, 1891, in Birmingham, the Southern Baptist Convention authorized the formation of a third board, the Sunday
School Board, to be located in Nashville, Tennessee. Though her
fellow Baltimoreans opposed forming another board, Annie
became a loyal supporter. She worked closely with James Marion
Frost and T. P. Bell, the early corresponding secretaries, for
many years. The Board had to compete with the established
American Baptist Publication Society for the privilege of supplying literature to Southern Baptist churches. Annie supported
the Sunday School Board even though her Levering cousins
backed the Publication Society and her own church used that
society's Sunday School literature. Frost gratefully acknowledged Annie's support many times. He later wrote: "From the
first the W. M. U. and its Secretary have been earnest supporters of this Board, and much of its success must be attributed
to them. Indeed they are so active in the work of all the boards
. . . and so helpful, that we have come to look upon the W.M.U.
as one of the most potent factors in every onward movement."[48]

Annie carried out faithfully the instructions of the WMU

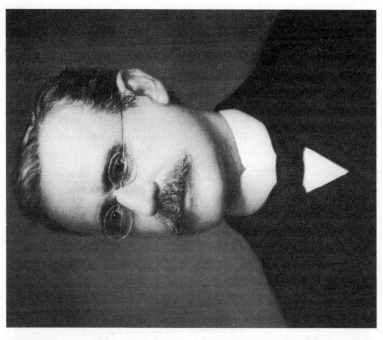

Left: James Marion Frost, Corresponding Secretary, Sunday School Board, 1891-93; 1896-1916. Right: T. P. Bell, Corresponding Secretary, Sunday School Board, 1893-96

executive committee. This involved writing many letters, in a day before typewriters. She corresponded regularly with the mission board secretaries, the states, and the missionaries. During the first year, Annie wrote personally 637 letters and 182 postcards. She doubled the letters written the second year, and in the third she got out 2,737. It is said that her writing hand was damaged permanently by this effort and never regained its strength. She got some relief in 1890 when the mission boards authorized purchase of a typewriter and employment of a salaried clerk to do routine work.[49]

Late in 1891 Martha McIntosh decided to decline another year as WMU president. There were indications then that Fannie E. S. Heck, president of the North Carolina Woman's Missionary Union, would be elected national president at the 1892 meeting. Annie wrote to Miss Heck to see if she would accept the position "should the ladies desire it."[50]

What had WMU accomplished in these three formative years? The new leader, Annie, had successfully worked new and untried fields. Annie built strong relationships with the two mission boards and the state WMU central committees. She and the organization found their way and began to shape the future. Publishing and literature distribution were put in place. Mission gifts increased from a total of $30,773.69 for both mission boards in 1889 to $38,990 in 1891. Each year at the Southern Baptist Convention, the mission boards applauded the efforts of the women in getting out missions information and in raising money.[51]

Though Annie was pleased with the initial successes, she was never satisfied. In 1889 at the WMU Annual Meeting, she urged the women not to be content, since they were still only averaging five cents each annually for missions. She called for united efforts and for the motto "Forward" to be blazoned on their banners, held high by leaders, and followed by members. In 1890 she stressed the opening of new doors in missions for women and the need to advance into the future. In 1891, calling for renewed effort fortified by prayer, Annie gave a reminder that the time was short.[52] The strong-willed young woman had taken charge well and emerged as a missions leader.

Notes (See pages 295-310 for Key to Sources.)

1. Minutes, the Woman's Meeting, Richmond, Virginia, May 14, 1888.
2. The organization was officially named Woman's Missionary Union, Auxiliary to Southern Baptist Convention, at the Annual Meeting in Fort Worth in 1890. Minutes, WMU executive committee, May 22, 1890. Hereafter cited as WMU minutes.
3. Annie Armstrong to T. P. Bell, September 16, 1890, FMB; Annie Armstrong to R. J. Willingham, March 30, 1895, FMB.
4. Minutes, the Woman's Meeting, Richmond, Virginia, May 14, 1888.
5. Ibid.; Constitution and By-Laws, 1888, WMU.
6. Interviews with Rosalind Robinson Levering, 1978, Elizabeth Marshall Evans, 1982, H. O. Walters, 1982, Robert R. Pumphrey, 1982, Virginia Atkinson, 1982; Memories by W. Clyde Atkins, June 11, 1975; Kate T. Davis, "I Remember Miss Annie," *Royal Service*, March, 1949; Harriett S. Levering, "A Sketch of 'Miss Annie,'" *The Window of YWA*, March, 1935.
7. Interviews with Rosalind Robinson Levering, 1978, H. O. Walters, 1982, Ethlene Boone Cox, *Following in His Train*, p. 66; Heck, *In Royal Service*, pp. 133-134, 165; "Memoirs of W.M.U. Annual Meeting, Memphis, Tennessee, May 11-13, 1889," *Report*, WMU, 1925.
8. *The Baptist Argus*, March 9, 1899, November 1, 1900; Boone, p. 66; Heck, pp. 133-134, 165; WMU minutes, June 9, 1888; *Reports*, WMU, 1889-1892.
9. *Report*, WMU, 1889; "Memoirs of W.M.U. Annual Meeting, Memphis, Tennessee, May 11-13, 1889," *Report*, WMU, 1925; *Encyclopedia of Southern Baptists*, 3:1612. McIntosh is listed as Martha E. McIntosh Bell in the *Encyclopedia*, as she later married T. P. Bell.
10. Martha McIntosh to Annie Armstrong, November 16, 1894, FMB; Annie Armstrong to R. J. Willingham, December 10, 1894, FMB. See chapters 8 and 10.
11. WMU minutes, 1888-1892.
12. Constitution, 1888, WMU; WMU minutes, 1888-1891; *FMJ*, June, 1891.
13. *Reports*, WMU, 1889-1891.
14. WMU minutes, June 9, 1888, January 24, 1890; HMB minutes, May 25, 1888; FMB minutes, June 4, 1888, March 4, 1890; H. A. Tupper to M. McIntosh, June 6, 1888, FMB; *Report*, WMU, 1889.
15. Annie Armstrong to Mrs. F. B. Davis, August 26, 1890, SWBTS; Correspondence, 1888-1906.

16. Minutes, the Woman's Meeting, Richmond, Virginia, May 14, 1888.

17. *Report,* WHMS, 1886; *The Baltimore Baptist,* February 10, July 28, 1887, June 21, 1888; Minutes, Mission Rooms Committee, 1886-1888; Secretary's book, Mission Rooms, 1888.

18. *Encyclopedia of Southern Baptists,* 3:1416-1417; *The Heathen Helper,* June 1883; WMU minutes, June 9, 1888.

19. Materials in WMU Scrapbook I, WMU; *Reports,* WMU, 1889-1890.

20. WMU minutes, December 12, 1889, January 24, September 11, 1890.

21. *The Baltimore Baptist,* June 10, 1890.

22. Ibid.; *Report,* WMU, 1890.

23. *Labor of Love, A History of Woman's Missionary Union Auxiliary to Alabama Baptist Convention, 1889-1939,* p. 40; Annie Armstrong to Mrs. F. B. Davis, November 4, 1890, SWBTS.

24. WMU minutes, October 15, 1890; *Report,* WMU, 1891.

25. *Reports,* WMU, 1890-1891.

26. WMU minutes, October 15, 1890.

27. H. A. Tupper to Annie Armstrong, July 24, 1888, FMB.

28. *Encyclopedia of Southern Baptists,* 2:1432,1510-1514; *The Heathen Helper,* June, 1883; Annie Armstrong to R. J. Willingham, January 19, 1894, FMB.

29. Lottie Moon to H. A. Tupper, 1886-1888, FMB; Allen, *The New Lottie Moon Story,* pp. 155-180; Bobbie Sorrill, "The History of the Week of Prayer for Foreign Missions"; *Baptist History and Heritage,* pp. 28-29.

30. H. A. Tupper to Annie Armstrong, July 24, 1888, FMB; H. A. Tupper to Lottie Moon, July 24, 1888, FMB; Lottie Moon to H. A. Tupper, August 27, 1888, FMB.

31. WMU minutes, October 11, 1888.

32. Ibid.

33. Ibid.; Week of Prayer for Foreign Missions materials, 1888, WMU Scrapbook I, WMU.

34. Lottie Moon to Annie Armstrong, January 9, 1889, FMB.

35. FMB minutes, March 7, 1889; T. P. Bell to Annie Armstrong, March 8, 1889, FMB; WMU minutes, January 31, 1889; *Report,* WMU, 1890.

36. *Reports,* WMU, 1889-1891; Annie Armstrong to H. A. Tupper, February 28, 1890, FMB; FMB minutes, April 7, 1890; H. A. Tupper to Annie Armstrong, March 23, 1891, FMB; Annie Armstrong to T. P. Bell, May 20, 1890, FMB.

37. Annie Armstrong to T. P. Bell, 1889-1893, FMB; Annie Armstrong to R. J. Willingham, January 19, 1894, FMB; *Encyclopedia of Southern Baptists,* 1:155.

38. WMU minutes, February 24, 1890, February 21, 1891.

39. Annie Armstrong to T. P. Bell, September 2, September 4, September 8, October 2, 1890, FMB.

40. Annie Armstrong to T. P. Bell, November 18, 1890, January 9, 1891, FMB; Annie Armstrong to H. H. Harris, November 28, 1890, FMB; H. A.

Tupper to Annie Armstrong, December 3, December 5, 1890, January 6, 1891, FMB; Annie Armstrong to H. A. Tupper, December 4, December 6, 1890, January 8, 1891, FMB; Annie Armstrong to R. J. Willingham, November 18, 1893, FMB.

41. Annie Armstrong to H. A. Tupper, February 26, March 20, 1891, FMB; WMU minutes, April 9, 1891.

42. WMU minutes, 1888-1891; Annie Armstrong to Mrs. F. B. Davis, August 26, August 29, October 22, November 4, 1890, SWBTS.

43. WMU minutes, October 11, 1888; *Report*, WMU, 1892.

44. *Reports*, WMU, 1889-1891.

45. WMU minutes, June 9, October 11, November 30, 1888; FMB minutes, June 4, 1888; H. A. Tupper to M. McIntosh, June 6, 1888, FMB; *FMJ*, July-December 1888; *Reports*, WMU, 1889-1891.

46. Ibid.; *The Baltimore Baptist*, March 21, 1889.

47. WMU minutes, May 22, June 12, September 11, October 9, 1890; Annie Armstrong to T. P. Bell, September 16, 1890, FMB; *FMJ*, March 1891.

48. *The Baltimore Baptist*, May 7, 1891; Scope and Content Note, Frost-Bell Papers, SSB; SBC Annual, 1905; J. M. Frost, *The Sunday School Board, Southern Baptist Convention, Its History and Work*, p. 44; Annie Armstrong to T. P. Bell, July 10, 1893, February 16, March 4, March 22, 1895, SSB; Annie Armstrong to R. J. Willingham, November 1, 1894, March 31, 1895, FMB.

49. *The Commission*, November 1938; WMU minutes, 1888-1891; *Reports*, WMU, 1889-1891; Annie Armstrong to H. A. Tupper, February 28, May 26, 1890, FMB; FMB minutes, March 4, 1890; WMU minutes, April 10, 1890.

50. Annie Armstrong to T. P. Bell, November 24, 1891, January 15, 1892, FMB; WMU minutes, November 12, December 10, 1891, February 11, 1892.

51. *Reports*, WMU, 1889-1891; SBC Annuals, 1888-1891.

52. *Reports*, WMU, 1889-1891.

5
Does a Pioneer Have It Easy?

By 1892 the pioneer leader and the young Woman's Missionary Union had proved their worth and could begin the process of growing up organizationally. As Annie wrote: "We are still in early youth." Everything had been untried, new, and exciting, every project a first during the first three years of Woman's Missionary Union's life. Though there were still new horizons, it was time to keep the momentum going. Perhaps more than vision and innovation, the leadership skill needed was know-how in forging better ways of getting the job done. Annie considered 1892-95 years of "pegging away on the same lines of effort, endeavoring to do more effective service."

There was still some opposition by pastors and leaders to a Southern Baptist women's organization. A strong, mature administrator was needed to persevere. Annie was such a leader. Bold and persistent, consistent and stalwart, she had the qualities of a true pioneer. She was a self-starter, could keep long hours, do many things, and stay with a task through completion. Most importantly, Annie kept constantly before her and others the purpose for which she and WMU, SBC, labored—missions.

Annie had well-established work patterns and personal habits. Her work was her life, and her goal, "the measure of the stature of the fulness of Christ" (Eph. 4:13). Though done on a volunteer basis, the work consumed her time. She often toiled late into the night or over weekends at home. Neither snowstorms, illnesses, nor vacations kept her from handling correspondence, distributing literature, or taking care of WMU business matters. She even admitted that on rare occasions she stayed home from church and wrote letters on Sunday. Her mother and sister Alice, with whom she lived, were her sounding boards and personal advisers. She also often talked with Eugene and Joshua Levering, her cousins, and the former her brother-in-law.[1]

Annie spent a great deal of time writing letters, many of which were lengthy. She might lay aside her pen on Christmas Day, but otherwise correspondence was a daily occurrence. She once told a mission board leader that she was impressed with the sixty or seventy letters he wrote in one day; she had only topped this with form letters. Annie usually wrote two or three times a week, and sometimes daily, to the corresponding secretaries of the Foreign Mission Board, Home Mission Board, and Sunday School Board. She wrote regularly to the state WMU workers and often to missionaries. She wrote to many persons concerning editorial and printing details and the other facets of the work. Her letters were usually long, wordy, and typed, but on weekends and while traveling she wrote by hand.

Annie's meticulous reports for these years give some indication of the magnitude of her correspondence. In May, 1892, she reported 4,077 letters for the previous year, 50 percent more than during 1890-91. In 1893 she wrote 17,718 letters, a 400 percent increase. In 1894 she wrote 15,255 letters, and in 1895, 8,152 letters. The load was especially heavy during a special campaign such as the Centennial of Missions in 1892 (one hundred years after William Carey had been sent out as a missionary from England in 1792). Annie also wrote many postcards and mailed untold amounts of literature.[2]

Noted for her competency in management and business, Annie gave careful attention to finances, reports, mailing lists, and other administrative details. She knew just how many leaflets were on hand. Because the Maryland Mission Rooms and Woman's Missionary Union, SBC, were different organizations, Annie was adamant that their business be kept separate. This was not a problem for her since she was corresponding secretary of both organizations, but it sometimes was a problem for others. The two organizations had the same address. Annie was careful to get accurate year-end reports to the boards on time. She hated to ask the boards for money and was extremely careful about how the money was spent and reported. She had a conviction that literature should be sold and not given away. She absolutely refused to take a salary for the work she did.[3]

There were many daily time-consuming details related to literature. Annie dealt with writers, printers, and editors. She solicited and edited manuscripts, had them reviewed by appropriate persons at the boards, and had them printed. She worried about paper, pictures, and the best possible price. Annie did not consider writing her forte, and she detested proofreading. She resisted glasses as long as possible for fear of mislaying or breaking them. Her sister Alice handled much of the writing and editorial work. Because she was so busy, Annie's reading often was hurried; she could only glance over WMU periodicals and other Baptist products. However, she did like to gather facts and information, which she called "cullings," for someone else to shape into good form.[4]

Though WMU, SBC, had a salaried clerk, volunteers usually addressed envelopes, got out special mailings, and handled literature distribution. Annie was conscious of every minute and always ready for volunteers. After Bible reading and prayer, she would assign the work in a systematic, organized way. She explained carefully the work to be done and how it would be used. Untiring herself, she usually got every ounce of energy out of the volunteers.[5]

The work was not all done from a desk. Annie spent many hours in committee meetings and conferences. The WMU executive committee and the Mission Rooms Committee, on which she served, met often. There were also planning meetings for the Woman's Baptist Home Mission Society of Maryland of which Annie was president. She helped the Maryland Foreign Mission Society in its operations. Often, when there was sickness in her sister Mamie's family or the Leverings were away, Annie acted for Mamie as treasurer of the Society. The Home Mission Society held all-day quarterly meetings, and the Foreign Mission Society met monthly. Annie presided over many missionary meetings in Baltimore and often spoke.[6]

Annie knew the value of personal consultation since persons could ignore or not answer letters. One summer during the early days of the Home Mission Society, Annie traveled and boarded throughout Maryland. To avoid criticism of those who believed women must be escorted, she would take friends with her. She spent her time contacting pastors and meeting ladies to promote missions and organize societies. The ladies usually would organize when someone explained how to conduct a meeting. Annie's visits were successful, for most of these organizations stayed in existence.[7]

Annie gave her major attention and support to the Foreign, Home, and Sunday School Boards. She was extremely loyal to the Southern Baptist Convention and its boards. She allied herself firmly with the Foreign Mission Board as it combated the Gospel Mission movement and with the Sunday School Board in its struggle for survival against the established American Baptist Publication Society. She was genuinely concerned about Maryland and other border states. Knowing about the work of both Northern and Southern boards, these states often divided their funds. When Eutaw Place Baptist Church, her church, was without a pastor in 1895, Annie desired deeply and urged that the church try to get a Southern man as pastor. She unashamedly advocated Southern Baptist causes, work, and literature in her church, in Maryland, and throughout the South.[8]

Annie liked to deal with the board leaders and others in a plain, candid, direct manner. There was no question about where she stood. Wanting to do what the boards wanted done and seeking their advice, opinions, and instructions, Annie asked them, therefore, to make specific and definite, not general, requests of her and WMU. She often spoke encouraging words and sent missionary letters to the secretaries of the boards. She inquired about their joys and problems.

Concerned about the heavy workloads of the secretaries, Annie many times offered assistance. Not long after Willingham took office at the Foreign Mission Board, Annie wrote: "If you will allow me to say it, I think you are making a mistake in having so little help. . . . Excuse plain speaking but I think in this matter I know a little of the strain you must be under and want to take the privilege of a friend and enter my protest against it." Annie expressed interest in the families of the secretaries and on occasion sent stamps, books, or other items to the children. The relationship between Annie and the corresponding secretaries was a brother-sister relationship. They called her "Miss Annie," and she called them "Brother."

An impatient woman, Annie was frustrated and sometimes angry when she did not get prompt replies from the men or when one sent an article late. She would write several times and sometimes send a telegram. On such occasions, she usually wrote harsh letters, then later apologized. Annie was extremely sensitive to criticism. At least once, and maybe more times during these years, she considered resigning. Annie empathized with the board leaders when they were criticized. She liked to discuss problem areas and major concerns facing WMU, the boards, or the Southern Baptist Convention in person. Considering the annual recommendations from the boards to WMU, SBC, extremely important, Annie made occasion to consult personally with the men and often invited them to Baltimore. During meetings, she made careful notes in a little notebook she carried. These notes were used by Annie as reminders, as speech material, and in making reports.[9]

Annie had some new relationships to build during the early 1890s. James Marion Frost, the Sunday School Board secretary, was only two years older than Annie. Rich in experience as a pastor, Frost had been a leading proponent for establishing the

Board. During his years of service from 1891 to 1893, and 1896 to 1916, he strengthened greatly the Board's publishing and educational efforts. He effectively stifled opposition and gained Southern Baptist backing. Annie believed strongly in, was intensely loyal to, and gave much support to the Sunday School Board. Not only did she promote the Board's work in writing and through speaking, Annie was instrumental in getting the Board to make annual recommendations to WMU. Frost acknowledged Annie's role and attributed much of the Board's success to her generous support.[10]

R. J. Willingham became corresponding secretary of the Foreign Mission Board in September, 1892, after pastorates in Georgia and Tennessee. For the first time, Annie was older than one of the corresponding secretaries, being senior to Willingham by four years. She had known him only slightly. Annie wrote Willingham immediately about the close link she saw between the Board and WMU. Wanting to learn his views and wishes and not make mistakes, she urged him to visit Baltimore as soon as possible for a personal conference. Annie offered to come to Richmond if need be. Though she was delighted that Willingham was at the Maryland Baptist Union Association meeting in October, Annie did not think their hurried talk between meetings was adequate.

In January, 1894, on behalf of the WMU executive committee, Annie invited Willingham to come to Baltimore in the near future to discuss the Foreign Mission Board recommendations to be presented at the WMU, SBC, Annual Meeting in May. After what she considered repeated delays and excuses on his part, Annie wrote Willingham a letter about the low estimate she considered the Foreign Mission Board placed on "the work done by those in charge of the Woman's Missionary Union and the Mission Rooms." She had hoped "to go forward more success-fully" when she could consult with a new secretary. In the letter Annie summarized her perception of Willingham's connection with WMU, SBC, since he took office. "You did not come to

R. J. Willingham, Corresponding Secretary, Foreign Mission Board, 1893-1914

Baltimore at the time spoken of; and when you were in Baltimore in October, it was the most hurried kind of talk we had together, and I must say to the Secretary of the W.M.U. altogether unsatisfactory. . . . I have never felt that Dr. Willingham understood the Woman's Work." She closed by asking whether he considered it unreasonable of her to request him to spend long enough in Baltimore to familiarize himself with the work done by WMU for foreign missions and to discuss his wishes for future areas of WMU support.

Willingham was astonished at Annie's letter. He claimed he had given her more time than any other one person since taking office. Comparing letters, postcards, and telegrams he had sent her with what she sent him, Annie did not agree. This concern was serious to her because WMU, SBC, had done so much to advance the cause of foreign missions. Nevertheless, Willingham came to Baltimore and met with Annie and the WMU executive committee in February.[11]

Apparently Annie and Willingham called a truce and managed to work together well for the next twelve years. At first Annie did not think Willingham understood all he needed to about the work of securing and distributing missionary literature. For awhile after their misunderstanding, she was restrained with him. She did not want him to have opportunity again to say she took too much of his time. Over the years, Annie came to like Willingham. She maintained a frequent and voluminous correspondence with him, she often sought his opinion, and they frequently conferred.[12]

Annie's energy never ceased to amaze others. In writing about the 1893 WMU, SBC, Annual Meeting, both Fannie E. S. Heck, WMU president, and a local newspaper reporter described Annie as indefatigable.[13] She was rarely stopped or even slowed down by illness, though she sometimes complained of colds, "grippe," rheumatism, and neuralgia.[14]

During the summers, at her family's insistence, Annie accompanied her mother and sister to the Maryland or North Carolina mountains or to seashore resorts in Connecticut or New Jersey. She kept up the work while on vacation, had the mail forwarded from Baltimore, took a typewriter and a quantity of leaflets with her, and engaged a stenographer. She continued answering letters and filling orders from the distant location. One summer while in the North Carolina mountains, Annie and Fannie Heck organized societies in two Asheville churches. Annie often conferred with persons in the area when possible about beginning women's missionary societies and Sunbeam Bands (organizations for children), publishing matters, and various missions projects. Though Annie did not enjoy the all-night train trips to the mountains or the way the work piled up at home while she was away, the change of pace and scenery must have been restful.[15]

During these precedent-shaping years, Annie worked with two national WMU presidents. Fannie E. S. Heck was elected WMU president in 1892 in Atlanta and served two years. Abby Murray Manly Gwathmey, elected in Dallas in 1894, served only one year. Annie wanted Fannie Heck to be president, considering her better fitted to hold the office than anyone Annie knew. Only thirty years old when elected, the single Fannie Heck was highly cultured and well educated. She had led the North Carolina WMU since it was founded in 1886, was present in the 1888 Richmond organizational meeting of the national WMU, and became a WMU, SBC, vice-president in 1891 after North Carolina joined the WMU.[16]

Because of family and personal illness, Miss Heck was not able to play the major role she thought the WMU, SBC, president should. She believed the people considered the president the head of the organization, and as such, the president should be informed about all the work, give constant time and counsel, and be a guiding hand in the organization's affairs. Fannie Heck's illness prevented her from coming to Baltimore from Raleigh often. She presided at only two WMU executive committee meetings during her first presidency. However, committee minutes were sent to her, and she sometimes made requests to the committee. Miss Heck came to Baltimore during the fall of 1892 to confer about the work. She and Annie also attended a meeting of the Woman's Missionary Societies of Virginia in Danville in November planned by the Virginia Central Committee. Miss Heck presided at the WMU, SBC, Annual Meeting in Nashville in 1893 but was unable to do so the next year.[17]

During Fannie Heck's presidency, WMU, SBC, played a major role in the Southern Baptist Convention's celebration of the Centennial of Missions in 1892. Also, the WMU moved headquarters to 9 West Lexington Street in September, 1892. Early in 1893 a column was begun in the *Foreign Mission Journal* for Sunbeam Band work. For years Miss Heck supplied the material for the Sunbeam Department in the *Journal*.[18]

Probably, only Fannie Heck's illness kept a potential storm from brewing to major proportions. Annie and Fannie thought highly of each other's abilities, and Annie was bitterly disappointed that Miss Heck could not continue to serve as national WMU president after two years. She considered Fannie Heck gifted and ready and willing to do God's work. In March, 1894, Annie went to Philadelphia, where Miss Heck had been sent for treatment, to see if she could convince Fannie to retain office. Though Fannie Heck did not express compliments often, she considered Annie a great leader and wrote a tribute in her history of WMU:

> Never was an organization more fortunate in its leader. . . . Miss Armstrong, energetic, resourceful, persevering, trained in the management of large affairs, of masterly mind and a born leader. It is not idle flattery, but within the truth to say that it would have been impossible to find a more faithful officer than Miss Armstrong. For eighteen years she gave herself wholly to the union—time, thought, strength and influence. No task was too hard, no journey too long, so it advanced the cause. All this was done without salary, the very suggestion of which she resented. To her more than to any one person, the Union owes its early growth.[19]

Fannie E. S. Heck, President, WMU, SBC, 1892-94; 1895-99; 1906-15

There was every possibility that these two leaders, each of whom saw herself as the head of the organization, might not be able to work in a dual leadership role and would clash. The major confrontation did not come until the late 1890s, but it was foreshadowed in March, 1894.

To understand the difference of opinion between Annie and Fannie Heck in 1894, it is necessary to understand a precedent WMU, SBC, established early for relating to the mission boards. Each year at WMU request, each mission board made recommendations at the WMU, SBC, Annual Meeting for the work it would like WMU to do during the next year. When adopted, these recommendations became the WMU plan of work for the year. In February, 1894, Annie wrote T. P. Bell, the corresponding secretary of the Sunday School Board, asking him to begin making Sunday School Board recommendations. Bell was familiar with this WMU custom from his days at the Foreign Mission Board. This action set the stage for trouble between Annie and Miss Heck that spring.

During their meeting in Philadelphia, Annie and Fannie Heck discussed the draft recommendations to be presented by the three boards at the WMU, SBC, Annual Meeting in May. This was the first time the Sunday School Board would make recommendations. Miss Heck questioned even having recommendations to WMU from the Sunday School Board. Since the Board was not approved of by some, Miss Heck thought having recommendations would put WMU in an unfavorable position and would also open the way for The Southern Baptist Theological Seminary to expect assistance from WMU.

Fannie Heck asked Annie who had solicited recommendations from the Sunday School Board. Annie did not admit that, on her own, without even consulting the WMU executive committee, she had asked the Sunday School Board to make recommendations. Since WMU was auxiliary to the Southern Baptist Convention, she reasoned that the Union should support all boards of the Convention, including the Sunday School Board. Annie refuted Miss Heck's arguments, believing that opposition to the Board was diminishing. Also, she reminded Fannie that Southern Seminary was not a board and did not have a parallel claim on WMU. She did not tell Miss Heck that the seminary was already making overtures to WMU. Annie did not argue her point since Miss Heck was not going to the Southern Baptist Convention in Dallas; therefore, Annie thought Miss Heck would have little opportunity to influence others.[20] The issue was stilled for a time since Miss Heck went out of office, but it would emerge again during her second presidency in the late 1890s.

In 1894 the women elected Abby Gwathmey WMU, SBC, president. A widow and the mother of nine children, the fifty-six-year-old Mrs. Gwathmey was chairman of the Virginia Central Committee. She was the daughter of Basil Manly, Sr., president of the University of Alabama. Her brother, Basil, Jr., was instrumental in founding The Southern Baptist Theological Seminary. Abby Gwathmey did not take an active role as president and did not come to Baltimore or chair a WMU executive committee meeting until March, 1895, nine months after her election. Though Annie believed Mrs. Gwathmey's heart was in the work, she wrote to Willingham: "I think perhaps the visit has led her to understand how the Woman's Work is conducted, etc., etc. better." Perhaps financial concerns and family troubles preempted Mrs. Gwathmey's time and energy. After presiding at the 1895 WMU, SBC, Annual Meeting in Washington, Abby Gwathmey gave up her national office but retained her state leadership position. Two years later, Annie considered Mrs. Gwathmey the most able state officer connected with the work, a woman who knew how to work and direct others.[21] Abby Gwathmey served ably as president of Virginia WMU from 1893 to 1897. By this time, because of the terms of Fannie Heck and Abby Gwathmey, Annie was becoming used to working with WMU, SBC, presidents who were fairly inactive. She had assumed the leading role in Woman's Missionary Union, SBC, and the executive committee.

Mrs. Abby Manly Gwathmey, President, WMU, SBC, 1894-95

Annie's major new undertaking for these years centered around the Centennial of Missions in 1892. Important as it was to inform Baptists about what had been done in missions in the past one hundred years, the Southern Baptist Convention Centennial Committee hoped to stir up the churches to more liberal and regular giving, to increase the present foreign missionary force by one hundred, and to enhance all missionary operations. The committee was made up of Thomas Treadwell Eaton, a Louisville pastor and editor of the *Western Recorder*; T. H. Pritchard, North Carolina pastor and associate editor of the *Biblical Recorder*; F. M. Ellis, Annie's pastor; H. H. Harris, Foreign Mission Board president; and I. T. Tichenor, Home Mission Board secretary.

Committee chairman Eaton asked WMU, SBC, in its annual meeting in Birmingham in 1891 to cooperate with the committee. The committee believed WMU was especially suited for reaching children and youth, launching a missions education campaign, and distributing leaflets and tracts. The women agreed readily to cooperate with the committee and the mission boards in this effort. The mission boards asked WMU to raise $250,000 to be used to build chapels and mission houses. Though the WMU executive committee did not think it wise to specify an amount, it agreed to raise as much of the $250,000 as possible.[22]

Annie proposed a certificate plan to the WMU executive committee. In subsequent months, she led the women to pull out all the stops and secured mission board approval of the plans. Women observed a week of prayer during the first week of January, 1892. WMU, SBC, prepared certificates of stock in the Centennial Chapel Building Fund at five dollars a share and chapel brick cards at ten cents each. Immediately after an appeal from the mission boards in state Baptist papers in February, WMU sent the materials to women's societies; the Maryland Mission Rooms sent materials to Sunday Schools for Children's Day programs. Many articles written by missionaries about the

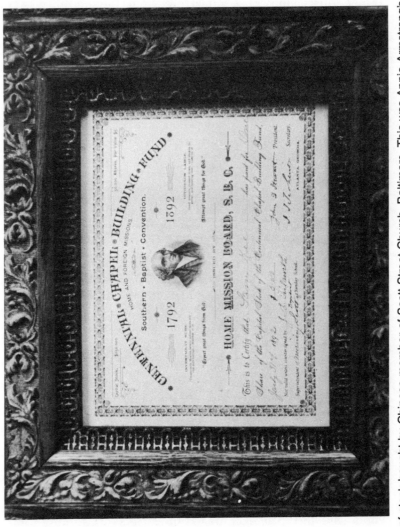

Share of stock bought by Chinese member of Scott Street Church, Baltimore. This was Annie Armstrong's idea for raising money for the Centennial Chapel Building Fund

need for chapels on the foreign and home fields were published in the state papers.[23]

Since this plan was a departure from the norm, it was important that the Mission Rooms, not WMU, SBC, distribute materials to Sunday Schools. Annie wanted to avoid opposition from critics of WMU to such a plan coming from WMU. Claiming that WMU had "developed the women and . . . not been detrimental to the churches," Annie hoped to convert the critics. It mattered not to her that she handled all the mailings from either WMU or the Mission Rooms; what mattered was the organization name on the return address. Annie devoted most of her energy during 1891 and 1892 to getting mailing lists, soliciting and editing articles and leaflets, preparing literature, and sending out thousands of letters. Dr. F. M. Ellis, on the committee, often went to bat for the women when they encountered difficulties. For the most part, the committee commended WMU for its good work.[24]

There was criticism during the centennial, some directed at the mission boards, some toward WMU, SBC. WMU faced criticism on two counts—going beyond what some considered the proper sphere for women and dictating to the church by distributing literature more widely than to the women and making an appeal for the centennial before the mission boards made their larger appeal for financial support of the entire missions enterprise. The criticism was unjustified because the Mission Rooms had distributed the literature to groups other than women's societies, and Annie had worked closely with the mission board secretaries on the timing of the mailings. Not everyone got behind the campaign to raise $250,000, though it was voted on at two Southern Baptist Conventions. Baptists were slow to give the money.[25]

Early in 1893 Annie was concerned over lack of progress in the centennial effort. She encouraged the state WMUs to use their influence. In March she and Mrs. James Pollard, WMU, SBC, recording secretary, attended a centennial meeting in Richmond. Lottie Moon spoke on foreign missions, and Annie on home missions. Annie gave three reasons for including home missions in the centennial movement: (1) God was bringing the nations of the world to America; (2) by helping home missions, the "foreign supply" was increased; and (3) the need for chapels and other aid, especially on the frontier, was immediate and distressing.[26] Annie was with Lottie Moon at least three other times during Miss Moon's furlough. Lottie Moon attended the 1892 and 1893 WMU, SBC, Annual Meetings and visited Baltimore.[27]

Annie was disappointed in the results of her two years of work in the centennial effort. After thousands of letters, mass distribution of literature, and numerous appeals in the state Baptist papers and board journals, the gifts were not large. Reported contributions through WMU to the mission boards from May, 1892, to April, 1893, were $62,326.75. This was higher than any previous year but nowhere near the goal. Annie felt the results should have been larger and indicated a lack of hearty cooperation. She could rejoice, however, that her church reached its $15,000 goal; $10,000 of this was given by Eugene and Joshua Levering, her cousins.[28]

Annie often agonized over Southern Baptists' lack of giving to missions. Once she stated that when she saw how difficult it was to secure money she thought about giving up trying to interest others in giving and using her own abilities to make money and contribute it personally to missions.[29]

In addition to chapel funds, the Home Mission Board requested WMU, SBC, to continue supporting and sending boxes of clothing and other supplies to frontier missionaries, aiding the Cuban School for Girls, doing missions work among the foreign population in the United States, and leading in observance of an annual Mission Day in Sunday School. In the foreign population, the Board included immigrants, Germans in Baltimore and other cities, Chinese in the cities, Cubans in Florida and other states, Mexicans in Texas and New Mexico, and the vast number of black women.[30]

Annie urged the women to send frontier boxes. On every possible occasion, she shared grateful letters from missionaries who received boxes and told of their work. She saw this project as mutually beneficial to the receiver and the donor. She got the Sunday School Board to send copies of all Sunday School publications to frontier missionaries. Annie was especially thrilled when frontier churches organized missionary societies or gave to missions.[31]

In a sense, Baltimore was a missions laboratory for working with special groups. Annie was instrumental in getting the Baltimore women, especially the Maryland Home Mission Society, involved locally in what is now called mission action. Eutaw Place Baptist Church had a Chinese Sunday School class. The work advanced when Lula Whilden, a former China missionary, was appointed to work with the Chinese. It must have excited Annie in 1890 when Dr. Ellis baptized Der Sang, the first Chinese convert from the Eutaw Place Sunday School.[32]

Annie asked the Home Mission Board to appoint a missionary to work with the great number of immigrants arriving in Baltimore from Germany. The Board appointed Marie Buhlmaier, who arrived in Baltimore from New York in October, 1893. Her first visit was to WMU, SBC, headquarters to see Annie, who became a good friend and associate. Annie immediately became Marie's advocate and adviser in the work; she felt she directed Miss Buhlmaier's work at the request of the Home Mission Board. Annie instructed Marie Buhlmaier not to overstep her bounds or get mixed up in matters that were not her business. She also got the Sunday School Board to supply Bibles, Testaments, and tracts to Miss Buhlmaier for her work.[33]

Annie led in starting work with black women in Baltimore. Constantly seeking new ideas about how best to do this work, she got the Sunday School Board to send Sunday School literature to missionaries with the blacks. The Baltimore women started mothers' meetings for the black women and industrial schools for the girls. They taught sewing and other skills and conducted religious exercises. Maryland Baptist leaders, including Annie, and the black pastors, started an orphanage for black children in Baltimore.[34]

Both mission boards were in debt in 1894. This greatly distressed Annie. WMU, SBC, quickly joined in the Southern Baptist Convention effort to wipe out the Foreign Mission Board debt during the summer. WMU agreed to raise $5,000, or one-sixth of the amount needed, by August. Goals were given to the states, and each woman church member, regardless of whether she was a society member, was asked to give one dollar. WMU met its goal and raised $397 more than asked for.[35]

In addition to debt reduction and chapel funds, the Foreign Mission Board asked WMU to support women foreign missionaries, to increase the missionary force in Japan, and enlarge and strengthen the work in China through the Christmas offering. The Foreign Mission Board also asked WMU to introduce an observance of Missionary Day in the Sunday Schools.[36]

When WMU, SBC, in 1894 voted to observe a week of self-denial, no one knew how significant this would later become for the Home Mission Board. At the time the vote was taken no date was set or object proposed. By early 1895 the Home Mission Board was in dire straits. Tichenor claimed the Board could not carry its present indebtedness through the coming summer and might have to discharge the missionaries. WMU stepped into the breach and inaugurated the third week in March, 1895, as a time of special prayer and effort on behalf of the work of the Home Mission Board; this week later became the annual Week of Prayer for Home Missions. Annie prepared and distributed literature. Because reports were not exact, the final results will never be known. However, more than the five thousand dollars asked for was contributed, and the Home Mission Board adopted a resolution of appreciation to WMU.[37]

Annie believed so strongly in the Sunday School Board that she established a strong relationship between that Board and WMU, SBC. She helped Frost in every way she could—offering him mailing lists and securing missionary material for *Kind Words, The Leader* (a Sunday School quarterly), and other periodicals. In 1894 Annie took charge of the Young People's Scripture Union, a daily Bible reading plan, in *Kind Words*. She backed the Board rather than the American Baptist Publication Society and encouraged use of Board publications. She asked Frost's opinion about many matters. On the other side, she asked him to send Sunday School literature to home and foreign missionaries and Bibles to Marie Buhlmaier, which he agreed to do.[38]

In 1893 Frost resigned to become pastor of First Baptist Church in Nashville. T. P. Bell, formerly at the Foreign Mission Board, became corresponding secretary of the Sunday School Board. Annie had mixed emotions about his appointment. She thought Bell's heart was in foreign missions, and she would have liked to see him as the Foreign Mission Board secretary, a position he had also been offered. However, she respected Bell's opinion and therefore gave him her full support at the Sunday School Board.

Annie liked working with Bell, thinking he understood her motives. She sought his advice on difficult problems probably more than she sought anyone else's. Best of all, Bell was prompt. In January, 1895, Bell married Martha McIntosh, the first president of WMU, SBC, which gave him additional ties with WMU.[39]

In 1894 Annie asked Bell to begin making annual Sunday School Board recommendations to WMU, SBC. Though Fannie Heck thought Annie had overstepped her bounds, the recommendations were presented at the WMU Annual Meeting in Dallas. The Board asked WMU cooperation in carrying out the request of the Foreign and Home Mission Boards that the Sunday School Board arrange for Missionary Day in the Sunday

Schools and for WMU aid in getting Sunday Schools to use Board publications.[40]

As she did with all requests from the boards, Annie took seriously the mission boards' request for WMU, SBC, to inaugurate a Missionary Day in the Sunday School. The goal was to give children missionary training and to raise an annual collection of money for missions, to be divided equally between the two mission boards. The Sunday School Board cooperated fully in this effort.

Annie wanted the first observance to be done well, since this would become an annual event. Since this project was not distinctive WMU work, she sought advice and opinions from the board secretaries about every detail. She believed they would have to make the appeal to the churches. Annie prepared a circular, letters, the program, and a pyramid-shaped mite box for the collections, and Sunday Schools ordered the materials.

The first Missionary Day in the Sunday School was observed on October 15, 1893. On that day, the program was conducted and the mite boxes distributed. The boxes were gathered on Thanksgiving Day or the Sunday before or after. Much literature was ordered for the observance. Annie felt good about her work and believed that when the day was established, much impetus would be given to missionary efforts.[41]

Missionary Day in the Sunday School had been a big job for Annie in 1893. She suggested that in 1894 the Sunday School Board take over its management; this proposal was agreed to by all three boards. Thus, in May, 1894, the Sunday School Board requested WMU's assistance in preparing for the next observance.[42] WMU, SBC, prepared the program, but this time materials were distributed by the Sunday School Board from Nashville. Annie felt definitely that the Board could do far better with this day than could WMU. In 1895, the Sunday School Board reported that as far as the Board could find out, at least $5,800 had been collected through this day for the mission boards.[43]

The previous year WMU, SBC, had asked the Sunday School Board for a regular appropriation to help pay WMU expenses. The request was "in view of said union's services rendered this board." The Board granted the request.[44]

During the 1890s, the young people's movement was emerging, and Annie became interested in it. Formed in 1891 as a national organization with headquarters in Chicago, the Northern Baptist Young People's Union of America (BYPUA) soon formed a "Department of the Green" in Southern territory. The BYPUA promoted the idea of young people's organizations in churches for Christian growth and loyalty, but a major attraction was the big convention held annually.

Between 1893 and 1895, the question of sponsorship of a young people's union by the Southern Baptist Convention was debated in annual sessions. Annie favored organization of a Southern young people's union, seeing such an organization as a good way to connect Southern Baptist young people with the Convention. She was most anxious, however, that the movement make missions prominent. Annie did not think it necessary to have a big annual meeting to feature missions; perhaps a general meeting every four years would be enough.

When the BYPUA proposed holding its 1895 meeting in Baltimore, Annie questioned the board secretaries about whether she should seek to prevent it. As a whole she opposed the Northern BYPUA and thought this meeting might be detrimental to Southern Baptist interests. Her opposition related to her feeling that the BYPUA alienated the youth from all existing organizations and emphasized "enthusiasm and talking" rather than work. After the meeting was scheduled, Annie sought advice about what WMU, SBC's, role should be if invited to participate; the WMU executive committee had divided opinions. Since Southern Baptist leaders seemed to be against the BYPUA, Willingham advised Annie for WMU, SBC, not to take any leading part in "mixed meetings"—meetings in which both men and women participated. Tichenor and Bell concurred. It was common practice for Northern Baptists to have women speakers in mixed meetings, especially at young people's meetings; most Southern Baptists, however, opposed this practice. The Baptist Young People's Union, Auxiliary to the Southern Baptist Convention (BYPU, not to be confused with the BYPUA, the Northern organization), was organized in November, 1895.[45]

Annie continued to encourage state WMU leaders in their work. She liked to help them, offer assistance in times of trouble, and present missions to them. She made several trips to WMU meetings in Virginia and began going occasionally to the District of Columbia. These trips were at her own expense, as were trips to the WMU, SBC, Annual Meetings. *The Religious Herald* once described Annie as the "oracle of the occasion." She was noted in the states for unraveling knotty problems and cheering discouraged persons. She evidenced much concern for the border areas such as Missouri and the District of Columbia, which she considered neutral territory for Northern and Southern Baptists. She coveted these areas for the Southern Baptist Convention and wanted to interest them in foreign and home missions work done by the Convention.[46] During these early years, Annie made only short trips by train except for the WMU, SBC, Annual Meetings each May.[47]

Annie was most concerned about the troubles Georgia WMU was having during 1894 and 1895 related to the Gospel Mission movement. Led by several China missionaries, including Tarleton Perry Crawford, Gospel Mission advocates were against conventions and boards. These missionaries, therefore, opposed the Foreign Mission Board and its policies. They favored direct support of missionaries by voluntary gifts from individuals, churches, and associations, rather than by the Board. Another Gospel Mission policy advocated missionaries living like natives on the field. Annie was of course supportive of the Foreign Mission Board and did all she could to offset Gospel Mission arguments. She called a meeting of the state central committees during the WMU, SBC, Annual Meeting in Dallas in 1894 and read to these WMU leaders a number of letters from Lottie Moon and other missionaries about the workings of the Gospel Mission members. Foreign Mission Board leaders had given her these letters. Annie thought the movement threatened women's work in Georgia, Kentucky, North Carolina, and South Carolina.[48]

Mrs. Stainback Wilson, the Georgia WMU corresponding secretary, became a Gospel Mission sympathizer and urged these views in *Our Mission Helper*, the Georgia WMU paper. She was aided by her sister, Mrs. C. E. Kerr, who managed the paper. Mrs. Wilson criticized Southern Baptist centralization and the mission boards. Gospel Missionites reasoned there would be no foreign missions debt if there was no Foreign Mission Board.

For the first time, Annie had to take strong action against a state leader. The problem in Georgia was a crisis in the work and called for decisiveness on her part. Annie prayed for guidance and sought and secured backing from Willingham, Tichenor, and Bell. They conferred with John B. Gibson, the Georgia secretary. The Georgia state board opposed the Gospel Mission movement, as did the SBC boards. Annie considered Mrs. Wilson most dangerous because she was well known and had a prominent role in WMU for years. Because she did not want foreign missions funds diverted into Gospel Mission coffers, Annie feared Mrs. Wilson's influence and that the Georgia paper's teachings would spread to other states. Mrs. Wilson resented Annie's interference, claiming this was state business.

Mary Emily Wright, vice-president of the Georgia Central Committee, and other Georgia WMU leaders opposed Mrs. Wilson's views. Miss Wright was also the Georgia vice-president for Woman's Missionary Union, SBC. She led the Georgia Central Committee to force Mrs. Wilson to take a stand, either for the Foreign Mission Board or the Gospel Mission. Mrs. Wilson, Mrs. Kerr, and six others resigned and formed a new organization which straddled the fence; it was in sympathy with the Gospel Mission and at the same time claimed to support the Southern Baptist mission boards. The Georgia state board and the Home Mission Board, both located in Atlanta, backed the original central committee. Led by Annie, the WMU executive committee in Baltimore recognized the Woman's Baptist Missionary Union of Georgia (the central committee) as the official organization and refused to send literature to Mrs. Wilson and her group for distribution.

The Georgia women feared trouble. Annie was asked but did not attend the Georgia WMU Annual Meeting in April, 1895. Things smoothed over, and the women wanted to avoid magnifying the problem by bringing in a national officer. Annie also feared trouble from Mrs. Wilson at the WMU, SBC, Annual Meeting in Washington in 1895. She prepared herself again with the missionary letters from China. She was concerned that there would be a move, although it did not materialize, to get WMU to recognize the Gospel Mission movement.[49]

By 1895 Annie felt that Woman's Missionary Union had moved from childhood into youth and was taking its proper place in the family. She and the organization were "pegging away" at missions efforts and would continue to go forward.[50] Further, Annie had experienced the reality that a pioneer does not have it easy. She had worked hard, accomplished much, and matured as a leader.

Notes (See pages 295-310 for Key to Sources.)

1. Annie Armstrong to T. P. Bell, September 30, 1890, January 9, 1891, January 15, 1892, FMB; Annie Armstrong to J. M. Frost, August 20, 1892, January, February 25, 1899, SSB; Annie Armstrong to H. H. Harris, August 7, 1893, FMB; *Reports*, WMU, 1893-1895.

2. Annie Armstrong to R. J. Willingham, March 14, 1895; other correspondence 1888-1906; *Reports*, WMU, 1892-1895.

3. Annie Armstrong to R. J. Willingham, November 28, December 21, 1893, January 9, February 15, March 17, March 20, April 20-27, 1894, March

30, 1895, FMB; Annie Armstrong to H. A. Tupper, February 19, April 9, April 26, 1892, April 28, 1893, FMB; Annie Armstrong to A. J. Barton, June 17, 1897, FMB; Alice Armstrong to T. P. Bell, March 3, 1894, SSB.

4. Annie Armstrong to T. P. Bell, March 17, 1894, SSB; Annie Armstrong to R. J. Willingham, March 6, 1894, April 17, 1896, FMB; other correspondence, 1888-1906.

5. Kate T. Davis, "I Remember Miss Annie," *Royal Service*, March, 1949.

6. Annie Armstrong to R. J. Willingham, April 26, 1892, February 9, February 15, 1894, July 7, 1896, FMB; *The Christian Index*, September 27, 1900; Annie Armstrong to H. A. Tupper, April, 1892, FMB.

7. Annie Armstrong to R. J. Willingham, July 19, 1897, FMB.

8. Correspondence with SSB, 1893; correspondence with FMB, 1894-1895; Annie Armstrong to R. J. Willingham, January 13, 1894, May 3, 1895, FMB; Annie Armstrong to T. P. Bell, July 10, 1893, February 16, March 4, March 22, 1895, SSB.

9. Annie Armstrong to H. A. Tupper, November 30, 1891, March 25, 1892, FMB; Annie Armstrong to R. J. Willingham, September 4, November 17, November 18, 1893, January, March 27, July 26, August 4, 1894, April 30, 1898, FMB; Annie Armstrong to H. H. Harris, July-September 1893, FMB; Annie Armstrong to T. P. Bell, June, 1893, February 13, 1894, June 12, 1895, SSB; Annie Armstrong to J. M. Frost, March 13, 1893, SSB.

10. *Encyclopedia of Southern Baptists*, 1:512-513; Annie Armstrong to J. M. Frost, June 23, 1893, SSB; SBC Annual, 1905.

11. *Encyclopedia of Southern Baptists*, 2:1502; Annie Armstrong to H. H. Harris, August 9, 1893, FMB; Annie Armstrong to R. J. Willingham, September 4, October 21, October 27, November 28, 1893, January, 1894, FMB; R. J. Willingham to Annie Armstrong, January 20, January 31, 1894, FMB; WMU minutes, February 13, 1894.

12. Annie Armstrong to T. P. Bell, February 5, March 13, April 11, 1894, September 3, 1895, SSB.

13. *Biblical Recorder*, May 31, 1893; *The Daily American*, May 13, 1893.

14. Annie Armstrong to T. P. Bell, January 15, 1892, FMB; Annie Armstrong to R. J. Willingham, December 21, 1893, January 3, December 27, 1894, August 29, 1895, November 13, 1896, January 27, 1897, FMB.

15. *The Baltimore Baptist*, August 13, 1891; Annie Armstrong to J. M. Frost, February 14, 1893, SSB; Annie Armstrong to H. H. Harris, July-August 1893, FMB; *FMJ*, September, 1893: *The Baptist*, July 26, 1893, August 22, 1894; *Missionary Talk*, September, 1893; Annie Armstrong to R. J. Willingham, November 17, 1893, July 26, August 4, September 1, September 2, September 12, 1894, July 19, 1897, June 6, 1900, April 30, 1903, FMB; R. J. Willingham to Annie Armstrong, June 22, July 19, August 6, August 27, 1894, FMB.

16. Annie Armstrong to T. P. Bell, January 15, 1892, FMB; Annie Armstrong to R. J. Willingham, March 17, 1894, FMB; *Encyclopedia of Southern Baptists*, 1:604; *Reports*, WMU, 1888-1892.

17. WMU minutes, May 1892-April 1894; *Report*, WMU, 1893; *The Religious Herald*, November 24, 1892; Annie Armstrong to Mrs. F. B. Davis, November 18, 1892, SWBTS; Fannie Heck to Annie Armstrong, March 27, 1894, FMB; Mrs. W. C. James, *Fannie E. S. Heck*, p. 66; *Biblical Recorder*, May 23, 1894.

18. WMU minutes, November 16, 1892; Annie Armstrong to Mrs. F. B. Davis, December 2, 1892, SWBTS; *FMJ*, September, 1892, January, 1893.

19. Annie Armstrong to T. P. Bell, February 16, March 13, March 24, 1894, SSB; Annie Armstrong to R. J. Willingham, March, 1894, FMB; WMU minutes, February 13, March 13, April 10, 1894; *Biblical Recorder*, May 31, 1893; Heck, *In Royal Service*, pp. 133-134.

20. Annie Armstrong to T. P. Bell, February 5, March 24, 1894, SSB.

21. *Encyclopedia of Southern Baptists*, 2:817-818, 4:2257; WMU minutes, May 1894-April 1895; Annie Armstrong to R. J. Willingham, March, 1895, October 11, 1897, FMB; *Report*, WMU, 1895.

22. *The Baltimore Baptist*, July 30, 1891; *Biblical Recorder*, August 5, 1891; *Western Recorder*, July 23, 1891; *OHF*, August, 1891; *Report*, WMU, 1891; FMB minutes, June 6, 1891; Annie Armstrong to H. A. Tupper, June 12, July 22, 1891, FMB; *Encyclopedia of Southern Baptists*, 1:385.

23. WMU minutes, 1891-1892; Annie Armstrong, "Centennial Appeal, WMU, SBC," WMU Scrapbook 2, WMU; Annie Armstrong to I. T. Tichenor, September 5, 1891, FMB; *Western Recorder*, January-February 1892, SBC Annual, 1893.

24. Annie Armstrong to I. T. Tichenor, September 5, 1891, FMB; WMU minutes, November 12, 1891, September 2, 1892; *Biblical Recorder*, July 22, 1891; *Western Recorder*, January 21, May 12, October-November 1892; F. M. Ellis to H. A. Tupper, December 29, 1891, FMB; *Report*, WMU, 1893.

25. WMU minutes, October 20, 1892; Annie Armstrong to T. P. Bell, February 25, 1892, FMB; Annie Armstrong to H. H. Harris, August 7, 1892, FMB; *Western Recorder*, March, October-December, 1892.

26. WMU minutes, January 10, 1893; Virginia WMU minutes, January 13, 1893; *FMJ*, March-June 1893; *The Religious Herald*, April 6, 1893.

27. *Reports*, WMU, 1892-1893; *FMJ*, June 1892, June 1893; *The Baltimore Baptist*, March 29, 1892.

28. SBC Annual, 1893; *Report*, WMU, 1893; *Western Recorder*, October 20, 1892.

29. Annie Armstrong to R. J. Willingham, March 30, 1894, FMB; Annie Armstrong to A. J. Barton, March 11, 1899, FMB.

30. *Reports*, WMU, 1894-1895.

31. *Reports*, WMU, 1893-1895; *OHF*, March, 1893; Annie Armstrong to Mrs. F. B. Davis, February 28, March 1, November 27, 1894, SWBTS; Annie Armstrong to J. M. Frost, August 1, 1892, February 14, 1893, SSB.

32. HMB minutes, November 11, 1887; SBC Annuals, 1888-1889; WMU minutes, 1892-1893; *The Baltimore Baptist*, October 2, 1890; undated article, minutes, Eutaw Place Baptist Church; minutes, WHMS, September 23, 1890.

33. WMU minutes, 1892-1893; *Report*, WMU, 1893; Marie Buhlmaier, *Along the Highway of Service*, pp. 8-9, 13-15, 80-81; Annie Armstrong to T. P. Bell, June 30, 1894, SSB.

34. Annie Armstrong to J. M. Frost, January 22, August 1, 1892, February 14, 1893, SSB; WMU minutes, 1892-1894; *FMJ*, February, 1894, March, 1896; Virginia WMU minutes, February 17, March 17, 1893; Annie Armstrong to R. J. Willingham, January 13, 1894, June 2, 1898, FMB; minutes, WHMS, January, 1896.

35. Annie Armstrong to T. P. Bell, January 15, 1892, FMB; T. P. Bell to Annie Armstrong, March 9, 1892, FMB; Annie Armstrong to H. A. Tupper, January 29, 1892, FMB; H. A. Tupper to Annie Armstrong, February 9, 1892, FMB; Annie Armstrong to Frank L. Butler, February 9, 1893, FMB; Annie Armstrong to H. H. Harris, August 29, 1893, FMB; Annie Armstrong to R. J. Willingham, December 26, 1893, January-March, August 11, September 1, 1894, FMB; WMU minutes, February 13, 1894; "Debt of the Foreign Mission Board," WMU.

36. *Reports*, WMU, 1894-1895.

37. *Reports*, WMU, 1894-1895; A. M. Gwathmey to Mrs. F. B. Davis, June 28, 1894, SWBTS; WMU minutes, December 11, 1894, March 12, 1895; Annie Armstrong to R. J. Willingham, March 8, 1895, FMB; *The Baptist Courier*, February 28, March 16, March 30, April 25, August 8, 1895; *Baptist Standard*, March 1, 1895; *FMJ*, February, July, 1895; *Royal Service*, February, 1938, "Indebtedness of the Home Mission Board," WMU; HMB minutes, May 4, 1895; minutes, WHMS, February 20, September 14, 1896.

38. WMU minutes, 1892-1893; FMB minutes, April 28, 1893; *The Baptist*, August 30, October 4, 1893; *OHF*, August, 1898; Annie Armstrong to J. M. Frost, March 13, 1893, SSB; Annie Armstrong to T. P. Bell, May 22, July 8, July 10, 1893, SSB; *Reports*, WMU, 1893-1894; Annie Armstrong to H. H. Harris, July-September, 1893, FMB; I. T. Tichenor to Annie Armstrong, July 7, 1893, FMB; Annie Armstrong to R. J. Willingham, September-November 1893, January 3, 1894, FMB.

39. Annie Armstrong to J. M. Frost, January 22, August 1, August 20, 1892, January 7, February 14, March 13, June, 1893, SSB; WMU minutes, November 16, 1892, June 12, 1894, January 8, 1895.

40. Annie Armstrong to T. P. Bell, June 12, 1893, SSB; Annie Armstrong to H. H. Harris, June 13, 1893, FMB; Annie Armstrong to J. M. Frost, November, 1896, SSB; *The Evangel*, January 30, 1895.

41. Annie Armstrong to T. P. Bell, February 5, 1894, SSB; SSB minutes, February 15, 1894; *Report*, WMU, 1894.

42. SSB minutes, April 21, May 19, 1894; FMB minutes, June 12, 1894; *Report*, WMU, 1894.

43. WMU minutes, May-June 1894; Annie Armstrong to T. P. Bell, June 12, 1894, SSB; Annie Armstrong to R. J. Willingham, July 26, August 25, 1894, FMB; FMB minutes, March 7, 1895; SBC Annual, 1895; *Encyclopedia of Southern Baptists*, 1:134.

44. SSB minutes, May 19, 1894; Annie Armstrong to T. P. Bell, June 12, 1894, SSB.

45. *American Baptist Year-Book*, 1893, 1900; Annie Armstrong to T. P. Bell, June 23, 1894, February 16, March 26, April 2, June 26, 1895, SSB; Annie Armstrong to R. J. Willingham, December 10, 1894, November 14, November 26, 1895, FMB; R. J. Willingham to Annie Armstrong, February 4, 1895, FMB; WMU minutes, January 8, March 2, 1895.

46. Annie Armstrong attended a women's meeting in Danville, Virginia, in November, 1892, the state convention in Alexandria, Virginia, in November 1894, and a quarterly mission society meeting in the District of Columbia in December, 1894. Annie Armstrong to Mrs. F. B. Davis, March 8, 1894; SWBTS; *FMJ*, December, 1892, March, May, June 1893, January, 1895; *The Religious Herald*, November 24, 1892; WMU minutes, December 8, 1892, December 11, 1894; Annie Armstrong to R. J. Willingham, November 9, 1893, November 9, November 23, December 10, 1894, March 1895, FMB; Annie Armstrong to T. P. Bell, March 22, 1895, SSB; *Reports*, WMU, 1893-1895.

47. *The Baltimore Baptist*, May 9, 1890; Annie Armstrong to Mrs. F. B. Davis, April 27, 1894, SWBTS.

48. *Encyclopedia of Southern Baptists*, 1:363-364, 571-572; Annie Armstrong to T. P. Bell, January 15, 1892, FMB; Annie Armstrong to T. P. Bell, January 15, 1892, FMB; Annie Armstrong to T. P. Bell, June 30, 1894, SSB; Annie Armstrong to H. H. Harris, July 29, 1893, FMB; Annie Armstrong to R. J. Willingham, September 21, 1893, FMB.

49. Annie Armstrong to T. P. Bell, June 30, December 22, December 24, 1894, March 22, 1895, SSB; Annie Armstrong to R. J. Willingham, August 1894-May 1895, April 11, 1896, FMB; R. J. Willingham to Annie Armstrong, December 31, 1894, FMB; WMU minutes, November 13, 1894, January 8, April 9, 1895.

50. *Report*, WMU, 1895.

6
Dreams Can Be Put into Action

Annie was "a dreamer in action." Seeing a need, she had the ability to dream, then move ahead in action to carry out the dream. During the latter 1890s, Annie had several dreams which came to reality. Seeing the need for WMU, SBC, work to "go forward" in new ways, Annie dreamed about and built strong relationships with key leaders in the Southern Baptist Convention and states. Wanting pastoral support for WMU, Annie put into action a new and strong relationship with The Southern Baptist Theological Seminary. Concerned about border areas, she strengthened ties between the District of Columbia, and Oklahoma and Indian Territory and the Southern Baptist Convention. Burdened for the blacks, Annie helped the black women organize for missions. Wanting to advance the work of the Southern Baptist boards, Annie dreamed about the establishment of an annuity plan for Southern Baptists and new excitement for already established missions projects. Wanting to strengthen the work in the states, Annie dreamed about more of her time spent in travel.

How does a dream get put into action? Annie had long believed that Woman's Missionary Union, SBC, needed the support of pastors. Therefore, she yearned for the cooperation of The Southern Baptist Theological Seminary faculty in Louisville, Kentucky. Long-term professor John Albert Broadus did not disapprove of WMU since his daughter, Eliza, was a Kentucky WMU leader. However, neither did he ever refer to women's work while teaching. At one time, Annie tried to get the aid of Franklin H. Kerfoot, her former pastor and now a professor, since he sympathized with WMU work. However, Annie indicated that Kerfoot was prone to become preoccupied with other matters and, no doubt, forgot her request.

When William Heth Whitsitt became president of the seminary in 1895 Annie saw this as her golden opportunity. She talked with Whitsitt about WMU work during the Southern Baptist Convention in Washington and agreed to keep him informed about the work. Her efforts paid off, and she made a believer out of Whitsitt. As soon as he got back to Louisville, Whitsitt talked with about 150 students about WMU and its work. He urged these students to organize missionary societies in their own churches that summer and to visit district associations and try to strengthen the work. Whitsitt felt sure this would ultimately increase contributions to missions work.[1]

Whitsitt did as he promised Annie. During the next seminary session, he presented the work of WMU during one of the seminary's missionary days. This presentation not only acquainted the students with the results of women's work but also disarmed possible prejudice against WMU. Later Whitsitt suggested guest speakers, usually Kentucky men in order to keep expenses down. Annie preferred the board secretaries, whom she considered the best-informed men about WMU work. When in 1897 Whitsitt asked WMU, SBC, to send a speaker, Annie secured T. P. Bell, then owner and editor of *The Christian Index*, the Georgia state Baptist paper. She reminded Bell that those who advocated WMU's cause at the seminary had to do so at their own expense.[2]

Mrs. Bell, formerly Martha McIntosh, WMU's first national president, accompanied Bell to the Southern campus in February. No doubt having gotten much information from his wife, Bell gave an excellent address about the history of the development of WMU, SBC, how it operated as an auxiliary, and the positive results. WMU agreed to print the address. Annie had some anxious moments during the Southern Baptist Convention in Wilmington in May when she went over the paper with Bell to correct what she considered inaccuracies. It was an awkward situation, since Martha McIntosh Bell had given the information which Annie considered incorrect.[3]

Annie built even more ties with Southern Seminary. She worked out a plan for the three Southern Baptist boards to send monthly literature free to the students and suggested that the seminary magazine carry monthly articles from the boards. In 1899 Annie, as well as the boards, began sending material regularly for *The Seminary Magazine*. Also, the seminary continued to feature WMU work during missionary days.[4]

Annie was interested in and sympathized with the seminary. However, she resisted a proposal from Whitsitt and Frost that WMU, SBC, support the student's fund and that Frost present this idea to the women at the WMU Annual Meeting in Wilmington in 1897. Annie thought this was unwise since she believed WMU, SBC, should limit its work to the three boards. Further, no seminary representative had ever spoken at a WMU Annual Meeting.

As always, Annie sought advice from the board secretaries and others, especially T. P. Bell. Bell agreed with her reasoning. Frost urged Whitsitt to watch for a chance to talk with Bell while in Wilmington about the idea of WMU, SBC, supporting a project for the seminary, since Bell "has more influence with Miss Armstrong than anyone else."[5]

After Whitsitt became president of Southern Seminary in 1895, a furor arose because of an article he published in *Johnson's Universal Cyclopaedia* in 1886. The controversy, called the "Whitsitt Controversy," raged for several years and centered on the historical article Whitsitt wrote which stated that believer's baptism by immersion was restored by English Baptists in 1641. This enraged persons who believed an unbroken succession of Baptist churches could be traced back to the apostolic era. Newspapers relentlessly attacked Whitsitt and the seminary. Annie felt the attacks on Whitsitt were outrageous. Appreciating the endorsement he had given WMU, SBC, and opportunities to present WMU work to the students, Annie hoped there would be no furor at the Southern Baptist Convention regarding the seminary or Whitsitt. To restore harmony and peace, Whitsitt finally resigned in 1899.[6]

E. Y. Mullins succeeded Whitsitt as Southern Seminary president. Annie had known Mullins when he pastored in Baltimore in the late 1880s and early 1890s. Also, she worked briefly with him when he was associate secretary of the Foreign Mission Board. Glad about the election, Annie wrote Willingham: "Few persons, I judge, can and do think more highly of Mr. Mullins in many ways than I do, but, I must acknowledge, it would never have occurred to me that he had the qualifications necessary to make him the 'ideal' president of a theological seminary in troubled times." Annie expressed, however, her "most unqualified admiration of Mr. Mullins' character, etc."[7]

Annie probably helped save the District of Columbia and Indian Territory as Southern Baptist missions territory during the early years of their development. Border areas could go either way, North or South. Annie led the District women to form their foreign missions society into one general organization which would contribute to home and foreign missions, and both Northern and Southern Baptist Conventions. She would have preferred complete allegiance to the South. However, this compromise caused less friction than having two completely separate organizations, one Northern and one Southern. Annie was elated when the churches contributed to Southern Baptist missions causes. She began reporting these contributions first at the 1895 WMU, SBC, Annual Meeting.

By inviting them to take part in Maryland Home Mission Society meetings and to visit her in Baltimore, Annie constantly encouraged the WMU workers in Washington, DC. Further, she arranged for Marie Buhlmaier to spend one day a week in Washington visiting Germans. Surely, she thought, Miss Buhlmaier's presence would inspire support for home missions.

Annie made several trips to Washington during the 1890s to help the District women with their organization.[8]

As soon as home missions work started in Indian Territory, Annie wanted missionary societies there to organize. Along with the frontier boxes to missionaries went encouragement to begin societies. Annie was immensely pleased when two Indian women, representing thirty societies, came as delegates to the WMU, SBC, Annual Meeting in Chattanooga in 1896. She saw the fruits of her labor when financial contributions began coming in to the boards. Annie believed the help extended to frontier missionaries would in time be returned a hundredfold to the mission treasuries. The work was strengthened greatly when the new wife of W. H. Kuykendall, Sunday School leader in Indian Territory, took charge of it.[9]

When Annie started working with the black women in Baltimore, she had no idea how this work would expand. Although *colored* was the term used in Annie's day, she usually referred to the blacks as "brunettes." Annie's attitude about blacks had been influenced early by her mother and Richard Fuller, her pastor. Mrs. Armstrong had always been considerate and fair with the family's household servants.

In late 1895 Annie addressed a Woman's Congress on Baptist Day at the Exposition in Atlanta on the topic, "Woman's Work in the Evangelization of the Homes of the Colored People." The Georgia Baptist women were concerned that Mary G. Burdette, corresponding secretary of the Woman's Home Mission Society of the North, would touch on social equality in her remarks. Annie thought Miss Burdette knew better; if not, however, she followed Miss Burdette, and would give the Southern viewpoint. There was much friction between Southern and Northern Baptists during this period over working with blacks.[10]

Annie's biggest challenge came in helping the black women organize for missions. In late 1896 L. G. Jordan, a National Baptist foreign missions leader, visited Annie to talk about organizing the black women. Considering this a "large opportunity," Annie was eager to assist. She agreed to help Jordan by writing for the *Afro-American Herald* and promised to attend the black women's meeting to be held in Washington in March. Annie saw this work not only as a way to develop the black women at home but the potential for future missionary workers for Africa.

Jordan asked Nannie Helen Burroughs, a young black woman from Washington, to write Annie about organization. Immediately after hearing from Miss Burroughs, Annie sought advice from Tichenor, Willingham, Frost, and others. Assisting the blacks was a big venture. She thought it would be wise to suggest locating the black executive committee in Baltimore. It would be much easier for her to assist the leaders there, and she claimed Baltimore had more blacks than any other city in the world.

Annie may not have realized it at the time, but she was dealing with potential greatness in Nannie Helen Burroughs. Miss Burroughs was not only destined to become the first corresponding secretary of the Woman's Convention, Auxiliary to the National Baptist Convention, a few years later, but would found a great school for black girls in Washington, DC.

In January, 1897, there was a four-hour conference between Annie, Jordan, Miss Burroughs, a black Baltimore pastor, and two WMU, SBC, executive committee members from the "committee on colored people." The group hammered out decisions and prepared a constitution, agreeing that the plan for general organization would come later. The plan called for the next National Baptist Convention to call on the women to organize; in the interim, leaders would seek to interest the women and pastors in missions. Jordan would print the constitution and bylaws in the *Afro-American Herald* and begin a women's department column largely prepared by Annie. A mass meeting would be held in Washington during the week of the United States presidential inauguration in March to interest black women in missions, and Miss Burroughs would try to get the Washington women to organize societies and be ready to unite with the general organization when formed.[11]

Annie wisely saw the need to work behind the scenes and remain out of sight. Instead of doing it herself, she sought to equip the black women to do the work. She saw, too, possible controversy with the American Baptist Publication Society about Southern Baptists assisting the blacks with their work. This work was extremely important to her, and she believed Southern Baptists could handle matters south of the Mason and Dixon line.[12]

The new work with blacks took a good bit of Annie's time. She conferred often with Jordan and sent monthly contributions to the *Afro-American Herald*. Annie also assisted a black woman in preparing programs for Missionary Day in the Sunday School.[13]

In June, 1897, Mary G. Burdette, the Northern Baptist women's leader, visited Annie to discuss the work with blacks and to review the Northern and Southern "sides." Annie and Miss Burdette, of course, differed. Annie stated that Southern Baptists were working directly with the blacks, not through employed missionaries, as were the Northerners. Miss Burdette thought Southerners were discourteous to Northern missionaries and should endorse the work of the Northern Baptists. Annie and Miss Burdette agreed that both groups should use their influence to get the blacks to do missionary work among their own people and to help them devise plans to do so. Annie thought Miss Burdette probably regarded her as an idealist and not practical.[14] Actually, it was the other way around.

Reports from the National Baptist Convention meeting in Boston in September, 1897, were bright. The blacks seemed increasingly to be turning to Southern Baptists for help. Jordan stopped to see Annie on his way home from the Convention, and they worked out some new plans. He visited her again in December and reported a split in the work. There still was much friction between Northern and Southern Baptists over the work, and this was causing difficulty for the blacks. Annie wrote several rather strong letters to the American Baptist Publication Society about the matter.

The WMU, SBC, executive committee endorsed all that Annie had done. The committee thought it would be wise to have women's organizations in the black churches.[15]

The young people's work was much on Annie's heart after the Baptist Young People's Union (BYPU) organized in Atlanta in November, 1895. Burdened that the young people be trained as workers, and not just be talkers and attend big meetings, she wanted the Sunday School Board to take over this work. Feeling keenly that the BYPU must be missionary, Annie led in working out a course of mission study that the Northern and Southern young people's organizations could both use. This course was based on the mission card topics selected by the Maryland Mission Rooms. She constantly proposed ideas for getting young people interested in missions.[16]

For years Annie wished that Southern Baptists would make provision in their wills for the work of the boards. In 1899 Annie worked out a proposal encouraging legacies to the boards. The first response came from Mrs. Anna G. Schimp, a Baltimore woman who would later be Annie's traveling companion; Mrs. Schimp decided to give the mission boards four thousand dollars each as a legacy. Anna Schimp, who did not want her name to be mentioned in public, later also offered the Sunday School Board one thousand dollars. The papers were properly drawn up and funds transferred. Annie felt that this will and annuity plan would be a model for others. The boards were extremely appreciative of Annie's role in instituting an annuity fund. Willingham told Annie it was "one of the biggest things that you have done in all your great work."[17]

In addition to dreaming of and activating new projects, Annie kept the WMU momentum going. In 1896 George Braxton Taylor, a Virginia pastor who founded Sunbeam Band work for children, resigned and turned the work over to the Foreign

Mission Board. The Board asked WMU, SBC, to assume responsibility, and WMU accepted. A Band Department column was already being prepared monthly for the *Foreign Mission Journal* by Fannie Heck. Soon, materials were printed, and states began to appoint Band superintendents.[18]

For the first time, during the summer of 1895, Annie wrote all the women foreign missionaries, acquainting them with WMU work. She asked them to respond with word about their work. This correspondence began a pattern of regular, personal communication from Annie to missionaries, in addition to the official letter of greeting sent each year from the WMU, SBC, Annual Meeting. The letters from missionaries were sent to state Baptist papers and often published. Annie also often enclosed a missionary letter when she wrote Willingham. She loved missionaries, usually referring to them as "our substitutes."[19] Giving practical expression to this love, Annie was a dreamer in action many times on behalf of missionaries.

In 1899 Anne Luther Bagby, missionary to Brazil, wrote Annie about a request which was "not made in order to test your love. We already have abundant proof of its genuineness." Ermine, the Bagbys' oldest daughter, was coming home for college. Anne Bagby asked Annie to arrange for someone to meet Ermine in New York and send her on to Annie in Baltimore. Annie could keep her until she could place Ermine in care of someone who was going to Waco, St. Louis, Dallas, or Atlanta. Annie asked Willingham for help. Since Ermine was eighteen and Annie's nieces made short trips alone, she inquired about the propriety of Ermine traveling unescorted. Because of her mother's illness, Annie eventually turned the whole matter over to Willingham, who took care of the situation.[20]

As much as Annie had to do, she constantly dreamed of new ideas. She planted many of her ideas in the mind of someone else, often a board secretary. When the idea was adopted, she was willing to let it go and have someone else implement it.[21]

WMU, SBC, headquarters moved from Lexington Street to 304 North Howard Street in 1896. Despite the ordeal of moving, Annie liked the new offices. WMU had three rooms, which gave her an office for the first time. Although the rent increased in late 1899, WMU decided to remain in these quarters.[22]

Overwork began to take its toll on Annie. When Fannie Heck became national WMU president again in 1895, she commented on Annie's strained look of overwork and sought to get her help.[23] Miss Heck believed WMU, SBC, could not get anyone else to take Annie's place if that person had a family. Annie gave her whole time without salary. She worked nonstop daily from seven in the morning to midnight. Often Annie referred to being tired or under pressure and thought she might like to be an office assistant at one of the boards and not have so much responsibility.

Pressure or controversy seemed to affect Annie. She complained occasionally of not feeling well, and neuralgia plagued her constantly, but she never missed work for more than a day or two until December, 1898, when she was confined at home for a week. Even then, the clerks came to her home daily so she could keep the work going.[24]

Annie admitted that she did not like to travel, especially alone, and preferred office work. She dreaded the accumulation of work when she returned home from a trip. Sitting in hundreds of meetings, Annie became weary and often had a headache afterwards.[25]

Annie continued to find great joy in working with and for the boards and sought their advice about everything. She considered herself "under orders" from her "bosses," the board secretaries, and liked to carry out details for them. Though she often gave them ideas, she stated repeatedly that she did not want to criticize or dictate policy. Her new ideas usually were designed to advance the work. For example, she devised a plan for getting the work of the three boards presented in district associations.

Several new convictions emerged in Annie's life during the

1890s. Annie believed that missions contributions should be given to the work of a board as a whole and not designated for special projects. She constantly battled against the tendency on the part of the women to designate money and resisted all efforts to get WMU, SBC, to support causes other than the work done by the Convention boards. Various persons bombarded her with appeals for colleges, Southern Seminary, even state missions. Her feelings about state missions caused some tension with the state secretaries. She faced a strong move on the part of the state Baptist secretary and others in Maryland to form a third women's society, one for state missions. Though Annie considered "this a very unwise movement" and claimed the women were already doing much for state missions, she joined the Woman's State Mission Society when it was organized early in 1899.[26]

The Foreign Mission Board was still in debt. Annie was concerned about the debt, the continuing influence of the Gospel Mission movement, and the precarious situation in China because of the war with Japan. She had many ideas to help erase the debt and put these ideas into action.[27] Also, Annie thought of ways to minister to and more effectively use foreign missionaries when they were on furlough.[28]

Some Brazilian churches were concerned with the Foreign Mission Board debt also. Brazilian missionaries notified Annie that Brazilian jewelry was being sent to her from a church in Brazil. The church wanted her to dispose of the jewelry and apply the proceeds toward the Foreign Mission Board debt. Annie was glad that the WMU, SBC, Executive Committee had passed a resolution several years earlier that the corresponding secretary was not to receive presents or articles for sale; otherwise she would be inundated with gifts, especially quilts. When the jewelry did not sink on a coffee vessel as Annie hoped, she joyfully sent it to the Foreign Mission Board.[29]

In July, 1897, the Foreign Mission Board did a special issue of the *Foreign Mission Journal* on missions history and women's work. Willingham innocently asked Annie for good photographs of Alice and herself. Annie, of course, refused in no uncertain terms. She told Willingham the stereopticon slide story from the Home of the Friendless and the decision she made twenty years earlier never again to have a picture taken of herself. Annie had strong feelings about women's pictures in print, writing: "I do not think such notoriety at all desirable for women."[30]

The next summer there was another special *Journal* issue in July. Willingham insisted on a picture of Annie seated at her desk. He thought Southern Baptists were entitled to see those who led them. Annie promised the picture, stipulating that "a position will undoubtedly be assumed which does not enable anyone to recognize the occupant of the chair." Annie sent the picture, as promised. It showed her at her desk, but the picture was taken from the back.[31]

Annie thought she saw a change in Willingham's way of looking at things in the late 1890s. He seemed to have a broader view of the work than before and spoke positively about Tichenor and the work of the Sunday School Board. Annie saw the potential for more harmony and union in what the three boards were doing.[32] Many times she herself unified and coordinated efforts on the denominational level. Not only did Annie build a good relationship with Willingham but also with his two associates, E. Y. Mullins in the mid-1890s and A. J. Barton later.[33]

Annie's love for home missions continued to grow. She was most concerned about the war in Cuba, the Spanish-American War. Marie Buhlmaier's work with Germans in Baltimore and Washington grew and even extended to Germans emigrating out of the country. Concerned about Marie's health, Annie got the Home Mission Board to approve an assistant for Miss Buhlmaier and the Sunday School Board to give more Bibles and Testaments for her work.[34]

John Eager, a missionary to Italy, preached often at Eutaw Place Baptist Church in Baltimore during the summer of 1896. As soon as Annie learned that the Eagers would locate in Baltimore, she urged him to start a work among the Italians.

Annie Armstrong at her desk in the office of the secretary of WMU, July, 1898, copied from the *Foreign Mission Journal*

Eager would return to Italy soon, but she thought he could begin the work and prepare it for someone else. Annie petitioned the Home Mission Board and secured funding for the Italian work. She got Frost to grant Bibles and literature and involved the Baptist Young People's Union in providing workers.[35]

After 1895 Annie tried to get the Week of Self-Denial observed as widely as possible. In 1897 a Virginia church objected to the week. Annie wrote the secretaries of the boards that the church's Woman's Missionary Society had claimed that a Week of Self-Denial is "unscriptural, tends to covetousness, and decreases receipts of the [Home] Board." The society sent resolutions to Annie, Tichenor, and the Virginia Central Committee. Annie thought F. C. McConnell, formerly at the Home Mission Board and now pastor of the Lynchburg church, had instigated the resolutions and would ventilate his opinion at the Convention. She considered McConnell not "overburdened with discretion." If McConnell spoke at the Southern Baptist Convention, Annie believed T. T. Eaton of the *Western Recorder* "will be delighted to take a hand in the fray." In spite of objections, the WMU, SBC, executive committee again considered and voted in May, 1897, to continue the week.[36]

There also was criticism of WMU, SBC, about the methods for sending and reporting boxes to frontier missionaries. Since Annie had been responsible for initiating and carrying out this work, she took the criticism personally and asked Tichenor to discuss the problem with the Home Mission Board. The Board needed to examine the methods and give her instructions. She offered to go to Atlanta, taking the books and all important papers. Tichenor assured Annie that the criticism was directed at the Board, not her. The Board appointed a committee to investigate thoroughly the methods and history of the box work.[37]

Annie was delighted when F. H. Kerfoot, who had been her pastor from 1877 to 1883, became corresponding secretary of the

Home Mission Board in September, 1899. Annie had long hoped he would go to the Home Mission Board, for she thought he had rare qualifications for the office. She wrote: "No truer, nobler man I believe lives than the one who is now asked to take this position." Concerned about the strain the Kerfoots had been under during the controversy at Southern Seminary where he was a professor, Annie hoped Kerfoot could stand his new pressure.[38]

Annie was responsive when the Sunday School Board asked for WMU, SBC, cooperation and support in several new areas of work. These projects included enlarging the Bible fund, Bible distribution, the Home Department in Sunday School, and sending boxes to frontier Sunday School missionaries. Although some persons felt that WMU had gone beyond the purpose for which it was organized when it presented the work of the Sunday School Board to missionary societies, Annie was convinced that this move was right and that WMU, SBC, was aiding the Board in the missionary features of its work. She admitted that the Bible work might be out of WMU's province but offered to do it to help Board interests.

Annie wanted to cement the connection between WMU, SBC, and the Sunday School Board. The best way she knew to do this was for the Board to pay an increased part of WMU's expenses. In turn, WMU helped with editorial work, distributed circulars, promoted Board literature, raised money for the Bible fund, and sent boxes to missionaries. In 1898 Children's Day was introduced to increase the Bible fund; Annie prepared the programs for the day. She thought WMU could help even more in the future by collecting money for Scripture distribution and publishing.[39]

When Bell resigned from the Sunday School Board in early 1896 to take over *The Christian Index*, J. M. Frost, whom Annie greatly respected, again became secretary of the Sunday School Board. Often Frost acted in a mediator role for Annie, and she had confidence in him. Apparently Frost respected Annie's abilities, too. When Frost gave Annie credit for her ideas, she wrote: "I do recognize that our Heavenly Father has given me quickness to bring forces together." She liked being a unifier and to do "such work as I am capable of without assuming responsibility."[40]

There was much correspondence between Annie and Frost about Bible distribution, boxes to Sunday School missionaries, using frontier missionaries as colporteurs, supplying literature to missionaries, Missionary Day in the Sunday School, the Home Department, and material for *The Teacher*. Annie, a great believer in the Sunday School Board's work, urged her own church to observe Missionary Day and have a Home Department. She was quite shaken when Frost discontinued *The Leader* about the same time the Southern BYPU organized and questioned his decision.[41] Frost appreciated Annie. In 1897 the Sunday School Board voted thanks to her for a particular action she took and "for her repeated acts of kindness to the Board."[42]

Annie had great concerns about Baptist work in Maryland and feared a move on the part of some leaders to separate from the Southern Baptist Convention. Many leaders were not acquainted with denominational affairs. What was needed, she felt, were pastors of experience and judgment. She often referred to the young pastors, whom she saw coming into Baltimore, as the "boy's brigade" or "juveniles."[43]

Because of her mother's feeble condition, Annie could not travel much. However, she kept up with state WMU work through letters, reports, and contacts at WMU, SBC, Annual Meetings. She devised a plan to get WMU work reported in district associations. Often she urged board leaders to talk about women's work and solicit the support of pastors when they spoke at state conventions. She especially wanted to strengthen WMU work in Virginia, Louisiana, and Mississippi, as well as the border areas of Missouri and the District of Columbia.[44] Annie met with the Virginia central committee in Richmond in late 1898 to help leaders work out some organization matters. She would have attended all the Virginia WMU Annual Meetings during these years if possible. Because of a study being made of Virginia's organization, in 1899 Annie sent to the meeting a paper she had written about the relation of WMU, SBC, to state organizations.[45]

Annie noticed an article in the *Florida Baptist Witness* in the summer of 1899, written by Jennie L. Spaulding, the Florida WMU corresponding secretary. Jennie Spaulding, with a Northern background, planned to introduce the Missionary Conquest Course offered by the Northern Baptist Young People's Union of America to associations in Florida. Annie was concerned that the Northerners were making inroads into Southern Baptist territory. She promptly urged Willingham and Frost to object to William N. Chaudoin, the Florida Baptist corresponding secretary. Chaudoin should talk with Miss Spaulding, she felt. Annie sent her views to Jennie Spaulding, and wrote E. E. Chivers, a BYPUA official, expressing her concern about the Florida situation. Though she wanted to say "hands off," she was a little more courteous. She thought Chivers was "undermining the work of the Southern Baptist Convention." Jennie Spaulding claimed she had a right to do what she thought wise in her own field. Not agreeing, Annie pointed out that Miss Spaulding was employed by the state board which received most of its money from the Home Mission Board. Annie proceeded to send a great deal of Southern Baptist literature to Florida.[46]

The Maryland Baptist Mission Rooms still issued programs quarterly, supported by monthly leaflets related to the prayer card topics. The rooms also circulated a catalog of all materials. In addition, Annie and her co-workers supplied a great deal of material to the Foreign and Home Mission Board journals and state Baptist papers. In 1898 Annie again sent copy to the Home Mission Board for *Our Home Field* when it resumed publication.

Annie hoped to do away with the women's papers put out by Kentucky, North Carolina, Missouri, and Texas WMUs, considering these papers "forlorn." She thought WMU could get all the coverage it needed through state Baptist papers and mission board journals.[47]

Annie could rejoice in the accomplishments of the 1890s. Maturing in leadership, Annie had grown tremendously in her ability to build strong relationships, to inspire others, and to unify national efforts. She was gifted in pulling forces together. Many dreams were put in action by Annie—new relationships with The Southern Baptist Theological Seminary and the state WMUs, new work with black women, and the beginning of an annuity plan. She saw, too, the work of the Foreign Mission Board, Home Mission Board, and Sunday School Board grow, and Woman's Missionary Union, SBC, mature as an organization.

Notes (See pages 295-310 for Key to Sources.)

1. W. H. Whitsitt to Annie Armstrong, May 23, 1895, SBTS; Annie Armstrong to R. J. Willingham, May 25, 1895, FMB; *Report*, WMU, 1896; *FMJ*, August, 1896.

2. *Report*, WMU, 1896; Annie Armstrong to R. J. Willingham, January 1, December 22, December 26, 1896, FMB; Annie Armstrong to J. M. Frost, January 26, 1897, SSB; *Biblical Recorder*, May 4, 1898; WMU minutes, January 12, February 9, 1897; *FMJ*, February, 1897.

3. WMU minutes, June 8, 1897; Annie Armstrong to A. J. Barton, May 13, 1897, FMB.

4. WMU minutes, March 9, 1897, February 8, 1898, September 12, 1899; *FMJ*, July, October, 1899, June, 1900; *The Seminary Magazine*, 1900-1904.

5. Annie Armstrong to J. M. Frost, April 9, 1897, SSB; W. H. Whitsitt to J. M. Frost, April 9, 1897, SSB; J. M. Frost to W. H. Whitsitt, April 20, 1897, SBTS; Annie Armstrong to R. J. Willingham, April 21, 1897, FMB.

6. Annie Armstrong to R. J. Willingham, April 21, April 23, August 16, 1897, January, 1899, FMB; *Encyclopedia of Southern Baptists*, 2:1496; Walter B. Shurden, *Not a Silent People, Controversies That Have Shaped Baptists*, pp. 21-32.

7. Annie Armstrong to R. J. Willingham, June 30, July, 1899, FMB.

8. WMU minutes, January-March, 1896; Annie Armstrong to R. J. Willingham, April 11, April 28, June 11, August 5, 1896, FMB; R. J. Willingham to Annie Armstrong, April 12, 1896, FMB; *Reports*, WMU, 1895-1896; *FMJ*, February, 1899; Dorothy Fisher Long, *This Glad Year of Jubilee*, p. 7.

9. WMU minutes, May 26, 1896; Annie Armstrong to R. J. Willingham, March 26, 1897, September 26, 1898, FMB; HMB minutes, October 3, 1899.

10. Annie Armstrong to R. J. Willingham, November 14, 1895, WMU minutes, October 8, 1895; Annie Armstrong to J. M. Frost, January 3, January 13, 1896, SSB.

11. Annie Armstrong to R. J. Willingham, November 13, November 28, December 10, 1896, January 6, January 19, March 22, April 28, 1897, FMB; R. J. Willingham to Annie Armstrong, December 12, 1896, January 7, January 22, 1897, FMB; Annie Armstrong to J. M. Frost, December 10, 1896, January 26, 1897, SSB; *Report,* WMU, 1898; Earl L. Harrison, *The Dream and the Dreamer,* pp. 9-13; Wharton, "One Woman's Vision," WMU.

12. Annie Armstrong to R. J. Willingham, January 19, February 5, 1897, FMB; Annie Armstrong to J. M. Frost, February 1, February 20, April 28, 1897, SSB.

13. Annie Armstrong to R. J. Willingham, March 22, April 28, 1897, FMB; Annie Armstrong to J. M. Frost, June 14, July 2, 1897, SSB.

14. WMU minutes, June 8, 1897; Annie Armstrong to J. M. Frost, July 2, 1897, SSB.

15. WMU minutes, 1897, January 11, 1898; Annie Armstrong to R. J. Willingham, September 28, December, 1897, January 17, 1898, FMB; Annie Armstrong to J. M. Frost, December, 1897, SSB; L. G. Jordan to Annie Armstrong, January 14, 1898, FMB; Annie Armstrong to O. F. Flippo, January 18, 1898, FMB.

16. Annie Armstrong to R. J. Willingham, November 26, 1895, February 13, April 11, May 18, August 24, 1896, January 21, August 19, 1897, June 24, September 19, September 30, 1898, September 19, 1899, FMB; Annie Armstrong to J. M. Frost, July 9, 1897, August 19, August 26, 1897, January 13, September 19, 1899, SSB; Annie Armstrong to E. Y. Mullins, January 18, 1896, FMB; B. D. Gray to Annie Armstrong, January 8, 1896, FMB; FMB minutes, October 1, 1898.

17. Annie Armstrong to R. J. Willingham, March 20, 1895, March 27, March 29, April 21, April 29, May 4, June 1, "Tuesday evening," July 6, 1899, FMB; R. J. Willingham to Annie Armstrong, April 26, April 28, 1899, FMB; Annie Armstrong to J. M. Frost, n.d., June 2, July 6, 1899, SSB; FMB minutes, April 11, April 27, May 30, 1899; HMB minutes, April 26, May 5, 1899, July 3, 1900; SSB minutes, May 6, June 1, August 16, 1899; *Report,* WMU, 1899.

18. FMB minutes, February 11, 1896; *Report,* WMU, 1896-1898; *FMJ,* June-July 1896; Fannie Heck to R. J. Willingham, March 27, 1897, FMB.

19. WMU minutes, September 24, 1895; Annie Armstrong to R. J. Willingham, August 1, 1898, August 26, December 12, 1899, FMB; *Reports,* WMU, 1897-1898.

20. Anne Luther Bagby to Annie Armstrong, July 10, 1899, FMB; Annie Armstrong to R. J. Willingham, August 8, August 21, 1899, FMB; R. J. Willingham to Annie Armstrong, August, 1899, FMB; R. J. Willingham to Ermine Bagby, August 22, 1899, FMB.

21. Examples: Annie Armstrong to R. J. Willingham, September 13, 1895, FMB; Annie Armstrong to J. M. Frost, March 24, December 16, 1897, SSB; WMU minutes, June 8, 1897.

22. Annie Armstrong to T. P. Bell, June 11, 1895, SSB; Annie Armstrong to R. J. Willingham, December 26, 1896, January 2, January 6, March 3, 1897, November 24, December 12, 1899, FMB; *FMJ,* February, 1897; Annie

Armstrong to J. M. Frost, November 24, 1899, SSB; WMU minutes, December 12, 1899.

23. Fannie Heck to R. J. Willingham, June 4, 1895, FMB; R. J. Willingham to Fannie Heck, June 4, 1895, FMB; Annie Armstrong to J. M. Frost, May 23, 1895, SSB; Annie Armstrong to R. J. Willingham, May 29, November 26, 1895; FMB; R. J. Willingham to Annie Armstrong, March 9, 1896, February 9, 1897, FMB.

24. Annie Armstrong to E. Y. Mullins, December 12, 1895, FMB; Annie Armstrong to R. J. Willingham, July 25, July 29, November 13, November 19, 1896, March 19, December 14, December 23, 1898, FMB; WMU minutes, January 10, 1899, *FMJ,* February, 1899; *The Religious Herald,* January 26, 1899; Minutes, WHMS, December, 1898.

25. Annie Armstrong to R. J. Willingham, November 14, 1895, September 20, 1897, March 7, 1898, April 12, 1899, FMB.

26. Annie Armstrong to R. J. Willingham, February 3, 1897, January 4, April 3, September 8, September 22, September 30, November 2, 1898, FMB; R. J. Willingham to Annie Armstrong, May 25, 1896, FMB; Annie Armstrong to E. Y. Mullins, October 9, 1895, FMB; Annie Armstrong to J. M. Frost, January 13, July 13, 1896, March 21, May 27, July 28, 1897, September 22, 1898, SSB; MBUA minutes, 1899; FMB minutes, May 25, 1896; Minutes, WHMS, January, 1899; Minutes, WSMS, 1900.

27. Annie Armstrong to R. J. Willingham, March 25, August 29, 1895, May 18, May 25, June 5, June 6, July 9, 1896; other correspondence, 1895-1897.

28. Annie Armstrong to A. J. Barton, January 10, 1898, FMB; Annie Armstrong to R. J. Willingham, August 1, September 16, 1898, FMB; Annie Armstrong to J. M. Frost, September 17, 1898, SSB.

29. Annie Armstrong to T. P. Bell, May 21, 1895, SSB; Annie Armstrong to R. J. Willingham, May 29, May 31, 1895, FMB; Annie Armstrong to E. Y. Mullins, September 26, 1895, FMB; E. Y. Mullins to Annie Armstrong, October 1, 1895, FMB.

30. R. J. Willingham to Annie Armstrong, May 21, May 24, July 5, 1897, FMB; Annie Armstrong to R. J. Willingham, May 22, July 1, 1897, FMB; Fannie Heck to R. J. Willingham, May 25, 1897, FMB; Annie Armstrong to J. M. Frost, August 17, 1897, SSB.

31. Annie Armstrong to R. J. Willingham, June 1, 1898, FMB; Annie Armstrong to J. M. Frost, June 1, June 6, 1898, SSB.

32. Annie Armstrong to J. M. Frost, January 15, 1898, SSB.

33. Annie Armstrong to R. J. Willingham, September 3, September 10, 1895, FMB; Annie Armstrong to A. J. Barton, September 28, 1896, FMB.

34. Annie Armstrong to R. J. Willingham, April 2, 1896, FMB; WMU minutes, September 14, October 12, 1897, May 17, 1898; HMB minutes, August 2, November 1, 1898; Marie Buhlmaier to Annie Armstrong, October 31, 1897, SSB; Annie Armstrong to J. M. Frost, November 17, 1897, September 17, 1898, SSB.

35. *The Evangel,* August 19, 1896; HMB minutes, December 14, 1896; Annie Armstrong to J. M. Frost, December, 1896, SSB; Annie Armstrong to

R. J. Willingham, August 3, 1896, FMB; WMU minutes, January 12, 1897, May 17, 1898.

36. Annie Armstrong to R. J. Willingham, March 22, 1897, FMB; Annie Armstrong to J. M. Frost, March 22, 1897, SSB; WMU minutes, May 10, May 21, 1897; *Reports,* WMU, 1898-1899.

37. Annie Armstrong to I. T. Tichenor, May 17, May 31, 1899, SSB; HMB minutes, June 2, December 12, 1899; WMU minutes, June 13, 1899.

38. Annie Armstrong to R. J. Willingham, July 20, August 28, 1899, FMB.

39. *Reports,* WMU, 1898-1900; Annie Armstrong to J. M. Frost, March 21, April 2, 1896, SSB.

40. Annie Armstrong to J. M. Frost, July 24, 1896, SSB.

41. Annie Armstrong to J. M. Frost, January 13, May-July, September 24, 1896, January 26, May 13, June 9, September 18, October 8, November 13, December 2, 1897, March 5, March 26, 1898, January 10, January 24, 1899, December 1, 1900, SSB; Annie Armstrong to R. J. Willingham, October 1, 1896, FMB; SSB minutes, April 21, 1898; Annie Armstrong to A. J. Barton, June 17, 1897, FMB.

42. SSB minutes, September 27, 1897.

43. Annie Armstrong to R. J. Willingham, February 3, February 17, March 13, 1896, February 3, March 3, September 3, 1897, FMB; Annie Armstrong to A. J. Barton, September 21, 1897, FMB; Annie Armstrong to J. M. Frost, September 13, September 15, 1899, SSB.

44. Annie Armstrong to R. J. Willingham, November 9, 1893, July 7, August 5, August 24, 1896, FMB; Annie Armstrong to T. P. Bell, August 9, August 27, 1895, SSB; *Reports,* WMU, 1898-1899; WMU minutes, September 14, 1897.

45. Annie Armstrong to R. J. Willingham, October 1, 1896, October 11, 1897, November-December, 1898, January 21, 1899, September-December, 1899, FMB; WMU minutes, December 13, 1898; January 9, 1900; Annie Armstrong to J. M. Frost, October 7, October 10, 1899, SSB.

46. Annie Armstrong to R. J. Willingham, August-September 1899, FMB; Annie Armstrong to J. M. Frost, August-September, 1899, SSB; Annie Armstrong to E. E. Chivers, August 30, 1899, SSB; E. E. Chivers to Annie Armstrong, September 6, 1899, SSB; Annie Armstrong to J. L. Spaulding, August 3, August 5, August 23, 1899, SSB; J. L. Spaulding to Annie Armstrong, July 15, August 31, 1899, SSB.

47. *Reports,* WMU 1898-1899; WMU minutes, September 14, 1897; M. M. Welch to Annie Armstrong, March 4, 1899, SSB; Annie Armstrong to M. M. Welch, March 6, 1899, SSB; Annie Armstrong to T. P. Bell, August 31, 1895, SSB; Annie Armstrong to E. Y. Mullins, September 12, October 26, November 27, December 12, 1895, FMB; Annie Armstrong to R. J. Willingham, June 4, 1894, FMB.

7
Did Troubles Get Her Down?

With a strong conviction that the Holy Spirit guided her thoughts and decisions, Annie faced each day and life situation with confidence. She believed if she were faithful and persevered in doing God's will and the work which he gave her to do, she could leave the results to him. Writing about her work, she said: "I am more and more persuaded that all that is required of those who have the work in charge is faithful seed sowing. The harvest is bound to follow." Though Annie had many trials and troubles during the last four years of the nineteenth century, she could say: "No matter how heavy the burden, daily strength is given, so I expect we need not give ourselves any concern as to what the outcome will be, but think 'go forward.'"[1]

Annie was a woman of prayer and Bible study, daily habits which sustained her in times of joy and difficulty. She believed in answered prayer and that the Lord would provide whatever was needed. With many familiar verses in her mind and heart, Annie could refer easily in writing or speaking to appropriate passages. Often she quoted verses such as these: "Fear thou not; for I am with thee: be not dismayed; for I am thy God: I will strengthen thee; yea, I will uphold thee with the right hand of my righteousness" (Isa. 41:10). "Not by might, nor by power, but by my spirit, saith the Lord of hosts" (Zech. 4:6). "As thy days, so shall thy strength be" (Deut. 33:25b). "Therefore, my beloved brethren, be ye stedfast, unmoveable, always abounding in the work of the Lord, forasmuch as ye know that your labour is not in vain in the Lord" (1 Cor. 15:58). In numerous devotions which she gave at committee or missionary society meetings, Annie read from passages about missionary laborers, Christian work, earnestness, trust, praise, and thankfulness. Her favorite passages seem to have been Psalms 46 and 91, John 14, Galatians 5, and James 1.[2]

During difficult times Annie relied on her faith, prayer, and assurances from the Bible. These convictions sustained her in times of trouble and strained relationships. Though Annie built strong relationships with Southern Baptist leaders and often unified denominational efforts, she was concerned about the Northern Baptists. Objecting to what she considered an intrusion by the Northern Baptists into Southern Baptist territory, Annie sometimes appeared negative in her dealings with Northern Baptist leaders. Her concerns grew out of her loyalty to the Southern Baptist Convention, on one hand, and, on the other, Northern Baptist actions which she considered detrimental to the work of Southern Baptists. These Northern Baptist actions related to distribution of Sunday School literature and various methods which seemed to Annie to harm the Sunday School Board. She was concerned, too, about Northern Baptist work with blacks, young people, and the border states and territories, production of the American Baptist Year-Book, and apparent Northern support of the Gospel Mission movement.

To illustrate how she thought Northern Baptist leaders were hurting Southern Baptist work, Annie compared the American Baptist Publication Society in Philadelphia with the Standard Oil Company. Annie wrote Frost: "It is with them the desire to monopolize and crush out and then act the part of benefactor—the same methods adopted by the Standard Oil Company."[3]

Annie was especially upset with A. J. Rowland, whom at one time she considered "a warm personal friend." Rowland, now in charge of the American Baptist Publication Society, had been a pastor in Baltimore and was possibly the friend who played the prank on Annie with her picture at the Home of the Friendless twenty years earlier. At least once during the 1890s Annie thought Rowland took advantage of a passing remark made by T. P. Bell when he was Sunday School Board secretary. She felt that Rowland capitalized on the remark and moved into Southern territory in an unscrupulous way. Managing to avoid Rowland at the Maryland Baptist Union Association meeting that fall, Annie had quite an altercation with his associate, O. F. Flippo. She also believed Rowland was out to crush the Sunday School Board and black Baptist publications.[4]

Why did Annie react to the Northern Baptists as she did and therefore appear negative and perhaps sometimes even hostile? To view properly Annie's reactions to Northern Baptists, it is necessary to understand the historical context. Baptists in the Triennial Convention, organized in 1814, parted ways in 1845, primarily over the slavery issue, and formed two conventions— the Northern Baptist Convention, with separate and independent societies for the various functions, and the Southern Baptist Convention, bound together as churches which cooperatively supported missionary, benevolent, and educational causes in a more unified way. Southern Baptists emerged from the Civil War struggling, impoverished, and with few missionaries; Northern Baptists, however, were strong and financially stable. The stage was set for a struggle between the two Conventions over territory and control.

The conflict between the stronger Northern Baptist Convention and the struggling, but emerging, Southern Baptist Convention can be seen in light of home missions and publishing efforts. Organized in 1832, the American Baptist Home Mission Society saw the whole continent as its mission field and expanded rapidly; its work included blacks and language groups. When I. T. Tichenor assumed leadership of the Southern Baptist Home Mission Board in 1882 and the Board began to expand its work, there was conflict with the Northern Baptists. Southern Baptists resisted Northern overtures toward union in home missions work. The American Baptist Home Mission Society and the Southern Baptist Home Mission Board, however, in 1894 made a comity agreement related to cooperative and combined efforts to assist National Baptists. In 1912 and 1914 (after Annie's years of service), Northern Baptists agreed to withdraw their work from New Mexico and Oklahoma in order to end competition with the Home Mission Board.

Organized in 1824, the American Baptist Publication Society engaged in publishing, Bible distribution, and Sunday School promotion. Until Southern Baptists established a lasting Sunday School Board in 1891, the Northern Baptist society had free rein throughout the United States. The society sent representatives to most Southern Baptist meetings, advertised widely, promoted the use of its literature in Southern Baptist churches, and established a number of branch offices in principal cities in the United States.[5] Close geographically to the publication society in Philadelphia and friends of former Baltimorean A. J. Rowland, many Maryland Baptist leaders, including the Leverings, supported the American Baptist Publication Society. Annie, with strong allegiance to the Southern Baptist Convention and its boards, resented what she considered the constant Northern Baptist intrusion into the South. With these feelings, she was most vocal about the Northern Baptist societies and leaders.

Annie's attitude about the American Baptist Publication Society was revealed when she proposed a Southern Baptist Convention almanac. Thinking that an almanac would show Southern Baptist unity and be educational, Annie sent Frost some examples and suggested that the Sunday School Board issue the almanac. Annie offered to gather the data and prepare a brief sketch of the Southern Baptist Convention and its agencies, and, if possible, a sketch of each state organization. She felt the Sunday School Board should send the almanac free to pastors and, possibly, Sunday School superintendents. The American Baptist Publication Society objected to the almanac since the American Baptist Year-Book seemed to meet this need. Annie claimed the almanac, which the Sunday School Board agreed to

Lansing Burrows, Recording Secretary, SBC, 1881-1919

produce, was not to take the place of the American Baptist Year-
Book but cover different ground.[6]

No doubt Annie was not pleased when Frost asked Lansing
Burrows, since 1881 recording secretary for the Southern Baptist
Convention, to be the editor of the Convention almanac. Burrows, also pastor of First Baptist Church in Augusta, Georgia,
was noted for getting the printed minutes of the Southern
Baptist Convention into delegates' hands immediately after the
meeting. Several years before her almanac proposal, Annie had
stated that she did not think the work should be crippled nor
reports hurried so Burrows could be "heralded over the country
as a phenomenal Secretary." Though the specifics were not
recorded, words flew between Annie and Burrows during the
Southern Baptist Convention in Washington in 1895. Annie
claimed she did not know what she had done to Burrows to make
him feel injured. Frost heard both sides and acted as peace-
maker, getting Burrows to apologize. Annie considered herself
the aggrieved party, thinking she had not done anything wrong,
nor had Burrows really apologized. Only Frost's levelheaded,
peaceful advice kept her from fanning the situation into major
proportions.[7]

Annie and Burrows had to relate to each other occasionally
because of the statistics and reports needed for the Southern
Baptist Convention Annual and the almanac. Neither seemed to
enjoy the experience. Burrows indicated Annie was not interested in "personal details." Annie wanted Burrows to appreciate
the fact that there was at least one person who was not willing to
overlook unnecessary rudeness; she claimed he did not know
how to treat a lady. She continued to resist sending him the
WMU, SBC, statistics when he wanted them, for it was impossible for her to secure final statistics from the states by that time.
For awhile there was an impasse. Annie finally agreed to send
Burrows reports by April 25, soon after she received them from
the states; however, she continually complained about this
process. Frost tried to get Annie to compliment Burrows on the

first almanac since she made positive statements about it. She refused, however, claiming Burrows did not care about her opinion.[8]

Annie's major trial of the late 1890s was with Fannie Heck, elected again as national WMU president in Washington in 1895. Miss Heck, known as modest, quiet, and dignified, with a calm and winning manner, believed the WMU, SBC, president's role should be a strong one, and she acted in that manner. This stance must have been difficult for the strong-willed Annie, for she had functioned without much contact with the WMU, SBC, president for three years. Miss Heck had been ill most of her previous term, and Mrs. Gwathmey did not assume an active role.

The initial confrontation between Annie and Fannie Heck came over the 1897 Sunday School Board recommendation at the WMU, SBC, Annual Meeting in Wilmington. The recommendation related to WMU cooperation in enlarging the Bible fund:

> Our Bible work has grown immensely this year, and we desire to see it still further increased. We earnestly wish that our Bible fund could be enlarged and should be glad of the co-operation of Woman's Mission Societies.[9]

There was much discussion on the floor of the WMU Annual Meeting. Miss Heck both privately and publicly opposed WMU, SBC, contributing to the Sunday School Board. Annie warmly advocated adopting the recommendation, but there were differences of opinion among WMU executive committee members. The Sunday School Board had earlier requested a specific amount, but the final motion asked only for WMU's cooperation.[10]

It was at this point that Annie admitted to Frost that the Bible fund work might be out of WMU, SBC's, area of work. However, she wanted to help Sunday School Board interests. Because Virginia was influential, Annie worried about Abby Gwathmey's and Virginia's objections to the fund.[11]

Annie endeavored during the next year to get out information about the Bible fund and to prepare for the next WMU, SBC, Annual Meeting. One state WMU, North Carolina, did not order the literature about the fund. Annie did not discuss the subject with Miss Heck, also president of North Carolina WMU, until Miss Heck came to Baltimore in January, 1898. On January 24, the day before a called WMU executive committee meeting, they had a heated discussion about the matter. Fannie Heck thought Annie had used her power to push Sunday School Board work and had implemented the 1897 Wilmington recommendation in a manner contrary to what the delegates had adopted. Miss Heck did not interpret "cooperation" as monied offerings, but as influence and promotion. Annie believed, on the contrary, that "cooperation" meant contributions as well as promotion and felt that she had interpreted the action correctly.

Annie thought Miss Heck had made a grave charge against her. She indicated a willingness for Miss Heck to present the matter to the WMU executive committee or during an annual meeting. Hurt, she wanted an opportunity to refute publicly the implication that she had used her authority to carry out her own wishes. Miss Heck considered it a personal matter between the two of them and did not bring it up to the committee the next day. From her knowledge of Fannie Heck, Annie felt sure Miss Heck would not again refer to the matter, nor make any public opposition to the upcoming 1898 Sunday School Board recommendations to WMU.[12]

In case the subject again came up, however, Annie urged Frost not to make any changes in the wording of the Sunday School Board recommendations to WMU, SBC, for 1898. She changed her mind about Fannie Heck's forgetting the matter, as Miss Heck brought it up again. Annie thought trouble was brewing and decided to ask Judge Jonathan Haralson, president of the Southern Baptist Convention and a member of the Supreme Court in Alabama, his opinion about whether she had acted in accordance with the recommendations adopted by the women in Wilmington. It was obvious that Annie would not back down from the position she had taken. She believed the women had agreed to make monied contributions to the Sunday School Board. Concerned when she learned that Miss Heck stopped in Richmond to see Willingham after she left Baltimore, Annie determined to prepare to the hilt for the 1898 WMU, SBC, Annual Meeting in Norfolk.

Willingham, opting not to take sides, hoped that Annie and Miss Heck would be able to work things out and agree on WMU, SBC, plans about Sunday School Board work. Judge Haralson sustained Annie's understanding of the recommendations about the Bible fund. He thought the actions at the last WMU Annual Meeting indicated funds or money. Annie had this information ready in case she had to use it but did not send Haralson's letter to Fannie Heck.

During the next few months, Annie agonized over the subject. She indicated to the WMU executive committee at a meeting, not attended by Heck, and to Frost, that she might not hold office the next year. Annie did her best to keep Frost on her side. She asked him not to write Miss Heck about the Sunday School Board recommendations to WMU, SBC, without letting her see the letter first. If Miss Heck made a private move to change the Board recommendations, Annie would call an extra session and put the whole matter before the WMU executive committee. Interestingly, none of the 1897 Sunday School Board recommendations ever were presented or referred to in North Carolina WMU meetings or reports.[13]

Fannie Heck tried to secure full information about the situation. She indicated that she thought Annie had influenced Frost and Mrs. W. J. Brown, the WMU, SBC, vice-president from Maryland, who was a personal friend of Annie's.[14]

Nothing happened at the WMU, SBC, Annual Meeting in Norfolk in May, 1898, to magnify the situation. Annie had arranged for the Sunday School Board recommendations to be brought the first session. If Fannie Heck opposed the recommendations, this would allow additional time for discussion.

Miss Heck made no comments one way or the other either in the WMU executive committee meeting or during the WMU Annual Meeting. The delegates approved the Sunday School Board recommendation asking for continued WMU, SBC, cooperation with the Bible fund. Annie indicated that the relationship between herself and Miss Heck was becoming more and more strained; she expected some decisive action before long.[15]

Decisive action was not long in coming. Miss Heck wrote Annie on May 13, reminding Miss Armstrong that she would neither be in Baltimore often nor attend most WMU, SBC, executive committee meetings. This placed her at a disadvantage in advising the committee as she should. To obviate this disadvantage, Miss Heck asked Annie to send her a detailed statement of agenda items a week before committee meetings. This would give her time to write the committee her opinion.

Annie refused Miss Heck's request. She based her refusal on the bylaw which stated that in the absence of the president, the vice-president from the state where the committee was located would take her place. This of course was the Maryland vice-president, elected by the Maryland women, not by the national WMU organization. Further, Annie reminded Fannie Heck that the committee's main work was to carry out recommendations from the three boards as adopted at the WMU, SBC, Annual Meeting. Since Miss Heck knew what these recommendations were, she was free to submit her views at any time.[16]

Miss Heck, astonished at Annie's refusal, wrote Willingham that she had at least two options. The first, which she felt sure Annie would prefer, was to resign without stating reasons. The second option, which she decided to take, was to have decided, once and for all, the meaning of the position of president of Woman's Missionary Union, SBC. Miss Heck felt she owed this to herself and to the future. She in no way agreed with the interpretation Annie had put on the constitution, nor did Martha McIntosh Bell, who also led in the 1888 Richmond meeting. Miss Heck intended to be the president and to have her views read at WMU executive committee meetings. It was clear to her that the executive committee controlled Union matters, and that Annie ran the committee. Further, the committee in essence decided who the Maryland vice-president and future committee members would be. This made the committee self-perpetuating. It seemed illogical to Miss Heck that the elected president would have no voice in the organization's affairs. Miss Heck believed Annie's actions were the result of a long, long course of disregard for the views of the president.

Fannie did not want to bring the matter before the Union in full session. She felt the personal issues would create a division, and this would be to the detriment of the work. Though she believed that Annie and Alice controlled the WMU executive committee and she probably would not get a fair hearing, that would be the forum she would use. Annie would probably overawe the committee by threatening to resign if her will were disputed. Miss Heck thought Annie had done that before. To delay, Miss Heck thought, would only be cowardly. She was willing to drop the whole matter if some kind friend would emerge to help Annie see and retract the false position she had taken in her interpretation of the constitution; however, she saw no such friend on the horizon.[17]

Both Annie and Fannie Heck sought advice from Willingham; however, he refused to take sides. He was careful to keep each woman informed. Annie asked Frost to take her side since the initial question at issue related to the work of the Sunday School Board. She believed thoroughly she was right and did not "propose to yield one iota."

In June, 1898, Miss Heck hit the problem head-on. She wrote a long letter to each member of the WMU, SBC, executive committee about the issue at hand, alerting them that she was asking the vice-president to bring it before the committee at its June meeting. Annie did not receive a copy of the letter. However, Miss Heck wrote her that she intended to refer the question of the role of the WMU, SBC, president as interpreted in the bylaws of the constitution to the WMU executive committee at its next session. The committee, without Miss Heck but with Annie, met on June 14. Annie was prepared with Judge Haralson's letters from February. A committee member moved that the matter be considered at the next Annual Meeting, but Alice, Annie's sister, quickly offered a substitute motion, which carried. She moved that the matter be tabled until September, since the WMU executive committee was unwilling to come to any conclusion until an expert decision was rendered by Judge Haralson.[18]

Annie felt she needed advice. Not having gotten much response from Willingham or Frost, she turned to Tichenor. He came to Baltimore to discuss the whole matter with her. She expressed the opinion that Miss Heck was acting in a strange way, calculated to do much harm. After the meeting with Tichenor, probably at his request, Annie sent Willingham and Frost numerous background documents—the correspondence from the previous February about the Sunday School Board recommendations, the constitution and bylaws, Miss Heck's letter to the WMU executive committee, and a letter she had just written to Judge Haralson. Annie sent Haralson copies of correspondence and asked him to interpret the bylaw clause which stated: "In her absence, the Vice President from the State where the Committee may be located shall take her place." She spelled out for him specific points on which the committee wanted opinions. Miss Heck also wrote Haralson.[19]

Haralson replied promptly, discussing the description of the duties of the president, vice-presidents, and corresponding secretary of WMU, SBC, as given in the bylaws. He made two points which were most significant. The term "shall take her place" meant *for the time*, to do any and all things the president might or could do if present; it did not mean displacement of or interference with the presidential office, or the responsibilities and prerogatives of the absent president. Also, Haralson indicated he could find nothing in the constitution or bylaws that would make it incumbent on the corresponding secretary to furnish the president the WMU executive committee agenda in advance. If this were done, it would simply be a matter of courtesy. Haralson thought that relations between the president and corresponding secretary of WMU had become strained and embarrassing, and not about "the weightier matters of the law." He urged both Annie and Miss Heck to let everything but the weightier matters be passed over.[20]

Tichenor, Willingham, and Frost met in July, apparently in Montgomery, Alabama. They wrote Annie and Fannie Heck, suggesting a conference to include the three of them, Judge Haralson, Miss Armstrong, and Miss Heck. Annie resented the implication that they placed her in the same category as Miss Heck but agreed to attend the conference and urged that it be held near Baltimore because of her mother's feeble condition. She suggested Washington. Annie hoped there would be no attempt to smooth matters over and that the men would judge plainly. No doubt she still considered herself right. Annie was troubled deeply. She wrote Frost: "I think I do see that God's hand is guiding in the way he is showing some of us what ought to be done under existing circumstances, but I fail entirely to see any signs of God's hand in what has occurred. I trust He will overrule it for good." Annie joined the others in the hope that the "Holy Spirit will be present and direct all" at the approaching conference.

Fannie Heck, too, agreed to attend the conference but requested it be postponed until after the first of September. She considered the question purely an official matter. She stated that everything was known already, she would not bring new evidence, and agreed with Haralson's interpretation. If the conference were held, Miss Heck thought the secretaries who asked for it should assume full responsibility for any action that followed. Annie made one more attempt in August to talk with Frost, asking him to visit with her in Baltimore before the meeting.[21]

The conference was held in late August, 1898, possibly August 23, in Norfolk, Virginia. Immediately afterwards, Willingham wrote the WMU, SBC, executive committee on behalf of the group. He stated that the conference had been "full and free" and that a settlement had been reached to which both Annie and Miss Heck agreed. He recommended that the committee take no further action and the matter be postponed indefinitely. The committee concurred. An official paper was drawn up, but it does not seem to exist in any archives or files. Apparently Miss Heck agreed verbally to decline reelection another year and to make her decision public the next March. She actually had decided this the previous May.

Annie stated she would not discuss what occurred before or during the conference with any WMU, SBC, executive committee members. She claimed the committee members tended to look at things through her eyes, and their decisions were largely hers. On this point she and Fannie Heck agreed. Annie did a lot of thinking during the next several months. She asked for opinions about whether the time had come for her to give up the work and allow for a change in policy and methods. At the time she could do this gracefully, without having to give a reason, because of the condition of her mother's health.[22]

There was great tension in the air between Annie and Miss Heck until the WMU, SBC, Annual Meeting in May, 1899. Little correspondence passed between them. Since Annie was a strong proponent of the frontier box work, it probably perturbed her when Miss Heck wrote in September, 1898, to inform Annie that North Carolina WMU would not send out letters from Sunday School Board missionaries about boxes. They would only give the names of home missionaries. Miss Heck remained firm in her conviction that WMU's purpose was to assist the mission boards, not the Sunday School Board.

Annie did not want, and apparently did not have, any dealings with Miss Heck during the fall and winter of 1898-99 but communicated through the corresponding secretaries of the boards. Annie tried to live up to the agreements reached in Norfolk the previous August.

In January, 1899, Annie began to verbalize her concern that Fannie Heck would renege on the agreement and not decline reelection. If Miss Heck did not live up to the agreement, Annie would give up the work. When she learned that Miss Heck planned to be in Louisville for the WMU, SBC, Annual Meeting, Annie decided not to go. With the strained relations between them, Annie did not want to be thrown with Fannie Heck at an Annual Meeting. On March 6 Miss Heck sent Annie a letter to present to the WMU executive committee. She notified the committee and would alert the states that she had decided the past May in Norfolk not to serve as president again. Annie decided she would go to Louisville after all, even if Miss Heck were present. She took her niece, May, and one of Joshua Levering's daughters with her. Annie wrote to Miss Heck in March about closing the year's accounts and making arrangements for the WMU Annual Meeting; she got no response.[23]

Miss Heck presided over the WMU Annual Meeting in Louisville. She was preoccupied, probably to some extent because her mother, who had accompanied her, was ill. The next seven years were silent between Annie and Fannie Heck. They apparently had little contact in the remaining years of Annie's service. Miss Heck continued to serve as the North Carolina WMU president but did not attend any WMU, SBC, Annual Meetings until 1906 when she was reelected president. She made no references to Annie in the women's department in the *Biblical Recorder*, nor did she print anything Annie had written, except for one annual report. From 1904 to 1906, Miss Heck served on the Advisory Board of the Margaret Home for Missionary Children, chaired by Annie. Therefore, they were thrown together on occasion.[24]

Things seemed to go from bad to worse during the controversy with Miss Heck. In late November, 1897, a fire threatened the Maryland Mission Rooms, completely burning a furniture store

across the street and killing a woman, though there was no
serious damage to the building where WMU, SBC, offices were
located. This was the second time in two months that WMU was
in danger of fire. The first time a fire next door occurred at night
and was quickly extinguished.[25]

Annie had personal troubles in addition to official ones. Since
1894 her aged mother had been feeble, and it had become
difficult to get or keep good domestic help.[26] Annie and Alice
took Mrs. Armstrong to Groton, Connecticut, the summer of
1895, thinking the sea air would do her good. The air did not
seem to help Mrs. Armstrong but aggravated Annie's neuralgia.
The next summer Mrs. Armstrong was too feeble to go to a
summer resort. While Mamie and Eugene Levering were in
Europe, Annie thought the change of moving into the Levering
home would help her mother. From that time on, Annie refused
to leave home unless it was essential and she could return
quickly.

Several times during the late 1890s Annie's mother was
critically ill, and Alice was not in good health. Annie had to keep
things running smoothly at home. The family had a scare in
August, 1898, when Mrs. Armstrong fell, cut her head badly,
and hurt her back. By the fall of 1899, when the situation was
critical, Annie secured nurses. Mamie was there most of the
time, which made it possible for Annie still to look after some of
the work. Mrs. Armstrong's death on November 15, 1899, was a
tremendous loss to Annie and Alice for they had always lived
with their mother. Though they considered several options, the
two sisters decided to remain in the home at 1423 McCulloh
Street where they had lived for thirty-six years.[27]

Sarah Jessie Davis Stakely (Mrs. Charles A.), wife of the pastor
of the First Baptist Church in Washington, was elected WMU,
SBC, president in Louisville in 1899. Annie had known Mrs.
Stakely for some time and felt she was the right person for the
position. Mrs. Stakely had greatly strengthened WMU work in
the District of Columbia. Annie had a few anxious moments

when Fannie Heck indicated to Mrs. Stakely that as national president she had often sent missionary letters to state Baptist papers. Considering this her business and not the president's, Annie took Willingham's advice and wrote to Mrs. Stakely that she would look after that part of the work since Mrs. Stakely had a family.[28]

In spite of the turmoil of the late 1890s, Annie could move into the twentieth century feeling good. She had worked for Southern Baptist unity at the national level. With the support of the Foreign Mission Board, Home Mission Board, and Sunday School Board, Annie did what she could to make Southern Baptist work strong even in the midst of keen competition from Northern Baptists. Though Annie and Fannie Heck, the two great WMU, SBC, leaders, had major differences of opinion, they came to an agreement which took into account what seemed to be best for Woman's Missionary Union at the time. Annie endured in spite of losing her beloved mother, a source of encouragement and inspiration for years. Mrs. Armstrong had modeled qualities of strength and faith evident in the life of her daughter.

Did troubles get Annie down? Though difficulties and conflicts perturbed her greatly, Annie continued to face the future with optimism, always believing that one needed to "go forward." She could look back on the past with a feeling of accomplishment, for she had been faithful to the task which God gave her to do. Facing the future, she could say: "Let us not be weary in well doing, but accepting from God each new day as a new opportunity, resolve there shall be no squandered hours, no wasted minutes."[29] She would continue to give her all.

Notes (See pages 295-310 for Key to Sources.)

1. *Reports*, WMU, 1894-1898; Annie Armstrong to R. J. Willingham, July 19, 1896, January 9, 1897, December 14, 1898, FMB; Annie Armstrong to A. J. Barton, April 7, 1897, FMB.

2. WMU minutes, 1889-1905; Minutes, Woman's Mission Circle and Ladies Foreign Mission Circle, Eutaw Place Baptist Church, 1890-1898; Annie Armstrong to H. H. Harris, August 9, 1893, FMB; Annie Armstrong to T. P. Bell, February 25, 1892, February 5, 1894, FMB and SSB; Annie Armstrong to R. J. Willingham, February 3, August 16, 1897, November 2, 1898, January 16, 1899, FMB.

3. Annie Armstrong to J. M. Frost, October 31, 1896, SSB.

4. Correspondence with R. J. Willingham, T. P. Bell, J. M. Frost, 1895-1899. For the Bell-Rowland story, see Annie Armstrong to E. Y. Mullins, December 31, 1895, FMB; Annie Armstrong to R. J. Willingham, March 3, April 17, October 29, 1896, FMB; Annie Armstrong to J. M. Frost, July 8, October 31, 1896, SSB.

5. *Encyclopedia of Southern Baptists*, 1:40-42.

6. Annie Armstrong to R. J. Willingham, January-March 1898, FMB; Annie Armstrong to O. F. Flippo, January 18, February 5, 1898, FMB; O. F. Flippo to Annie Armstrong, January 28, 1898, FMB; Annie Armstrong to J. M. Frost, April 2, 1898, SSB; Annie Armstrong to A. J. Rowland, March 30, April 2, 1898, SSB; A. J. Rowland to Annie Armstrong, March 31, April 4, 1898, SSB.

7. Annie Armstrong to R. J. Willingham, March 20, 1894, FMB; Annie Armstrong to J. M. Frost, May-September, 1895, SSB; J. M. Frost to Annie Armstrong, June-August, 1895, SSB; Annie Armstrong to Lansing Burrows, July 24, 1895, SSB.

8. Annie Armstrong to J. M. Frost, October 20, October 24, December 30, 1897, January 29, February 12, February 28, April 8, April 11, April 14, 1898, SSB; J. M. Frost to Annie Armstrong, February 12, 1898, SSB; WMU minutes, June 8, 1897.

9. *The Evangel*, May 19, 1897; *Reports*, WMU, 1895, 1897.

10. *Reports*, WMU, 1897; WMU minutes, April 13, May 21, June 8, 1897; Annie Armstrong to J. M. Frost, January 24, 1898, SSB.

11. Annie Armstrong to J. M. Frost, June 9, July-September, 1897, January 24, February 18, 1898, SSB.

12. Annie Armstrong to J. M. Frost, January 24, January 29, February 2, 1898, SSB; Annie Armstrong to R. J. Willingham, February 3, 1898, FMB.

13. Annie Armstrong to J. M. Frost, February-April, 1898, SSB; J. Haralson to J. M. Frost, February 16, 1898, SSB; J. Haralson to Annie Armstrong, February 16, 1898, SSB; Annie Armstrong to R. J. Willingham, February 18, 1898, FMB; WMU minutes, April 12, 1898.

14. Fannie Heck to R. J. Willingham, April 5, 1898, FMB.

15. *Reports*, WMU, 1898; Annie Armstrong to J. M. Frost, April-May, 1898, SSB.

16. Fannie Heck to Annie Armstrong, May 13, 1898, SSB; Annie Armstrong to Fannie Heck, May 20, 1898, SSB.

17. Fannie Heck to R. J. Willingham, May 25, 1898, FMB; Fannie Heck to WMU executive committee, June 10, 1898, SSB.

18. Fannie Heck to R. J. Willingham, May, 1898, FMB; R. J. Willingham to Fannie Heck, May, 1898, FMB; R. J. Willingham to Annie Armstrong, May-June, 1898, FMB; Annie Armstrong to R. J. Willingham, June, 1898, FMB; Annie Armstrong to J. M. Frost, June, 1898, SSB; WMU minutes, June 14, 1898.

19. Annie Armstrong to R. J. Willingham, June, 1898, FMB; Annie Armstrong to J. M. Frost, June, 1898, SSB; R. J. Willingham to Annie Armstrong, June, 1898, FMB; R. J. Willingham to Fannie Heck, July, 1898, FMB.

20. J. Haralson to Annie Armstrong, July 5, 1898, SSB.

21. Annie Armstrong to J. M. Frost, July-August, 1898, SSB; Annie Armstrong to R. J. Willingham, July-August, 1898, FMB; R. J. Willingham to Annie Armstrong, August, 1898, FMB; R. J. Willingham to J. M. Frost, August, 1898, FMB; R. J. Willingham to I. T. Tichenor, August, 1898, FMB.

22. R. J. Willingham to WMU executive committee, August 25, 1898, FMB; Annie Armstrong to R. J. Willingham, August-September, 1898, FMB; Annie Armstrong to J. M. Frost, August-September, 1898, January, 1899, SSB; WMU minutes, September 13, 1898.

23. Fannie Heck to Annie Armstrong, September 26, 1898, March 6, 1899, SSB; Fannie Heck to J. M. Frost, September 26, 1898, SSB; Annie Armstrong to R. J. Willingham, November 2, 1898, February-April, 1899, FMB; Annie Armstrong to J. M. Frost, January-April, 1899, SSB; Fannie Heck to WMU executive committee, March 6, 1899, SSB; Annie Armstrong to Fannie Heck, March 28, 1899, FMB; Annie Armstrong to I. T. Tichenor, April 8, 1899, FMB and SSB; Fannie Heck to R. J. Willingham, April 26, May 3, 1899, FMB.

24. *Biblical Recorder,* May 24, June 7, 1899, 1899-1906; *Reports,* WMU, 1900-1906; Annie Armstrong to R. J. Willingham, May 19, 1899, FMB.

25. Annie Armstrong to R. J. Willingham, November 26, 1897, FMB; Annie Armstrong to J. M. Frost, November 23, December 20, 1897, SSB.

26. Annie Armstrong to R. J. Willingham, September 12, September 26, 1894, March 16, January 16, 1899, FMB; Annie Armstrong to J. M. Frost, April 18, 1898, SSB.

27. Annie Armstrong to T. P. Bell, June, 1895, SSB; Annie Armstrong to R. J. Willingham, 1894-1899, FMB; R. J. Willingham to Annie Armstrong, August 24, 1895, FMB; Annie Armstrong to J. M. Frost, 1898-1899, SSB; WMU minutes, October 13, November 10, 1896, November 14, 1899; Minutes, Eutaw Place Baptist Church, November, 1899; Certificate of Death, Mary Elizabeth Armstrong, November 15, 1899; Land Records #1871, Folio 61-62, October 17, 1900, Superior Court, Baltimore, Maryland.

28. Annie Armstrong to R. J. Willingham, May 19, July 27, July 29, 1899, FMB; R. J. Willingham to Annie Armstrong, July 28, 1899, FMB.

29. *Report,* WMU, 1898.

8
New Visions, New Frontiers

January, 1900, ushered in the turn of a new century. Annie herself was almost half a century old. How did she face this new century? Did she reflect on the past or look forward to new visions and and new frontiers in the future? Was she tired or renewed to "go forward"?

Annie seemed eager to enter the new century. In spite of difficulties, she claimed the past year had been the best ever in the history of Woman's Missionary Union, SBC. She was encouraged that women better understood the work, carried out the plans, and were anxious for information. She believed, however, that her efforts of the nineteenth century were only beginnings. They were pioneer efforts, and greater work was called for on her part in the twentieth century. She wrote: "As pioneers of the 20th Century, we face responsibilities for helping to lay a foundation for far *greater work* than was possible by Southern Baptists in the past. With hearty enthusiasm, let us follow our divine leader, and by unity of plans, by systematic, proportionate giving, and by personal activity, 'Ring out the old, old story, Ring in Thy Kingdom Come.'"[1]

Annie desperately needed a rest. The doctor had warned her more than a year earlier to rest for several months. Because of Mrs. Armstrong's condition she had not left Baltimore for a vacation for several summers. Also, stress, such as she experienced in the late 1890s, took a physical toll. WMU, SBC, leaders recognized Annie's condition. The women voted wisely at the 1900 WMU Annual Meeting that Annie rest during the month of

August. All communications would cease with the WMU executive committee that month, states having secured needed supplies in advance.

Alice, Annie's sister, refused to leave Baltimore unless Annie went with her. Reluctantly, Annie agreed to go with Alice to Virginia during July and August. In July they closed the house and took board near Culpeper with Rebecca Norris, sister of Jane Norris Hartwell. Annie had the office mail forwarded to her and traveled back and forth to Baltimore at regular intervals. She did not consider this a vacation, as it was harder for her to keep up with the work. However, it was a change of air, and she was relieved of housekeeping duties.

Annie detested housekeeping and cooking. She never had to do much of it, however, as the Armstrong sisters had a cook. They were often plagued with servant problems, and Annie once wrote to Willingham about having to get up at an uncanny hour to make the fires and do the housework before going to the Mission Rooms because the servant had quit. During those times, Alice did the cooking. When both Alice and Mamie were gone for several weeks during summers, Annie would close the house and move to a boarding house. In 1903, Annie and Alice began to board in their own home with a Presbyterian minister and his family. The minister's wife took charge of the home.[2]

Too much was going on in 1900 for Annie to rest. Southern Baptists were launching the New Century Movement, a special emphasis related to the beginning of the twentieth century. In 1898 the Southern Baptist Convention named a committee, chaired by Home Mission Board secretary F. H. Kerfoot, to "elicit and combine the energies of the whole denomination in the sacred effort for the propagation of the gospel." The campaign's primary effort was to enlist churches not giving anything to state, home, or foreign missions.[3]

Kerfoot visited Annie early in 1899 to secure her support. She liked and respected Kerfoot, agreeing to help him on two conditions. First, she wanted it understood that she would work under his direction. Willing to do any amount of routine work as long as he directed it, Annie was not eager to take on more responsibility. Her second condition was to be allowed to secure an additional typewriter and clerk. The boards must pay these expenses, but the expenses would not be credited to WMU, SBC. It was not unusual for Annie to say she wanted to take "orders" from a board secretary before making decisions about Southern Baptist Convention matters. In years past she had gone to leading Baltimore pastors for advice but thought the current ministers were not sufficiently acquainted with denominational affairs. Nor were WMU executive committee members good advisers since they tended to look at things through her eyes. Perhaps Annie simply wanted to put WMU, SBC, on firm footing in case of criticism or would rather someone else take the risks. However, she herself intimated on more than one occasion that the men usually did as she requested. In this case Annie used her influence, and WMU, SBC, voted at the 1900 WMU Annual Meeting to cooperate in the New Century movement.[4]

The Southern Baptist Convention appointed a Committee on Cooperation, chaired by Kerfoot, to devise the New Century plans. Kerfoot visited Annie again in June, 1900. She resisted committing WMU, SBC, to anything specific at that time, feeling that any action was premature until the committee first decided what the plans would be and who would direct the work. Annie foresaw months and years of persistent effort if the Convention objective were to be accomplished.

Kerfoot invited Annie to the meeting of state Baptist convention secretaries in June so she could hear the discussion. Before agreeing to go she sought advice from Willingham and Frost. Willingham saw no need for her to go to the meeting since the committee had not yet laid out its plans. Frost advised her to go and was disappointed when she did not. Annie offered to attend the committee meeting in August with Mrs. Charles A. Stakely, the WMU, SBC, president, and Kerfoot agreed that this was a good idea.[5]

Annie and Mrs. Stakely went to the meeting at Old Point Comfort, Virginia, on August 2. The Committee on Cooperation asked WMU, SBC, to use its influence to stimulate people to give regularly and proportionately to Southern Baptist causes, to use Southern Baptist literature, and to organize missionary societies. Annie and the president agreed that WMU would do its best to increase the number of societies and to urge women to help their pastors carry out plans for a "New Century" meeting in every church. Supporting these plans wholeheartedly, Annie got out a letter immediately to societies about the plans.[6]

Since in some states not even one-tenth of the churches had societies, Annie saw the challenge in enlargement. Virginia, the best organized WMU state, where more money was raised for the boards than anywhere else, had societies in only half the churches. At this time there were almost nineteen thousand Southern Baptist churches. Believing in the end result, Annie poured her heart and soul into this work. She began a rigorous schedule of travel for the next six years to organize societies, often accompanied by Mrs. Anna Schimp who gave the money which started the annuity fund. This Swiss-born woman traveled at her own expense and relieved Annie of travel arrangements. She, too, was devoted to missions and wanted to see missions work so she could pray and give more intelligently.[7]

As she had promised Kerfoot, Annie did much of the routine, detailed work related to contacting churches. With amazing ability to keep up with a multitude of data and many large and small details, she duplicated lists of churches and church clerks supplied by Lansing Burrows and the times and places of the district associational meetings in each state. Annie used these lists extensively and gave them to state WMUs. She prepared literature for women to use in helping their pastors hold New Century meetings. Surveying pastors to see if they had societies in their churches, she followed up with contacts to key women.[8]

By May, 1901, Annie reported encouraging results. In just eight months, 480 societies and 136 Sunbeam Bands had been organized. Annie's spirits were dampened somewhat when F. H. Kerfoot died in June, 1901. He had once been her pastor, as well as the spearhead of the New Century movement.[9]

Annie proposed another idea for the Home Mission Board in 1900—a Church Building Loan Fund. Liking the idea, the Board appointed a committee to develop a plan. Due largely to Tichenor's efforts, the Home Mission Board had earlier had such a fund; however, it had been discontinued when many persons feared that the raising of money for a loan fund would over-shadow other missions undertakings.

As far back as the 1892 Centennial of Modern Missions, Annie encouraged such a fund. Her heart was stirred by the frontier, and she saw the need to help struggling churches to build. When, in 1900, an anonymous donor gave one thousand dollars to the Woman's Baptist Home Mission Society of Maryland for the Church Building Loan Fund of the Home Mission Board, this was all Annie needed. She went to work, was able to secure thirty-five hundred dollars more from Baptist women for the fund, and urged the states to contribute one thousand dollars each. Because of her insistence, the Home Mission Board reinstituted the Church Building and Loan Fund.[10]

The next year Annie suggested a plan for increasing the fund by raising more money from missionary societies. Not taking action on her plan, the Home Mission Board agreed that the women ought to raise money any way they could. Annie thought that had Kerfoot lived, he would have inaugurated a plan to greatly increase the fund because he had been much interested in it and believed that through building churches "the home base of supplies" would be enlarged. Annie agreed with Kerfoot's views. Early in 1902 she tried to get the Board to establish a fund known as the Kerfoot Memorial Fund. Annie must have been heartsick when the Board declined taking this action.[11]

Annie did all she could to further the building and loan fund. When she heard that John D. Rockefeller might be interested in aiding Southern Baptist work to the tune of $250,000, Annie thought she might be able to get an interview with him. As exciting as this would have been, there is no record that such an interview ever took place.[12]

In 1903 the Home Mission Board asked WMU, SBC, to inaugurate a Tichenor Memorial Fund in connection with the building and loan fund. The fund already had over five thousand dollars, most of it furnished by WMU through Annie's efforts. At the WMU, SBC, Annual Meeting that year, Annie spoke most feelingly about the death of I. T. Tichenor. She paid tribute to his far-reaching work as secretary of the Board, having worked closely with him since 1882. She was persuasive, and the women adopted the Board's recommendation that WMU raise twenty thousand dollars for the Tichenor Memorial Fund.[13]

Annie continued to encourage Marie Buhlmaier in her work with German immigrants, making frequent references to Miss Buhlmaier stopping in to visit with her. She often petitioned the Home Mission Board on behalf of Miss Buhlmaier—more salary, days off, a vacation, increased appropriations, and an assistant for the work—and had the nerve to persist until action was taken. Annie had utmost admiration for Marie Buhlmaier. Spending an afternoon with Miss Buhlmaier at the immigrant pier, Annie was moved with compassion when she saw fourteen hundred "healthy, hearty-looking specimans [sic] of humanity" disembark from one vessel with so few material goods. She wrote:

> Most of the men carried in their hands a box or valise of some description; the women, on their backs, bundles of clothing. As I watched the registration, when they have to show to the inspector what amount of money they have, it was only one that I noted who had over $10. . . . When I went to the part of the building where the baggage had been put, there were probably not over twenty-five trunks or hampers and about the same number of sacks of clothing. . . . It was to me pitiful, indeed, to think of those hundreds and hundreds of people coming to a strange land, and having so little to start life with.

Annie watched Marie Buhlmaier welcome and minister in love

to the immigrants in many ways and give them copies of "God's word."

Recording immigrant statistics for Baltimore carefully in the little notebook she carried with her, Annie also wrote down her belief about the opportunity of working with immigrants:

> Our Opportunity. God has two distinct methods of propagating His gospel. 1st. by sending Christian people to heathen people. 2nd. By sending foreigners to Christian people.
>
> Men and means were not forthcoming fast enough for the great work of foreign missions, so God turned the stream this way and sent great masses of the unevangelized to come in contact with Christian civilizations. Is not God sending this message to us—"Here are these people; I have taken them from the overcrowded countries where they were living, and sent them to you that you may mass your forces and lend a hand to them.[14]

Annie's enthusiasm for helping the blacks never lessened. She gave her full support to the mothers' meetings and industrial schools for blacks in Baltimore, keeping up with their progress and consulting often with leaders. Believing this work extremely important, Annie secured a small Home Mission Board appropriation for each of the schools.[15]

In September, 1900, in Richmond, the black women organized as an auxiliary to the National Baptist Convention. They invited Annie to be present at the organization meeting. She must have been torn, for she was on an extended trip to Indian Territory at the time. Both of these causes were dear to Annie.

Nannie Helen Burroughs, the new corresponding secretary of the Woman's Convention, sought Annie's assistance. Since the black women wanted to pattern after WMU, SBC, Annie gave her all to Miss Burroughs and other black women during the formative years of their work. Miss Burroughs invited Annie to speak at the annual meeting in Cincinnati, Ohio, in September, 1901, on the topic "Why and How"—why a woman's organization and how one worked. Annie hesitated in accepting the invitation. She foresaw resentment from the two Northern women's home mission societies, both of whom were doing much work with the blacks. Also, she did not agree with the accepted Northern practice of having "mixed meetings" attended by both men and women.[16]

Believing as did many prominent Southern Baptists that women should not take part in "mixed public exercises," Annie thought this practice might possibly harm women's missions work in the South. Men were not allowed in meetings Annie planned or where she spoke. Nor did she permit WMU, SBC, to plan meetings for mixed audiences. When Annie invited the board secretaries, men missionaries, or other men to speak at WMU Annual Meetings, she made it clear that they were to leave immediately after their addresses. The only exception Annie ever made to her rule was to speak in coeducational schools or colleges where men were present. She rationalized that in this case, she was simply, for the time, replacing a female teacher.[17]

Annie accepted the invitation to speak at the National Baptist women's annual meeting in 1901 with the condition that when she spoke only women would be in the audience. Believing that her role in this meeting was the most important step she had taken since she became corresponding secretary of WMU, SBC, she did not want to do anything to harm this effort.[18]

Wanting to better understand the work, Annie did her homework before going to Cincinnati. On a visit to Nashville in August she met with black women from societies in nine churches. She talked with Mrs. V. W. Broughton, the recording secretary of the Woman's Convention, Auxiliary to the National Baptist Convention, who lived there. She visited the Negro publishing house and talked with black men missions leaders about ways to help the women. Annie saw two Negro schools in Nashville, Fisk University and Roger Williams.

Many things impressed Annie about the black women's meeting. She noted the quality of leadership she saw and the progress the black women had made. Believing it was important to help these women develop a good program of missions work, Annie predicted that the black people of America would largely do the missions work in Africa. No men were present when Annie spoke. Mrs. Anna Schimp was quite amused when one of the black women went to the gallery to escort two men out after the presiding officer had repeatedly requested them to leave. Annie missed this episode because she was sitting on the front row and did not want to turn around.

To the black women Annie was a symbol of what a woman could do. They considered her inspirational, caring, and full of encouragement. Eager to get the women's work closely identified with that of the National Baptist boards, Annie had a long interview with R. H. Boyd, secretary of the Home Mission Board, while in Cincinnati. She must have enjoyed writing to Frost that Boyd wanted her to be a "big sister" to the women, in the same way that Frost was a "big brother" to him.[19]

Nannie Helen Burroughs paid tribute to Annie for what she did during and after the Cincinnati meeting. Years later Miss Burroughs wrote:

> Miss Annie W. Armstrong—the trail blazer in Christian cooperation between white and Negro Baptist women of the South . . . guided us in the completion of the organization of the Woman's Convention, Auxiliary to the National Baptist Convention. No woman in America has ever done more to encourage Negro Baptist women in their work. . . . It was she who offered the prayer for divine guidance at the close of our first day's session. Her presence was a benediction. She stayed with us, and took part. In the afternoon, she delivered one of the most inspiring addresses of the entire Convention.

Annie had encouraged the black women to advance and offered to assist them in carrying forward their work.[20]

Not long after the 1901 black women's convention Annie recommended that the Home Mission Board pay partial salaries of two black women missionaries to work among the black women in the Southern states, one a general missionary and the other the position held by Nannie Helen Burroughs. R. H. Boyd had promised to pay half the salary of the general missionary, and Annie felt sure she could get someone to pay half of Miss Burrough's salary. The Home Mission Board referred this request to a committee, chaired by T. P. Bell, a board member. Annie asked Frost to intercede with F. C. McConnell, now secretary of the Home Mission Board, and to write Bell. If the Home Mission Board did not see the possibilities of this work, she hoped the Sunday School Board would.[21]

The Home Mission Board did not immediately approve Annie's request. Bell reported for the committee to the Board that they did not have sufficient information as to the projected work. Nor had they received communication or a direct application from the National Baptist Home Mission Board. This might have been Bell's way of telling Annie to mind her own business, and she was sure the action was the result of his influence. Angry over this action, Annie wrote emphatically in a letter to Tichenor, Home Mission Board secretary emeritus, that the committee could have told her that the National Baptists had to apply. Apparently the necessary contacts were made, for the next March the Home Mission Board approved appointment of two black field missionaries.[22]

Annie often spoke at meetings of black women and continued to encourage the leaders. In June, 1902, she met with Mrs. Shirley Layten, the National Baptist Woman's Convention president, and advised her strongly to relate to and support the boards of the National Baptist Convention. Urging the black women not to be independent, Annie suggested they ask the boards for annual recommendations, as WMU, SBC, did. As she saw the fruits of her labor, Annie thrilled during the next few years over the progress the black women made in missions efforts. They again asked her to address their annual meeting in 1903, but she was traveling to Indian Territory at that time.[23]

For years, Annie had a special place in her heart for Oklahoma and Indian Territory. At the urging of missionaries in these sections, who for years had been inviting her to come, and over the protest of her sister, Annie made an extensive four-thousand-mile, forty-day trip to Oklahoma and Indian Territory during August and September, 1900.[24]

This long trip was made possible when the Southern Baptist Convention mission boards agreed to pay Annie's travel expenses. Willingham and Kerfoot had trouble convincing Annie to agree to this policy. For years, she had seen the need for states to have expense funds and felt, therefore, that if her expenses were met, state WMU officers would no doubt feel that a similar provision should be made for them. Fearing adverse criticism if board money was used, Annie was reluctant to receive travel money and still refused a salary.

Mrs. Charles A. Stakely, the WMU, SBC, president, conferred with Willingham and Kerfoot. Somehow she managed to convince Annie to agree to allow the boards to meet her travel expenses. When Mrs. Stakely announced this decision at the WMU Annual Meeting in Hot Springs in 1900, the delegates were glad. They saw that Annie would advance WMU work and promote the New Century movement through her travels.[25]

Annie stated three purposes for going to Oklahoma and Indian Territory—to gain personal knowledge of the frontier field, to be in the Indian Territory when the two conventions there consolidated, and to present New Century plans to state WMU central committees on the way to and from Oklahoma. At the time, there were two conventions in each territory, one cooperating with the American Baptist Home Mission Society of New York and the other with the Southern Baptist Home Mission Board. Missions work was hampered by controversies created by these rival conventions. As Baptist work matured in the territories, there was a move toward unification. The year 1900 marked the beginning of a process which led to final unification in 1906. In 1900 the two conventions in each territory, Oklahoma and Indian Territory, united to form one convention in each, with dual alignment and cooperation with both the Northern Home Mission Society and the Southern Baptist Home Mission Board. Each church would decide where its contributions would go.

Since the general conventions were consolidating, Annie wanted to help bring about harmonious plans for organizing women's societies, some now related to the Woman's Baptist Home Mission Society of the West (Northern Baptist) and some to WMU, SBC. If she were not at the meetings, she feared the Northern sisters would preempt the ground since they appointed missionaries in the territories.[26]

A trip of this magnitude was a new experience for Annie. Before going, she sought advice from Willingham about the physical rigors of travel, expenses, clerical rates on trains, and the itinerary. She was excited and anticipated the experience, though she was not a good traveler. Trains were not electrified or air conditioned in those days. It was no easy matter to prepare for a long trip; things must be left in order at home, and Annie always made it a practice to get the work done ahead and literature printed and mailed out to the states before leaving.

The indefatigable secretary left Baltimore on August 20, 1900, accompanied by Anna Schimp. En route to Oklahoma, they stopped in Louisville and St. Louis to meet with the Kentucky and Missouri WMU central committees. Annie discussed with the committees many phases of the work—correspondence, postage, and finances. Speaking at a women's meeting in Louisville, Annie anticipated with excitement her upcoming trip to the West. She also reported on the status of women's work at present and dreamed about possibilities for the future. Having been concerned about women's work in Missouri for some time, Annie was most eager to stop there. She was burdened over the "deplorably small" contributions from the state to Southern Baptist work and the support being solicited by and given to the Northern Baptists. Her heart went out always to the border states.[27]

Oklahoma and Indian Territory made indelible impressions on Annie. The one-hundred-plus-degree temperatures were oppressive, though the nights were cool. Annie noted especially the almost total absence of trees, the blinding sun, and the dusty roads. Via train, two-horse carriage, and horseback, Annie visited many small churches, women's meetings, missionaries, the mining sections, and two Indian agencies. She gave her best efforts toward encouraging the missionaries and organizing societies. Seeing firsthand the hardships and personal sacrifices of the pioneer missionaries, whom she called "our substitutes," Annie reaffirmed her strong support of the frontier boxes. She noted, too, that these struggling churches were not able to give much money to the Home Mission Board. No doubt because she had seen the needs firsthand, her heart was stirred to bigger and better efforts in the future.

Both Annie and Mary G. Burdette, corresponding secretary of the Northern Woman's Home Mission Society, were at the Oklahoma Convention in Durant on September 7. The Oklahoma women held three general meetings—one for those working in connection with Southern work, one for those working with Northern work, and a joint meeting. Agonizing over what would happen, Annie gave advice and counsel. Because the general convention consolidated, the women also agreed to form one general organization with dual alignment. Annie left the meeting feeling that Southern Baptists must be alert and not allow the territories to become Northern territories. Because the Northern Baptist women appointed missionaries who organized societies and Southern Baptists had no organizer, she feared Northern supremacy. For the next few years Annie believed that she would have to do the organizational work in the territories for Southern Baptists, with the societies and churches in the territories operating "under the watchcare of Southern Baptist Convention officers."[28]

After leaving Indian Territory, Annie met with most of the state WMU central committees. Her itinerary took her through Dallas, Little Rock, Memphis, Nashville, Birmingham, Atlanta, Greenville, Charlotte, and Richmond. With a lot of time to think and dream as the train rolled through the Southland, Annie spoke at a number of missionary rallies and meetings at various stops. During the forty days she was gone, Annie attended fifty-nine meetings and made thirty-nine addresses. She kept exact records in her notebook about her travels. Challenging her audiences about the work of WMU, conditions in war-torn China, and her recent experiences in Oklahoma and Indian Territory, she urged the women to do even more for the spread of the gospel during the new century. Annie spoke from her heart about causes dear to her and pleaded with the women to organize more missionary societies.[29]

Seeing the work in Oklahoma and Indian Territory firsthand, reporting on her experiences to women throughout the Southland and her own state Home Mission Society, and reflecting on the needs, Annie must have intensified her prayers for the missionaries and their work. No doubt she also sought intercession from others, believing: "Whatever may be our circumstances in life, may each one of us really believe that by way of the Throne we have *unlimited power*. Would that we could realize that the success of missions and our prayers are linked together." Too, she believed that God heard prayers for the "substitutes." She wrote: "Loyalty to the missionaries demands that we shall give support by prayer even as we in their places would wish to be supported." That same year (1900) Annie began sending letters to the wives of frontier missionaries, as well as to the women foreign missionaries.[30]

Because of her trip West, Annie made additional special trips to Georgia and Virginia the next spring to interest the women in those states in supporting a missionary each in Indian Territory. Both Annie and Mrs. Charles A. Stakely, the national WMU president who now lived in Montgomery, Alabama, attended the Georgia WMU Annual Meeting in March, 1901, at Valdosta. Having been especially moved by the people in the mining camps, Annie spoke on the New Century movement and the conditions she had seen in Indian Territory. She presented the idea, and the Georgia women agreed to support a missionary to Indian Territory.

Mrs. Charles Stakely, President, WMU, SBC, 1899-1903

Annie got the maximum mileage out of any endeavor she attempted. On the way to and from Georgia, she visited cities in Georgia and South Carolina. While in South Carolina, Annie spoke at several Week of Self-Denial meetings, the annual observance for home missions which she had been instrumental in starting. She told of her experiences in the West and the needs of frontier missionaries. In April she met with the Virginia WMU Board in Richmond to challenge the women about the needs and work in the mining district of Indian Territory. She was persuasive, and the Virginia board agreed to support a second missionary to this area.[31]

The next month, Annie, Mrs. John A. Barker of Virginia, and Mrs. J. D. Easterlin of Georgia went to Atlanta to confer with the Home Mission Board about several matters. The three women sat in an adjoining room until they were called in to the Board meeting. Annie presented three items, all of which were referred to committees. The first told of the offer from the women of Georgia and Virginia to support two missionaries to the mining district in Indian Territory. She also raised questions about the work with black women and about frontier boxes. Wanting to know whether the Board thought WMU's management and methods of handling box work were satisfactory, she requested further instruction about the boxes. There had been some questions about placing a money value on the boxes.[32]

T. P. Bell, editor of *The Christian Index*, was particularly antagonistic about the boxes. Bell, who once had been a top administrator at both the Foreign Mission Board and Sunday School Board, was now a member of the Home Mission Board. Having been told the previous fall that Bell, once a favorite of hers, was not altogether favorable to WMU work, Annie was anxious, for she considered any attack on WMU an attack against herself. In an article in an October, 1899, issue of *The Christian Index* entitled "The Woman's Missionary Union, A Critic's View," Bell offered three suggestions for improvement—to study the missions work of other Christian groups in addition to Southern

Baptists', to avoid the tendency of multiplying special days or weeks for missions objects, and to motivate giving out of love rather than from a fund-raising method.

In the April 11, 1901, issue of *The Christian Index*, a month before Annie's visit to the Home Mission Board, Bell attacked WMU's emphasis on home missions over foreign missions. He criticized particularly the sending of boxes to frontier missionaries, four-fifths of whom he claimed were not on the frontier. He also took exception to Annie having secured the promised support of two missionaries for Indian Territory from the women in Georgia and Virginia.

Annie was amazed at Bell's attack and saw him as a completely different person than he had been six to eight years before. She and others conjectured that his real attack was against Kerfoot. Annie sent a telegram to Bell, asking him to print an article from her in reply to his article, which he agreed to do. Many friends were astonished at the mildness of Annie's article. It was not her nature to be mild when the beloved work was criticized.

In a second article which Bell agreed to print, Annie referred to the assistance of WMU, SBC, to the Sunday School Board as well as the Home Mission Board. She wrote Frost that Bell certainly had not been averse to this assistance when he was corresponding secretary of the Sunday School Board.[33]

The feud carried over to the Southern Baptist Convention in New Orleans in May. Some state Baptist papers reported that this meeting marked the beginning of a reaction against national WMU leadership. The papers claimed that WMU leaders did not seem content to develop the women in the churches but were trying to direct Convention operations.[34] Perhaps there was some justification for their accusations. In reality, Annie was influencing missions work by her suggestions to the mission boards.

Annie was perturbed after the Southern Baptist Convention. She never liked misunderstandings and misrepresentations, and the statements being made by the press and some of the men were almost more than she could bear. It tore at her very being to be criticized for influencing the work of her beloved Home Mission Board.

Bell did not relent. In the June 20, 1901, issue of *The Christian Index*, he published an article by Annie about stewardship. In the article Annie also gave comments of appreciation for WMU, SBC, from Willingham, Kerfoot, and Frost at the Southern Baptist Convention in New Orleans. Though he endorsed the expressions of appreciation in an editorial, Bell wrote that he felt free to criticize WMU because of his long friendship with the organization. He believed WMU was drifting too far away from its original purposes and plans. Georgia WMU passed resolutions of support for the WMU, SBC, policy of receiving and considering annual recommendations from the three boards. In essence, these resolutions were also in support of Annie. Annie considered circulating the resolutions to each state WMU central committee but followed Tichenor's advice not to do so.

Annie thought she had Bell figured out. By attacking her, Bell was in reality attacking Kerfoot, who advocated a "home base of supplies"; everyone knew of Annie's devotion to Kerfoot. Having tried to advance the work of each board, Annie did not believe Bell had grounds for his criticism. Her record of the past twelve years proved that she promoted foreign missions and the work of the Sunday School Board as much as she did home missions. Annie claimed that Bell continued to place obstacles in the way of progress and wrote: "My only explanation of his conduct is that his mind has become unbalanced." Bell's antagonism toward Annie did not die down and perhaps influenced others.[35]

In the midst of this debate, the Home Mission Board on July 2 approved recommendations about box work. The Board committee praised Annie and the women for cash gifts and boxes given in support of home missionaries. Having seen the need firsthand the past fall, Annie continued to stay in constant touch with frontier missionaries and societies about the need for frontier boxes, and the work progressed well. Later that year the Home

Mission Board agreed to appoint the two missionaries to the mining district of Indian Territory, the support provided by Georgia WMU and Virginia WMU. In April, 1902, two missionaries were appointed: Kate D. Perry of Texas and Kate Hanson of Washington, DC.[36]

Dr. F. C. McConnell, Home Mission Board secretary after Kerfoot, invited Annie to join the Frosts and others on a trip to Cuba in January, 1902. Though Annie would have loved to see the work which she had encouraged for so long, she had to decline because WMU, SBC, was in the process of moving headquarters to 304 North Howard Street.[37] The only trip Annie ever made out of the country was to Mexico later that year.

In 1901 a change was made for Annie when the publishing work of the Maryland Mission Rooms, for which she was corresponding secretary, was transferred to the Sunday School Board and Home Mission Board. For five years Annie had looked forward to the day when the Sunday School Board would take over the Mission Rooms and discussed the possibility with Frost and Willingham. She hoped the Sunday School Board would be the general publishing agency for Southern Baptists in the future, perhaps with branches in different cities.

While discussions were taking place over the years in Maryland Baptist Union Association meetings about management of the Mission Rooms, Annie was laying a foundation behind the scenes for the Sunday School Board by making the work strong. She saw the potential of a branch office remaining in Baltimore until it was deemed wise to transfer the operation to Nashville. Maryland Baptists, however, would not favor such a move, as the Mission Rooms had always been "Baptist Headquarters" to them.[38]

In the fall of 1900, the Maryland Baptist Union Association, believing the work would be enlarged and more effective, voted to transfer the work and assets of the Mission Rooms to the two mission boards. The Association stipulated that if, with WMU, SBC, as agent, the mission boards found the work too burdensome they could make a change to another agency. Though the Mission Rooms Committee had actually suggested that the assets be transferred to WMU, Annie reminded them that WMU did not receive funds but simply acted as an agent for Convention boards.

Annie went to Richmond to confer with Willingham and his associate, E. E. Bomar, about the transfer, though she still thought it would be wiser to place the Mission Rooms under the Sunday School Board. In late December, on behalf of the Mission Rooms Committee, Annie wrote to Willingham and Kerfoot recapping the history and offering the mission boards the assets and work of the Mission Rooms. While Kerfoot was in Baltimore in January, he and Annie discussed fully the future of the Mission Rooms.[39]

When the Foreign Mission Board declined Maryland's offer, Annie was "astonished, grieved, and hurt"; it had never occurred to her that the boards would refuse the offer. The Foreign Mission Board indicated that it felt the work could be done better by the Sunday School Board in connection with WMU, SBC. Willingham wrote Annie that he was surprised at the Board's action. In February, Annie presented the transfer proposal to Frost for official action by the Sunday School Board.

That spring the Home Mission Board and Sunday School Board accepted the property, trust fund, and work of the Mission Rooms, with WMU, SBC, as agent. Visiting Baltimore in April, 1901, for the formal transfer, the corresponding secretaries of the two boards agreed that Annie would continue to contribute her services and manage the business of the Mission Rooms. Until March, 1906, when the two boards turned the work, now called the Mission Literature Department of the Southern Baptist Convention, back over to the Maryland Baptist Union Association, Annie ran the work and made annual reports to the Home Mission Board and the Sunday School Board. The boards frequently acknowledged Annie's interest and efficiency in carrying out this work.[40]

In the early 1900s Annie and Frost began to have some differences of opinion. Finding from her 1900 trip to the West that a person needed some time when traveling to rest and not meet people, Annie had a conversation with Frost about the virtues of staying in hotels versus homes. She stated that in the future she would not urge the board secretaries to accept invitations to her home; however, she also stated that Frost and I. J. Van Ness, his associate, could always make her home their Baltimore headquarters. Van Ness was new and had hoped to be in Annie's home while at the Maryland convention that fall. Apparently misunderstanding Annie and taking her at her word, Frost told Van Ness of his conversation with Annie. She was offended when Frost wrote that they wanted to establish "other centers of acquaintance . . . and be more serviceable to the work." She abruptly referred Van Ness to the Maryland convention committee on hospitality.[41]

In spite of differences, Frost appreciated Annie for her support of the Sunday School Board. He said that Annie had

shown rare ability and tact in helping this work to a noble success. While holding with equal, almost jealous care, and with an absolute impartial hand the interests of the home and foreign boards, she has never failed to give her support in every possible way to making the Sunday School Board also a mighty agency for furthering all the work of the Convention.[42]

Annie constantly had new ideas for the Sunday School Board. Thinking the idea might get Southern Baptists reading about missions, she proposed missionary circulating libraries and asked the Board to make a grant of books. She pursued the idea relentlessly, even though Frost was not responsive. Also approaching Willingham and McConnell, Annie claimed she had the ability to keep at something until she accomplished the "object in view."[43]

A concern of Annie's was the lack of adequate promotion given by Frost and the Sunday School Board to Missionary Day in the Sunday School. Unless Frost got behind Missionary Day and

Children's Day, she did not think it worthwhile for her to continue preparing the programs. Annie spoke to Frost about this concern frequently, but it did not seem to do much good. Thoroughly outdone with Frost about Missionary Day, she thought her persistence annoyed him. Annie asked Willingham to "talk some quite plain English" to Frost about Missionary Day. Since Frost now had associates to help him, she thought she could back off from providing manuscripts.[44]

In spite of Bell's accusations that Annie favored the Home Mission Board, she balanced her interests well among the three boards. As an example of her interest in foreign missions, in April, 1900, Annie and a number of other Southern Baptist representatives attended the Ecumenical Conference on Foreign Missions in New York. Annie met many delegates from around the world. Her quick mind must have been stimulated as foreign missions was discussed from all viewpoints.[45]

Foreign missions became even more personalized for Annie in 1901. On April 18 the Foreign Mission Board appointed Dr. Philip S. Evans and his wife, Mary Grace Levering Evans, for medical work in China. Annie was close to Mary Evans, the daughter of Joshua Levering and her second cousin, who had at one time been on the WMU, SBC, executive committee. Eutaw Place Baptist Church had a big farewell service for the Evanses in July. Thinking this occasion might increase the church's interest in foreign missions, Annie had given Junius W. Millard, her pastor, ideas for the service.[46]

Maryland Baptists became personally interested in providing the funds for building a suitable house and dispensary for the Evanses in Yang Chow, China. Annie helped Mrs. John Eager, president of the Woman's Foreign Mission Society of Maryland, promote this effort by writing letters for Mrs. Eager's signature and sending them out.[47]

During this period Annie led in encouraging new foreign missions efforts. In late 1903 she asked Willingham to consider the advisability of the Foreign Mission Board asking WMU, SBC, to secure the support needed for all schools, except theological schools, on foreign fields. She had seen this as a plan successfully used by other denominations. After the Board agreed, Annie devised a plan for securing the money which she thought would create interest and give "definiteness to the work." Her plan was to obtain from each missionary in charge of a school information about the school and possible projects for which money could be appropriated (desks, native teachers, and so on) and the missionary's agreement to write a quarterly letter to her which she could copy and send to each contributing missionary society or Sunbeam Band. In order to send regular information, Annie proposed keeping careful records of organizations which contributed for the support of schools. She reiterated that she was not trying to decide missions policy, only to secure funds.[48] Even though Annie promoted approved Board projects, she believed the first priority was missionary salaries and urged persons to make general, not designated, contributions for missions causes.[49]

After her initial long trip to Oklahoma and Indian Territory in 1900, Annie traveled extensively. She could now do this for three reasons—her mother's death in 1899 freed her from home cares, the boards were paying her travel expenses, and the New Century movement, with its goal of a women's missionary society in every church, necessitated personal contact.

In 1901 Annie made two trips, each of several weeks duration. The first trip was to Georgia, South Carolina, and Virginia during the spring when she was soliciting interest in support of two women missionaries to Indian Territory. That summer Annie set out on several short trips and one long trip, which included Virginia, Tennessee, Kentucky, and Maryland. In June she spoke at an associational workers' conference in Manassas, Virginia.[50] No sooner had she returned to Baltimore from Virginia than Annie went to several meetings in and around Rockville, Maryland.[51]

In August and September the tireless Annie spent fifty days traveling 2,250 miles to thirty places in southwest Virginia, Tennessee, Kentucky, and Maryland. She went mostly to associational meetings but conducted other business along the way— conferring with Frost in Nashville, meeting with state WMU central committees when possible, and speaking at the National Baptist women's meeting in September. Annie always made every minute count. Somehow she managed to stay fresh and inspiring in spite of rigorous travel, unusual rains, and diminished audiences. Always grateful to her many hostesses, she thanked the state WMU workers who had carefully planned her itinerary. The fact that she would take a tour during the sultry month of August put new life and energy into the women with whom she met.

The Tennessee WMU planners had a surprise for Annie. Without her knowledge or consent, they planned that she spend one week at Monteagle, a mountain resort in East Tennessee. There she had opportunity to rest and to confer with Mrs. Charles Stakely while the Stakely family vacationed. Annie seemed to be in closer contact and accord with Mrs. Stakely than with former WMU, SBC, presidents.

Women were impressed with Annie. They saw her as modest, cultured, and consecrated. Annie loved close contact with the women and wanted to meet as many as possible. She seemed to have a knack for encouraging them and offering fresh ideas.[52]

Annie made two lengthy trips in 1902. Beginning in February, she and Mrs. Schimp made a twenty-one-day trip of 3,300 miles which took them to a number of places in Louisiana and Florida, with brief stops in Alabama and Georgia for conferences with Dr. McConnell and Mrs. Stakely. Since Annie had never met the workers in Florida, the major purpose of the trip was to visit that state. Because of cold rains and a bout with neuralgia, this trip was the most trying one Annie had made. When she received a telegram in Florida from Mamie about the serious illness of Alice, her trip was cut short. Annie took the next train to

Baltimore. Alice was quite ill, probably with either pneumonia or typhoid fever, and Annie shared the nursing duties until Alice improved.[53]

During the summer of 1902, Annie made her second trip to Oklahoma and Indian Territory, spending time in Missouri, Texas, and Mexico on the way home. Her purpose was to cultivate the work in Indian Territory and to save that region for Southern Baptists, not to visit the missionaries or see missions work. She wanted the women in the territory to realize that there was a work for them to do. Traveling 8,500 miles, and away from home eighty days, Annie had many interesting experiences on this trip, including a train wreck in Mexico. Another time she took a train that had been held up only four hours earlier by train robbers. She met with extremes in temperature and saw life in many forms—the western part of the new strip in Oklahoma, a Mormon hotel, and a Mexican palace.[54]

Annie kept copious notes in her little notebooks during her travels. She was deeply moved with the needs of both home and foreign missionaries. While on the frontier, she observed extreme poverty, hardships, difficulties, and many miles without missionaries or churches. In Mexico, Annie saw the needs and witnessed Roman Catholicism in its expressions there. When she returned home she wrote a number of articles about her experiences in Mexico—her memories, Mexican superstitions, and what it meant to be a Roman Catholic in Mexico. She spoke to many groups about Mexico and Indian Territory.[55]

Annie was quite candid about why she made the trip to Mexico—she wanted to silence the critics, including T. P. Bell, who accused her of working for home missions and not foreign missions. Since she had made a trip to Oklahoma and Indian Territory during the summer of 1900 and planned to go again in 1902, she wanted to show in some way that she was equally as interested in foreign missions and not give just cause for criticism. She could think of no better way to get people to see her interest in foreign missions than by going to Mexico. She was most concerned, however, about how much this trip would cost.[56] Annie had another chance to leave the country when Joshua Levering invited her to accompany the Levering family party in May, 1903, to visit the Evanses in China; they would also stop in Japan and many other countries around the world. No doubt Annie did not want to be gone that long, for the Leverings did not return home until December.[57]

Annie made three long trips during 1903. In the spring she traveled 5,250 miles in a fifty-two-day sweep which included Virginia, Georgia, Alabama, Mississippi, Louisiana, Florida, and South Carolina. This time she traveled without Mrs. Schimp. In addition to the meetings in white churches, Annie held a number of meetings with black women and visited several colleges.[58]

Wanting to visit North Carolina, Tennessee, Arkansas, and Kentucky, Annie offered to spend up to two weeks in each state visiting societies. In August, 1903, she made a three-thousand-mile trip to five states, most of the time spent in Tennessee. During this trip Annie attended the Missionary Conference at Lookout Mountain, which related to young people's work, and the Baptist Young People's Union of America (BYPUA) meeting in Atlanta.[59]

Because of her interest in the age group between Sunbeam Band and Woman's Missionary Society, Annie attended the Missionary Conference and the BYPUA Convention. She was eager to interest young people's unions in Southern Baptist work and sought to get the young people involved in missions projects. She worked with the Foreign, Home, and Sunday School Boards in appealing to the Southern Baptist Young People's Union to contribute money for a project related to each board—schools in Mexico and other countries, church houses in Cuba, mission Sunday Schools, and the Bible fund. She devised a plan to get missions information to the unions regularly. To keep them in touch with Southern Baptist work, a quarterly letter would go to each BYPU from one of the board secretaries or Annie, enclosing a missionary letter giving information about the field.[60]

After returning home the end of August, 1903, Annie set out again for the West. She spent forty days and traveled 4,350 miles to Missouri, Indian Territory, Oklahoma, and Arkansas. Because the Northern Baptist women missionaries were traveling and organizing societies in Indian Territory, Annie believed it was essential to be at the annual meeting of women in Indian Territory.[61]

Her deep desire to relate the District of Columbia firmly to Southern Baptist work led Annie to visit Washington frequently. Also, she loved the Virginia WMU, calling it the banner state in missions and number of societies, and went to that state often. Annie helped the Virginia women work out their state organization, and each year from 1900 to 1903 spoke at the Virginia WMU Annual Meeting. Lottie Moon was also at the 1903 meeting.[62]

In her dual leadership role as a national and state WMU leader, Annie traveled a good bit in her native state of Maryland. Her trip to the Eastern Shore in November, 1901, made a lasting impression on her. Annie made a difficult four-day stay in that section. Accompanied by Mrs. Schimp, she met ladies at six churches, mostly in the country. She had to travel by train and drive many miles in a buggy to do this. One day she had breakfast at one place, dinner at another, and supper at a third. One point was reached at three o'clock in the morning, and another time she slept in a home in a room with four windowpanes out, though ice was forming.

Annie was impressed that city folk did not realize how difficult it was for the women in country churches to hold regular meetings in winter months. Thinking again of the frontier missionaries who suffered great privations during travel over country roads, through heat and cold, often insufficiently clad, she came home from the Eastern Shore more determined than ever to urge women to send frontier boxes.[63] Annie attended many district meetings throughout Maryland. As a member of the Foreign

Mission and State Mission Societies, and president of the Home Mission Society, Annie was always at the annual meetings of these societies in November. She often invited the board secretaries as speakers.

Common threads ran throughout Annie's travels. Making careful preparations, she got the literature edited, printed, and mailed out to states in advance. The work was always done ahead when Annie left Baltimore. Itineraries were carefully arranged with the state WMU workers, who most often traveled with Annie. Sometimes she talked with them into the small hours of the night. Always mindful of expenses, and trying to keep these as low as possible, she stayed in homes most of the time.

Annie had a purpose for each trip she took. Many times it was to organize or to encourage the missionary societies. She tried hard to transform ladies' aid societies into missionary societies. Always promoting missions, the work of the boards, and personal commitment to and involvement in missions, she encouraged women and suggested missions projects for them to do. Annie was a loyal friend and co-worker to members of the state WMU central committees. Enjoying being with missionaries herself, Annie liked for women to hear missionaries, as missionaries usually spurred them on to better support. Since Annie thought that the next best thing to a "live meeting" with a missionary present was a missionary letter, she took many letters with her.[64]

Annie worked extremely hard while she traveled, usually making an address every day, sometimes more. In addition to church and associational meetings, she visited a number of women's colleges and met with black women as often as possible. She had only two expressed rules—to see as many women as possible and to defer to custom and allow no gentlemen to be in the meetings. She was a gifted speaker, interesting, and charming. It was easy to observe Annie's bright intelligence, clear thought, complete grasp of a subject, and zeal for missions. After Annie's visit to Florida, Mrs. W. D. Chipley, a Florida WMU leader, wrote: "She is a wonderful woman and a most delightful one, too. It was a great privilege and a great joy to be with her. . . . I am sure we have not anywhere a wiser, nobler, more consecrated Christian than she is and the good she has done our cause by these visits is incalculable."

A student at Roanoke Female College in Danville, Virginia, remembered Annie as "an attractive lady" who appealed to the students to continue their education for service in God's Kingdom. Feeling as if Annie were a friend talking to her personally about the ideal of service in God's work where she was, the young woman that day decided to continue her education for missionary service.[65]

Annie seemed to know the concerns of each state. In the District of Columbia, Missouri, and Indian Territory, she promoted Southern Baptist work and tried to get these areas behind that work. She got the boards to send missions literature free for a year to societies in Oklahoma and Indian Territory. Because of her long-term relationship with the missionaries, she believed she had an influence in these areas. Annie stated that if she were given the opportunity of being the secretary of WMU work in Oklahoma and Indian Territory, she would gladly give up her other duties and take this position. She believed that if she could give full time to this territory for five years, the women and girls would do as much for the boards as did the Eastern states. This area was her first love, and in essence, she functioned as the WMU secretary for Indian Territory and the District of Columbia.

Annie was concerned about the tendency of some of the men to push state missions and encourage contributions from the societies to these causes. She believed, however, that WMU was organized to aid Southern Baptist causes, not state missions.

Annie was also concerned about actions by the American Baptist Publication Society to put workers, funds, and headquarters in key locations such as Dallas and St. Louis. Annie was leery of cooperative work with the Northern Baptists, which she thought always meant "Northern supremacy." When the South Carolina State Board employed a woman missionary jointly with the Woman's Home Mission Society of Chicago, she watched carefully and wrote letters. She did not understand why South Carolina did not seek help from the Home Mission Board. Annie was distressed, too, by the lack of missions giving to Southern Baptist work in some of the churches and states.[66]

Annie opposed WMU, SBC, workers receiving a salary unless it was absolutely necessary. She had three reasons for this view—(1) "For nearly 15 years I have tried to teach the principle of women giving their work without remuneration"; (2) "It would open the door for state officers to expect payment for their services"; and (3) "It would probably be thought if the secretary were to receive a salary, office expenses should decrease." Annie believed that the one who led must do more "in *every* direction" than she asked of anyone else.[67] Her leadership stance was to invite Baptist women to come with her rather than asking them to do something she would not do.

The question of paid or unpaid officers was not considered by WMU, SBC, in its early years. Nor had it ever come up during a WMU Annual Meeting. Somehow Annie and Alice managed to live their entire lives without salaries, nor had their mother ever worked. They had income, probably from property, for at least by 1900 they owned their McCulloh Street home free and clear.

The WMU, SBC, executive committee first urged Annie to accept a salary in 1900. She refused. Willingham, unknown to Annie, learned of various shrinkages in her income. Perhaps he found this out from Joshua Levering, her cousin and long a Foreign Mission Board vice-president. In late 1902 Willingham conferred with Frost and McConnell, especially wanting Annie cared for. They believed it only right that Annie receive some compensation for her services. Willingham wrote the WMU, SBC, executive committee that the Foreign Mission Board recommended that $750 a year be appropriated to the WMU, SBC, corresponding secretary, the three boards to make equal appropriations. They had not consulted Annie, since she was personally involved.

When Willingham wrote Annie in November, 1902, and sent her a copy of his letter to the WMU executive committee, the whole question pained her. It was well known that she had never received a salary or approved of one being paid. Annie wrote the WMU, SBC, vice-presidents in December: "It has been the joy of my life to give my services freely, and my hope never to be required to take one." She asked Mrs. Stakely, the WMU, SBC, president, to present the matter at the next WMU Annual Meeting in Savannah with the understanding that the matter was to be considered on its merits, apart from the person involved. Her one concern was whether this was best for the work. Annie feared not, for in states where an officer received remuneration there was much expense. She saw no way to decrease WMU, SBC, expenses, nor would receiving a salary enable her to do any more work. If need be, she could seek other fields for remuneration. Annie believed she must be excused from the 1903 WMU Annual Meeting so the question could be considered objectively.[68]

Annie must have been an emotional wreck throughout the winter and spring because of the uncertainty of her future. Would the delegates in Savannah vote a salary? She did not intend to go to the WMU Annual Meeting, until she learned just sixteen days before the meeting that Mrs. Stakely, the WMU, SBC, president, could not be there.[69] Mrs. Stakely wrote Annie in April that she could not be at the meeting because of "her present condition," the expression used in that day when one was expecting a baby. Thinking she should let the vice-presidents know why Mrs. Stakely would not be in Savannah and why Annie changed her mind when she had so positively stated earlier that she would not be present, Annie sent a copy of Mrs. Stakely's letter to the WMU, SBC, vice-presidents. Annie also wrote Mrs. Stakely of her astonishment that Mrs. Stakely had not told Annie she would not be in Savannah in February when Annie passed through Montgomery.

Dr. Charles A. Stakely, now pastor of the First Baptist Church in Montgomery, sent a short, curt note, apparently to a number of people. He wrote that Annie's action in sending his wife's private letter to the WMU vice-presidents and her statement about her visit to Montgomery in February were resented by the Stakelys as "offensive and humiliating." Annie claimed there was nothing in Mrs. Stakely's letter to indicate it was to be regarded as confidential and thought she was doing the right thing when she sent out copies to let Mrs. Stakely "speak for herself." It was a delicate matter, and Annie sought Willingham's advice. He urged her not to read Mrs. Stakely's letter publicly but thought it would be all right for her to show it to the WMU executive committee quietly. Perhaps it might be wise for her to show the letter to several of them privately and let them explain the matter to others. The WMU executive committee went on record in approving Annie's actions and disapproving Dr. Stakely's communication.[70]

Annie followed the correct procedure and enlisted Mrs. John H. Eager, the Maryland vice-president, to preside at the WMU, SBC, Annual Meeting in Savannah. Though she was in feeble health, Mrs. Eager wanted to "help Miss Annie." It was an embarrassing position for Annie during the WMU Annual Meeting to read the November 4, 1902, letter from Willingham to the WMU executive committee about a salary and her response of December 15, 1902. She then left the meeting. The women voted almost unanimously to attach a salary to the office of corresponding secretary. Only South Carolina was opposed. Annie was again nominated as corresponding secretary. Since she was in the hotel during the election, the women sent for Annie and stood and sang the doxology as she entered. The action taken on the salary was reported widely in state Baptist papers, most indicating they thought Annie deserved a salary.[71]

Annie asked Mrs. Eager to call a WMU, SBC, executive committee meeting in June, during which she declined to receive a salary. Though the executive committee reaffirmed its conviction that the corresponding secretary should receive a salary, it felt, however, that there was nothing to do but yield to Annie's determination to decline the salary. The committee sent communications from the committee and Annie to the state Baptist papers and to the boards.[72]

Through the ups and downs of her experiences as a leader of Southern Baptist women, Annie was extremely close to her family. The Armstrong sisters lived well and had many joys. At one point the sisters boarded temporarily because of a scarcity of coal. Though their house was robbed once and most of their jewelry stolen, this loss did not bother Annie because she did not wear much jewelry. In 1900 the Puritan Printing Company, which did much printing for WMU, SBC, and the Mission Rooms, asked Annie to head up the company. Though she was tempted so she could make money for the boards, Annie declined the offer. She claimed that if she had been a man she would have been successful in business, for she had much ability along these lines.

Mamie and Eugene Levering lived nearby, and Annie counted on them. Often she sought out Eugene, or his brother Joshua, for advice about business or personal matters. No doubt Annie enjoyed her nephew and nieces, as well as Joshua's large family. Often the family held gatherings at Eugene and Mamie's.[73]

Annie continued always her active participation in the life of her church, in the three Maryland women's missionary societies, and in Baltimore affairs. She had long been connected with the Woman's Interdenominational Missionary Union in Baltimore. In 1901 she let the union elect her president so she would have opportunity to suggest various lines of work, such as with the black women. Annie was faithful to her church, continuing to teach the Infant Class, belonging to a missionary society, attending prayer meeting, and giving suggestions to her pastor.

Eutaw Place Baptist Church was noted throughout the Southern Baptist Convention for its interest in missions and its large contributions. Annie's influence was keenly felt in her church.[74]

As the year 1903 ended, Annie could look back with satisfaction on the new frontiers she had crossed since the turn of the century. She led in the establishment of the Church Building and Loan Fund. She greatly assisted the black women in organizing for missions. She got the Maryland Mission Rooms under the management of the Sunday School Board and the Home Mission Board. Promoting missions more than ever, she traveled extensively throughout the South and West, organizing societies and strengthening missionary work. She visited Mexico and made three trips to Oklahoma and Indian Territory. She laid the groundwork for later plans for organizing girls and young women for missions. Annie had crossed many frontiers and had inspired thousands to join her in new visions.

Notes (See pages 295-310 for Key to Sources.)

1. *Report*, WMU, 1900.

2. Ibid.; *The Baptist Courier*, May 31, 1900; Annie Armstrong to R. J. Willingham, April 14, June 18, 1900, August 4, August 14, 1903, May 24, July 6, 1904, FMB; Annie Armstrong to J. M. Frost and I. T. Tichenor, June 18, 1900, SSB; 1900 Census Schedules of Maryland, Ward 15.

3. *Encyclopedia of Southern Baptists*, 2:959-960.

4. Annie Armstrong to F. H. Kerfoot, January 9, 1899, SSB; F. H. Kerfoot to Annie Armstrong, January 2, 1899, SSB; Annie Armstrong to R. J. Willingham, September 13, 1899, FMB; Annie Armstrong to J. M. Frost, September 15, 1899, December 5, 1903, SSB; HMB minutes, January 3, 1899; *Report*, WMU, 1900.

5. Annie Armstrong to R. J. Willingham, June 5, June 11, 1900, FMB; Annie Armstrong to F. H. Kerfoot, June 7, 1900, FMB; Annie Armstrong to E. E. Bomar, July 17, 1900, FMB; WMU minutes, June 12, 1900.

6. Annie Armstrong to J. M. Frost, July 22, August 14, 1900, SSB; *FMJ*, September, 1900.

7. *Baptist and Reflector*, January 10, 1901; Levering, "A Sketch of 'Miss Annie,'" *The Window of YWA*, March, 1935.

8. WMU Minutes, October 9, 1900, February 12, 1901; *Report*, WMU, 1901; Annie Armstrong to J. M. Frost and F. H. Kerfoot, October 3, 1900, SSB;

Annie Armstrong to J. M. Frost, October 8, 1900, SSB.

9. *Report*, WMU, 1902; Annie Armstrong to E. E. Bomar, March, 1902, FMB.

10. HMB minutes, March-April 1900; *Encyclopedia of Southern Baptists*, 1:282; *Report*, WHMS, 1900; *FMJ*, July, 1900; *Southern Baptist Witness*, April 20, 1905; SBC Annual, 1900; WMU minutes, June 12, 1900; Annie Armstrong to E. E. Bomar, "Sunday Night" (1900), FMB.

11. HMB minutes, July 2, 1891, January 7, March 4, 1902.

12. Ibid., October 3, November 5, 1901; Annie Armstrong to E. E. Bomar, "Sunday Night" (1900), FMB.

13. SBC Annual, 1903; *Report*, WMU, 1903; *Baptist Standard*, May 21, 1903.

14. HMB minutes, July 3, 1900, June 30, December 1, 1903; Annie Armstrong to R. J. Willingham, December 2, 1897, FMB; Annie Armstrong to E. E. Bomar, February 8, 1902, FMB; Annie Armstrong Notebooks, WMU; Minutes, WHMS, September, 1898.

15. HMB minutes, October 3, 1899.

16. WMU minutes, November 13, 1900, February 12, 1901; HMB minutes, May 22, July 2, 1901; Annie Armstrong to E. E. Bomar, March 4, 1901, FMB; Nannie H. Burroughs to Annie Armstrong, July 11-12, 1901, SSB; Annie Armstrong to J. M. Frost and M. M. Welch, July 12, 1901, SSB; M. M. Welch to Annie Armstrong, July 12, 1901, SSB.

17. Annie Armstrong to T. P. Bell, February 16, 1895, SSB; Annie Armstrong to R. J. Willingham, March 24, 1896, June 17, 1898, January 24, 1899, January 5, 1900, August 10, Thanksgiving, November 28, 1903, FMB; WMU minutes, June 13, 1898; *Central Baptist*, October 1, 1903.

18. Annie Armstrong to J. M. Frost, July 11-12, 1901, SSB.

19. Ibid., September 13, September 20, 1901; Annie Armstrong to E. E. Bomar, September 18, 1901, FMB; WMU minutes, October 8, 1901.

20. Nannie H. Burroughs to W. Clyde Atkins, January 28, 1939, Eutaw Place Baptist Church.

21. Wharton, *Fruits of the Years*, p. 26; HMB minutes, October 3, 1901; Annie Armstrong to J. M. Frost, October 11, October 22, 1901, SSB.

22. HMB minutes, November 5, 1901, March 4, 1902; WMU minutes, November 12, 1901; Annie Armstrong to I. T. Tichenor, November 9, 1901, SSB.

23. Annie Armstrong to R. J. Willingham, June 2, 1902, January 29, 1903, FMB; Minutes, MBUA, 1902; WMU minutes, February 10, 1903; Annie Armstrong to E. E. Bomar, August 21, 1903, FMB.

24. *Report*, WMU, 1901; Annie Armstrong to R. J. Willingham, January 21, 1899, FMB.

25. Ibid.; Annie Armstrong to J. M. Frost, March 21, 1896, SSB; Annie Armstrong to R. J. Willingham, March, July 23, 1900, FMB; R. J. Willingham to Annie Armstrong, March 17, 1900, FMB; R. J. Willingham to F. H. Kerfoot, May 22, 1900, FMB; WMU minutes, June 12, 1900; *FMJ*, July, 1900.

26. Annie Armstrong to R. J. Willingham, June 6, July 23, 1900, FMB; *Report*, WMU, 1901; *Encyclopedia of Southern Baptists*, 2:1028-1031.

27. Annie Armstrong to R. J. Willingham, January 21, January 24, 1899, July 23, 1901, January 20, February 29, August, 1903, FMB; R. J. Willingham to Annie Armstrong, 1901-1902, FMB; Minutes, WHMS, 1900; *Religious Herald*, September 30, 1900; *The Baptist Argus*, August, 1900; *Western Recorder*, August, 1900; Levering, "A Sketch of 'Miss Annie,'" *The Window of YWA*, March, 1935.

28. *FMJ*, October-November 1900; Minutes, Woman's Missionary Society of the Indian Territory, September 7, 1900, quoted in a letter from J. M. Gaskin to Eula Mae Stewart, November 13, 1981; "A Message to the Baptist Girls of Virginia," 1902, WMU Scrapbook 2, WMU; Annie Armstrong to R. J. Willingham, January 4, July 18, 1902, FMB; Annie Armstrong to J. M. Frost, May 24, 1902, SSB; *The American Indian Voice*, January-February 1958; Annie Armstrong Notebooks, WMU; Minutes, WHMS, November 15, 1900.

29. *The Baptist Courier*, September-October 1900; Virginia WMU minutes, September 21, 1900; *The Christian Index*, September 27, 1900, *Western Recorder*, August 16, 1900; Annie Armstrong Notebooks, WMU.

30. *Reports*, WMU, 1897-1898, 1900; Minutes, Woman's Mission Circle and Ladies Foreign Mission Circle, Eutaw Place Baptist Church, 1890-1898; Annie Armstrong to R. J. Willingham, June 28, 1897, FMB.

31. HMB Minutes, October 3, 1899; WMU minutes, February 12, March 12, April 9, 1901; *The Baptist Argus*, April 18, 1901; *The Christian Index*, June 11, 1903; *The Baptist Courier*, April 11, April 25, June 6, 1901; Annie Armstrong to J. M. Frost, April 8, April 10, 1901, SSB; *FMJ*, April, July, 1901.

32. HMB minutes, May 22, 1901.

33. Annie Armstrong to I. J. Van Ness, October 27, 1899, FMB; Annie Armstrong to J. M. Frost and Mrs. Northen, October 10, 1900, SSB; Annie Armstrong to E. E. Bomar, March 7, 1901, FMB; Annie Armstrong to R. J. Willingham, October 31, November 3, 1899, April 22, May 3-4, 1901, FMB; Annie Armstrong to J. M. Frost, April-June 1901, SSB; Annie Armstrong to T. P. Bell, April 22, 1901, SSB; T. P. Bell to Annie Armstrong, April 24, 1901, SSB.

34. *Biblical Recorder*, May 22, 1901.

35. Annie Armstrong to R. J. Willingham, June 4, July 3, July 16, 1901, April 3, May 4, 1902, May 2, 1903, FMB; Annie Armstrong to J. M. Frost, July 1, July 16, 1901, SSB; *The Christian Index*, October 26, 1899, June 20, 1901; WMU minutes, June 17, 1903.

36. HMB minutes, June 7, July 2, October 3, 1901, April, 1902, June 30, December 1, 1903; WMU minutes, June 11, 1901; Annie Armstrong to J. M. Frost, July 1, July 16, 1901, SSB; Virginia WMU minutes, 1901-1902; Annie Armstrong to I. T. Tichenor, November 9, 1901, SSB; Annie Armstrong to R. J. Willingham, January 15, 1903, FMB.

37. Annie Armstrong to J. M. Frost, December 28, 1901, SSB; Annie Armstrong to R. J. Willingham, January 2, 1901, January 3-4, 1902, FMB;

Annie Armstrong to E. E. Bomar, January 2, 1902, FMB; WMU minutes, June
11, 1901, January 14, 1902.
    38. Annie Armstrong to R. J. Willingham, May 31, 1895, October 29, 1896,
November 24, 1899, FMB; Annie Armstrong to T. P. Bell, September 3, 1895,
November 24, 1899, SSB; Annie Armstrong to J. M. Frost, November, 1896,
SSB; R. J. Willingham to Annie Armstrong, November 25, 1899, FMB.
    39. Annie Armstrong to J. M. Frost, November, 1900, January, 1901, SSB;
Annie Armstrong to R. J. Willingham, December 29, 1900, FMB; Annie
Armstrong to F. H. Kerfoot, December 29, 1900, FMB.
    40. R. J. Willingham to Annie Armstrong, January 9, 1901, May 26, 1902,
FMB; Annie Armstrong to E. E. Bomar, January 11, 1901, FMB; WMU
minutes, February 12, 1901; HMB minutes, January 5, 1901, June 6, 1902;
SSB minutes, February 14, April 15, May 2, 1901, May 22, 1902; Annie
Armstrong to J. M. Frost, February 7, 1901, SSB; SBC Annuals, 1901-1906,
Report, WMU, 1901; *FMJ*, August, 1901; Minutes, MBUA, 1901; Transfer of
Maryland Baptist Mission Rooms to Home and Sunday School Boards, SBC,
March 18, 1901.
    41. Annie Armstrong to J. M. Frost, October, 1900, SSB; Annie Armstrong
to I. J. Van Ness, October 8, 1900, SSB.
    42. *FMJ*, August, 1901; *Arkansas Baptist*, August 7, 1901.
    43. Annie Armstrong to R. J. Willingham, May 26, 1902, FMB; R. J.
Willingham to Annie Armstrong, June 10, 1902, FMB; Annie Armstrong to
E. E. Bomar, June 14, June 17, 1902, FMB; Annie Armstrong to J. M. Frost,
June 4, 1902, SSB.
    44. Ibid., April 29, May 3, June 2, June 9, 1902, May 29, August 10, 1903;
R. J. Willingham to Annie Armstrong, December 22, 1902, FMB.
    45. WMU minutes, November 8, 1898; *Report*, WMU, 1898; R. J.
Willingham to Annie Armstrong, March 14, 1900, FMB; Annie Armstrong to
R. J. Willingham, March 24, April 6, 1900, FMB; Annie Armstrong to E. E.
Bomar, March 7, 1901, FMB; *FMJ*, September, 1899, April-June, 1900.
    46. *FMJ*, May, September, 1901; SBC Annual, 1901, Annie Armstrong to
R. J. Willingham, July 18, 1901, FMB.
    47. Minutes, MBUA, 1902-1903; Annie Armstrong to R. J. Willingham,
January 3, January 6, 1903, FMB; R. J. Willingham to Annie Armstrong,
January, 1903, FMB.
    48. Annie Armstrong to R. J. Willingham, May 19, 1902, January 8, June 24,
August 14, October 23, November-December 1903, FMB; Annie Armstrong to
E. E. Bomar, October 17, November 19, 1903, FMB.
    49. R. J. Willingham to Annie Armstrong, May 5, 1903, FMB; Annie
Armstrong to R. J. Willingham, January 5, May 22, 1903, FMB.
    50. *The Religious Herald*, July 11, 1901.
    51. *FMJ*, November, 1901.
    52. Ibid.; *The Religious Herald*, November 14, 1901; *Florida Baptist
Witness*, October 9, 1901; *Baptist and Reflector*, August-September 1901; *The
Baptist Argus*, July-October 1901; *Western Recorder*, August-September

1901; Annie Armstrong to R. J. Willingham, September 18, 1901, FMB.

53. Annie Armstrong to R. J. Willingham, January 9, January 18, "Friday Night" (February), March 17, 1902, FMB; *FMJ*, May, 1902; *The Baptist Chronicle*, March 20, 1902; *Florida Baptist Witness*, February-March 1902; Annie Armstrong to J. M. Frost, March 18, March 21, 1902, SSB.

54. Annie Armstrong to R. J. Willingham, May 14, July-September 1902, FMB; Annie Armstrong to J. M. Frost, May 24, October 6, 1902, SSB; *Central Baptist*, July-October 1902; WMU Minutes, October 14, 1902; *FMJ*, November 1902-February 1903; Annie Armstrong to E. E. Bomar, January 6, 1903.

55. *FMJ*, December 1902-February 1903; *The Baptist Argus*, October 23, 1902; Annie Armstrong Notebooks, WMU.

56. Annie Armstrong to R. J. Willingham, January, 1902, FMB.

57. Annie Armstrong to R. J. Willingham, April 12, December 23, 1903, FMB; *FMJ*, May, 1903.

58. *FMJ*, May, 1903; Annie Armstrong to E. E. Bomar, February, 1903, FMB; Annie Armstrong to R. J. Willingham, February-April 1903, FMB; WMU minutes, April, 1903; *The Baptist*, February-April, 1903; *The Baptist Chronicle*, March-April, 1903; *Florida Baptist Witness*, March-April, 1903; *The Baptist Courier*, March-April 1903, *Southern Alabama Baptist*, February, April, 1903. Records indicate that Annie visited these colleges during 1903: Hillman College, Mississippi; Judson College, Alabama; Winthrop College and Benedict College, South Carolina. She was on the Carson-Newman College campus in Tennessee during August, 1901, and was entertained in the home of the president of Ouachita College in Arkansas in September, 1903.

59. Annie Armstrong to R. J. Willingham, May 20, July-August 1903, FMB; *FMJ*, September, 1903; *Baptist and Reflector*, July-August 1903.

60. Correspondence with R. J. Willingham, 1903, FMB; correspondence with J. M. Frost, April, 1903, SSB; L. O. Dawson to Annie Armstrong, April 13, 1903, FMB; *Report*, WMU, 1903.

61. *FMJ*, November, 1903; *Central Baptist*, August-October 1903; Annual, Oklahoma Baptist State Convention, 1903; *The Baptist Argus*, December 17, 1903; *The Baptist Advance*, October 29, 1903; Annie Armstrong to R. J. Willingham, August 27, 1903, FMB.

62. The Virginia WMU Annual Meetings were in Danville in November 1900, Culpeper in 1901, South Boston in 1902, and Norfolk in 1903. Minutes, Annual Sessions of Virginia, 1900-1903; Annie Armstrong to E. E. Bomar, November 12, 1900, February 18, 1903, FMB; *FMJ*, December, 1900, July, December 1901; *The Religious Herald*, November 15, 1900, November 21, 1901, November 20, 1902, November 19, 1903; WMU minutes, November 15, 1900, February 12, April 9, November 12, 1901, December 16, 1902; Annie Armstrong to R. J. Willingham, November 8, 1901, February 4, February 9, November, December 17, 1903, FMB; R. J. Willingham to Annie Armstrong, January-February, 1903, FMB.

63. Annie Armstrong to J. M. Frost, November 20, 1901, SSB; Annie Armstrong to R. J. Willingham, November 21, 1901, FMB.

64. Annie Armstrong to R. J. Willingham, January 5, 1903, FMB; R. J. Willingham to Annie Armstrong, January 19, 1903, FMB; Annie Armstrong to R. M. Inlow, January 15, 1903, FMB; R. M. Inlow to Annie Armstrong, January 7, 1903, FMB; E. E. Bomar, January, May 18, 1903, FMB.

65. *Florida Baptist Witness*, April 15, 1903; *Western Recorder*, September 26, 1901; Noland Hubbard Bowling to the author, February 21, 1983.

66. Annie Armstrong to R. J. Willingham Thanksgiving Day, 1900, July 5, 1902, January 28, February 4, February 12, April, July 31, 1903, FMB; R. J. Willingham to Annie Armstrong, January 30, 1903, FMB.

67. Annie Armstrong to R. J. Willingham, March, 1900, FMB; Annie Armstrong to E. E. Bomar, November 17, 1902, FMB.

68. 1900 Census Schedules of Maryland, Ward 15; Annie Armstrong to R. J. Willingham, October 11, 1897, December 15, 1902, FMB; Annie Armstrong to J. M. Frost, n.d., (1902), SSB; Annie Armstrong to vice-presidents, December 13, 1902, SSB; R. J. Willingham to Annie Armstrong and WMU executive committee, November 4, 1902, FMB; WMU minutes, June 12, 1900, January 13, 1903; SSB minutes, March 13, 1902; FMB minutes, November 3, 1902; *FMJ*, July, 1903; Virginia WMU minutes, February 13, 1903.

69. Annie Armstrong to E. E. Bomar, January 7, February 28, April 28, 1903, FMB; Annie Armstrong to R. J. Willingham, February 15, April 21, April 30, 1903, FMB; R. J. Willingham to Annie Armstrong, April 22, 1903, FMB.

70. Annie Armstrong to R. J. Willingham, May 4, 1903, FMB; R. J. Willingham to Annie Armstrong, May 4-5, 1903, FMB; Annie Armstrong to vice-presidents, April 22, 1903, FMB; Annie Armstrong to Mrs. Stakely, April 23, 1903, FMB; Charles A. Stakely to (no addressee indicated), May 1, 1903, FMB; WMU minutes, March, 1903. The minutes are apparently dated incorrectly; the meeting was held in *May* in Savannah.

71. Annie Armstrong to R. J. Willingham, May 2, 1903, FMB; R. J. Willingham to J. M. Frost, May 18, 1903, FMB; *Report*, WMU, 1903; *Baptist Standard*, May 21, 1903; *FMJ*, June, 1903; *The Religious Herald*, June 25, 1903; *Biblical Recorder*, May 13, June 24, 1903; *The Christian Index*, July 2, 1903; *The Baptist Advance*, June 24, 1903.

72. Annie Armstrong to R. J. Willingham, June 13, June 17, 1903, FMB; WMU minutes, June 17, 1903; SSB Minutes, July 2, 1903; HMB minutes, June 30, 1903; FMB minutes, July 2, 1903; *The Baptist Courier*, June 11, 1903; *Florida Baptist Witness*, August 12, 1903; *The Religious Herald*, July 2, 1903; *Southern Alabama Baptist*, June 24, 1903.

73. Annie Armstrong to R. J. Willingham, November 30, 1900, January 6, December, 1903, FMB; Annie Armstrong to E. E. Bomar, January 26, 1903, FMB; Annie Armstrong to J. M. Frost, November 30, 1900, SSB.

74. Annie Armstrong to J. M. Frost, February 7, 1899, February 8, 1900, October 11, 1901, SSB; correspondence, 1900-1903.

9
When Annie
Stood Up

During the early 1900s Annie's energies were sapped and diverted from other pursuits by the controversy over founding a Southern Baptist training school for women. Though it is difficult to understand the dynamics surrounding the controversy, it is clear that Annie disapproved of a training school in connection with The Southern Baptist Theological Seminary at Louisville. This conviction led ultimately to the end of her long service as corresponding secretary of WMU, SBC, and other leadership positions.

A training school for women was not a new idea. Northern Baptists founded training schools in Chicago in 1877 and Philadelphia in 1892. As early as 1895 Texas WMU passed and sent to Annie as corresponding secretary of WMU, SBC, a resolution encouraging the establishment of a centrally located training school. Annie read the Texas resolution to the WMU executive committee. Feeling that it was not wise at the present to undertake this new work, she stated that they could recommend the Chicago and Philadelphia training schools.

It is interesting that Annie was willing to recommend Northern training schools, since she usually adamantly opposed cooperation with Northern Baptists. Too, the Northern Baptist training schools advocated practices which Annie opposed, such as women speaking before men in prayer meetings. Annie tried to discourage the Texas women from pursuing the idea of a training school. Though Willingham agreed with her at the time, he indicated that later, as the work developed, it might be best for Southern Baptists to have one of these schools.[1]

The training school idea emerged again in 1900. Dr. Ezekias Z. Simmons, missionary to China since 1870, had observed the difficulties women missionaries had because of poor preparation. While on furlough he campaigned extensively for a training school. Apparently he wrote the WMU central committees in the states and tried out the idea on Willingham. In February, Simmons talked at length with the Southern Seminary faculty about a training school for women in Louisville. Though President E. Y. Mullins was out of town, he heartily favored the idea, as did the faculty. Also while in Louisville, Simmons interested the women's missionary societies at Walnut Street and Broadway Baptist Churches in the project. His idea was to get the Louisville Baptist women to rent and furnish a house near the seminary where most of the teaching could be done.[2]

Eager for the training school to open the next fall, Simmons continued his campaign by writing Annie to secure her interest. Opening a training school was a big undertaking, and each denominational leader wanted to know what the other thought. Much correspondence passed between Baltimore, Richmond, Atlanta, Nashville, and Louisville that spring, the leaders conferring when possible. In February, Annie wrote Willingham: "You are perfectly right when you say that I do 'heartily favor the idea of having a training school.' It is what I have long desired and felt that it *must come*, but whether Mr. Simmons is adopting the wisest course in trying to arrange for the opening of a school next fall, without the matter having been very thoroughly considered and information secured from those who have done this kind of work, as to what it involves, etc., I very seriously doubt."[3]

In her usual thorough manner Annie sought to find out all she could about training schools and wrote to a number of key leaders—Willingham, Frost, Kerfoot, Tichenor, Mrs. Stakely, Mrs. Gwathmey, Eliza Broadus of Kentucky, and others. Annie also got data from Mary G. Burdette and Mrs. J. N. Cushing, who ran the training schools in Chicago and Philadelphia.

Meanwhile, Annie thought Simmons should be silenced until all the information was in and conclusions drawn by those who would be responsible for a school. From her study, Annie drew some conclusions. She believed that if a training school were established, it would be of more service to the cause of home missions, and maybe even the Sunday School Board, than to foreign missions. She also concluded, as did Kerfoot, that it was not wise to take this step at the time. Unless someone donated a lot of money and the women took hold of the idea vigorously, it would be hard to make a success of a training school.

Annie shared these conclusions with Willingham when he was in Baltimore in March and kept the WMU, SBC, executive committee fully posted. On April 10 the committee took action opposing starting a training school at the present time. If the question came up at the Southern Baptist Convention in Hot Springs and delegates favored Simmons's proposition, the committee did not favor a training school being located in Louisville.[4]

Willingham, Frost, Kerfoot, and Mullins discussed the training school question with Simmons during the Georgia Baptist Convention in April, 1900. They agreed for Simmons to confer with Kerfoot and Willingham, and through them, the Foreign and Home Mission Boards, about the advisability of a training school. Simmons prepared a proposal for the boards and, at the suggestion of Dr. and Mrs. T. P. Bell, wrote a circular letter to Baptist schools to canvass for students.

After talking with Simmons, Willingham realized how strongly Simmons felt about the matter. Simmons firmly believed that a training school would be started west of the Mississippi River if Southern Baptist leaders did not take hold of the idea and start one more in the center of Southern Baptist territory. Willingham advised caution when Annie asked about sending the correspondence relating to the training school to the state WMU central committees. He thought such agitation might precipitate state action before SBC leaders were ready. He also believed that if the training school question came up in

Hot Springs it would be referred to a committee.

Several times Willingham urged Annie to talk with Simmons, suggesting she either ask Simmons to stop off in Baltimore or talk with him when they were both at the Ecumenical Conference on Foreign Missions in New York. Disgusted because Simmons had talked freely all over the country and written countless letters about his proposition, Annie did not want to talk with him. Annie wrote Willingham that a missionary told her "that the missionaries in Canton fully recognized that Dr. Simmons is a man of schemes." Though the missionary had not used the word *schemes*, Annie claimed that it expressed the idea. She believed Simmons was being unreasonable and that many of his statements were inaccurate. Also, Eliza Broadus, close to The Southern Baptist Theological Seminary because of her late father, did not confirm the faculty support claimed by Simmons or encouragement from the Louisville women. Nor did any of the WMU leaders Annie contacted approve of Louisville as the location. Most of them indicated they thought the idea of a training school superfluous since there were already several such schools in existence.

Deferring to Willingham's advice, Annie did not send copies of the correspondence about training schools to the state WMU central committees. No doubt Annie considered this decision unfortunate, for since a training school was for women, she believed they should have a voice and wanted to know how the central committees felt before she went to Hot Springs. The men did not disagree with her in this latter sentiment. Both the Virginia and Kentucky WMU central committees passed resolutions against starting a training school.

As Annie freely expressed her opinions, she gave another clue as to her increasingly negative feelings about the training school idea. Not wanting to place young women in a position where jokes would be made about them, she thought Simmons's comment that the original plan was for missionaries to go by twos was an example of the kind of comments the secular press would exploit. Annie believed in candor and was not noted for her tact or diplomacy. Because Annie's letters sometimes seemed harsh, Willingham urged her to talk with Simmons, an "old and valued missionary," rather than writing him. He himself had learned to soften responses and become less sharp. Willingham believed that Simmons was not familiar with all of the denominational machinery or the many factors involved but was simply promoting an idea in which he believed.[5]

Annie neither wrote nor conferred with Simmons before the 1900 Southern Baptist Convention. However, she did see him and described their meeting:

> At Hot Springs I had a very plain talk with Mr. Simmons, and told him that unless he expected to carry on a training school himself, that it certainly was unwise for him to present the matter until those who had charge of the work had had an opportunity to consider the advisability of same. I went over with Mr. Simmons point by point the ground he had taken, and I think he realized that he had not informed himself as thoroughly as he should have before presenting the subject.[6]

For all practical purposes, the matter was temporarily laid to rest at the 1900 Southern Baptist Convention. The Foreign Mission Board and the Southern Seminary trustees had both referred the question to committees, and it had not been brought up by the Home Mission Board.

Annie was a little annoyed to learn that J. W. Millard, her pastor, had been the one to present the matter to the seminary trustees when he had never discussed the issue with her. When she questioned him, Millard said the matter had been brought to his attention by a seminary professor and struck him as a good idea. Annie did not like being placed in a position of seeming antagonism to a plan which appeared to have been endorsed by the secretaries of the three boards and the seminary president, presented by the pastor of the Eutaw Place Baptist Church, and endorsed by the Home Mission Board president. Also, B. H. Carroll of Texas, noted educator and denominational leader, had written Joshua Levering, a Southern Seminary trustee, that he thought the committee should get the views of the WMU, SBC, leaders, notably Annie. Carroll asked Levering to show Simmons' plan to Annie and to get her recommendations, but Annie indicated she had already made her feelings clear.[7]

From Annie's vantage point, not much happened until 1903. Meanwhile, Southern Seminary moved ahead, and by the 1902-03 school year admitted to classes young women who were planning to be missionaries. These women were not considered students.[8]

Annie saw the handwriting on the wall and realized that she needed to get in control. Little did she know at the time that the proposal she made in 1903 would lead ultimately to her downfall. She did see, however, the need for a training school. Both mission boards needed more women missionaries, and increased gifts to foreign missions made this possible for the Foreign Mission Board.

In April, 1903, Annie wrote to the board secretaries and proposed a plan to bring about the establishment of a training school: "I appreciate that you recognize the need for this, perhaps even more fully than I do, so it is not necessary for me to take your time or mine in advocating such a departure." Annie would get one of her workers to present a resolution at the WMU, SBC, Annual Meeting to appoint a committee to confer with the secretaries of the Home and Foreign Mission Boards and report in May, 1904, as to the desirability of having a training school "under the auspices of the Woman's Missionary Union," and, if favorable, suggest the location. Until an endowment could be raised, Annie believed the training school could be supported by students in Baptist colleges or women's schools.

Not favoring Annie's idea about support from college students, Willingham suggested a slight change in Annie's proposal, which was the plan ultimately adopted. In the 1903 WMU, SBC, Annual Meeting in Savannah, WMU adopted a resolution that the Southern Baptist Convention appoint a committee of seven, three to be the board secretaries, to confer with a WMU

Mrs. John A. Barker, President, WMU, SBC, 1903-1906

committee of the same size to consider a training school. This resolution followed the presentation of a paper, "The Demand for Trained Women Workers," in which Mrs. George W. Truett of Texas advocated the establishment of a training school by Southern Baptists.

The WMU, SBC, resolution was also adopted by the Southern Baptist Convention. Included on WMU's committee were Annie, Mrs. John A. Barker, who had been elected president in Savannah, and five other women.[9] The Convention named W. J. Northen from Georgia, a Southern Seminary trustee, as chairman, and included Willingham, McConnell, and Frost on the committee. Meeting before leaving Savannah, the joint committee agreed that more needed to be done to prepare young women for the missions field. The committee discussed location, curriculum, and finances, and appointed three subcommittees. Northen named Annie as chairman of the committee on curriculum, with Willingham, McConnell, and Mrs. W. D. Chipley of Florida as her committee.

Seeking input from various sources, Annie got a large number of prospectuses from different mission boards which had training schools and from Southern Seminary. She asked her curriculum committee to examine this information carefully and give her their opinions about the curriculum for the proposed school. During the year Annie visited four training schools of different denominations to study their work and secured catalogs from others; only one of the schools was connected to a theological seminary. Though the curriculum committee did not meet, members sent their input to Annie, and she prepared a draft report for their review.

Twice during the 1903-04 school year, the Southern Seminary faculty offered WMU, SBC, its classrooms for lectures for the proposed training school. Stating that the seminary trustees voted two or three years earlier to establish a training school department in connection with the seminary, E. Y. Mullins wrote an article in the April 7, 1904, issue of *The Baptist Argus*, giving reasons for selecting Louisville as the location of the department. Therefore, Mullins wrote, in essence a training school was already in Louisville, and he thought the seminary was the place for it. *The Baptist Argus* printed a number of other articles advocating a training school.[10]

During the same time, Elridge B. Hatcher, Maryland Baptists' state secretary, was advocating Baltimore as the location for a training school. He secured the endorsement of the Ministers' Conference and got the Woman's State Mission Society behind the idea. The Social Union tried to raise money as an inducement to getting the school in Baltimore. Annie claimed she had nothing whatsoever to do with the Baltimore proposal and did not want to be identified with it. Since she was a member of the joint Southern Baptist Convention-Woman's Missionary Union committee, she refused to give an opinion.[11]

W. J. Northen reported in Nashville in May, 1904, to the Southern Baptist Convention for the joint training school committee. Since Southern Seminary had not given notice before the appointment of the committee in 1903 that there was already a Training School for Women Missionaries in connection with the seminary at Louisville, and since President Mullins had publicly announced this school in the April 7, 1904, issue of *The Baptist Argus*, the committee recommended taking no action and leaving the subject with the seminary. Annie had offered these resolutions to the committee and said later that she "fully acquiesced" in the decision to leave the matter with the seminary "for the present." Though Annie did not support the action, Frost, also a committee member, offered a resolution that the Southern Baptist Convention commend the work Southern Seminary was doing and encourage the seminary to enlarge and better equip the work of the Training School Department.[12]

Perhaps because they were local institutions not related to the Southern Baptist Convention, most people did not seem too concerned or know much about the two training schools already operating during these years. Neither was under the control of or endorsed by WMU, SBC. One training school was in Dallas and the other in Baltimore. Robert Cooke Buckner, who ran an orphans' home in Dallas, saw the need to train the girls in the home who wanted to be missionaries. Gaining the support of some Texas pastors, Buckner opened a missionary training school in connection with Buckner Orphans Home in 1904. Later that year Texas WMU appointed a committee to promote the Woman's Baptist Missionary Training school, and the Texas Baptist Convention endorsed the project.[13]

In March, 1905, pastors opened a training school in Baltimore. The Maryland men had agreed earlier that if the Southern Baptist Convention did not open a training school in Baltimore, they ought to have one of their own. Annie was against this idea and wanted WMU workers and persons interested in the Southern Seminary training school to know her views about the Baltimore school. She wrote: "I had nothing whatever to do with this nor will it have my support or help." Believing the Baltimore pastors had not used their best judgment in proposing a training school, she thought it was all they could do to keep the Baltimore work going and out of debt following the terrible fire Baltimore suffered in February, 1904.

Endorsed by the Maryland Baptist Union Association and the Woman's State Mission Society, which raised money for current expenses, the Baltimore training school had as its purpose training women city missionaries. The women did missions work in the city while training. The school was discontinued in May, 1906, and did not reopen until 1917.[14]

After the 1904 Southern Baptist Convention, the Kentucky Baptist women got behind the proposed training school at Southern Seminary 100 percent. Spurred by Eliza Broadus, who had changed from earlier opposition to a training school, the women led in securing and furnishing a home for young women in Louisville. Appointing a local committee to take charge, the Louisville women involved many women in other states in the project.

Left: F. H. Kerfoot, Annie's pastor, Eutaw Place Baptist Church, 1877-82; Corresponding Secretary, Home Mission Board, 1899-1901; Center: F. C. McConnell, Corresponding Secretary, Home Mission Board, 1901-03; Right: B. D. Gray, Corresponding Secretary, Home Mission Board, 1903-28

Because of numerous inquiries, E. Y. Mullins gave a status report about the Training School Department at Southern Seminary. The number of women taking courses in the school had increased steadily, and Dr. W. O. Carver was offering a class in practical missions methods. Since the Southern Baptist Convention had made no change in the training school department, the department was operating as before. In 1904-05, Mullins spent seven months abroad, so he was somewhat removed from what became a growing controversy.[15]

Kentucky WMU support for the training school and home grew steadily throughout the year, as did the feeling that WMU, SBC, should support the school. Mrs. George B. Eager, wife of a Southern Seminary professor and chairman of the Louisville women's committee for the home, wrote an article in the February 23, 1905, issue of *The Christian Index* about the school and the home for young women. Her article, asking for support of the home, was endorsed by T. P. Bell.

Annie, who called the training school now under Southern Seminary the "so-called training school," was trying to avoid anything that would make her vulnerable. Not wanting training school proponents to have an excuse to ask WMU, SBC, for aid to Southern Seminary, she was careful in working with Willingham about WMU support of schools overseas to limit the support to all schools except for theological seminaries.[16] Annie did not want to be accused of supporting theological institutions overseas, but not at home.

Since Frost had been on the Southern Baptist Convention committee that recommended taking no further action, Annie did not think he should have made the additional resolution in May, 1904, commending Southern Seminary for its training school and encouraging its enlargement. She was upset with Frost and wrote him a sharp letter in March, 1905. Reminding Frost that she had not had his support during the controversy with Fannie Heck, even though Annie was behind the Sunday School Board, she told Frost she did not think she had his support now. For the next year, Annie kept on bringing up Frost's action at the 1904 Southern Baptist Convention.[17]

Control was beginning to slip out of Annie's hands. In the spring of 1905, Mrs. S. E. Woody, secretary of the Louisville committee for the home for the training school, wrote Willingham and B. D. Gray, now Home Mission Board secretary, to get them to recommend the training school to WMU, SBC. Stating that the Home Mission Board made only recommendations about its own work, Gray declined to take the action requested by Mrs. Woody. Gray considered that the Southern Baptist Convention action in May, 1904, had removed the training school from connection with the Home Mission Board.[18]

The Louisville training school home committee also wrote to the WMU, SBC, vice-presidents in April, enclosing a copy of Mrs. Eager's article in *The Christian Index* and seeking their support. Annie thought it ridiculous that the committee made a distinction between the Southern Seminary training school and the home for young women. Five of the WMU, SBC, vice-presidents, including Eliza Broadus, asked Mrs. John A. Barker, national president, to include the home on the 1905 WMU, SBC, Annual Meeting program. Refusing this request on the grounds that the whole matter had been referred to Southern Seminary, Mrs. Barker stated, however, that the subject could be brought to the floor by resolution.

Annie was incensed that those trying to create public sentiment for the training school wrote to everyone but her. The Louisville women's committee did not even send her a copy of the letter which they wrote to the WMU, SBC, vice-presidents. Nor did Mullins write Annie, though he was advocating support of the training school at all turns. While not receiving one letter from training school supporters, Annie knew what was going on because some of the vice-presidents kept her informed.

Perhaps those in favor of the training school ignored Annie because of her power and influence. Also, she proved in May, 1904, that she could take an innocent statement, such as the one

Mullins made when he referred to a training school department at Southern Seminary, and use it to accomplish her purposes. In the 1904 Southern Baptist Convention, by influencing the joint training school committee to defer the subject to Southern Seminary, Annie effectively stopped any action which might lead to WMU, SBC, management of a training school.

Just in case she needed it, Annie prepared a thorough paper giving the complete history of the training school movement. She asked Willingham how he would feel if a similar effort were being made to engage the Foreign Mission Board in some work and he did not know about it. She wrote: "It savors very much of political wire pulling and I would say to you without the shadow of a doubt if the Woman's Missionary Union is prepared to endorse such actions they will at the Annual Meeting in Kansas City have to select another Corresponding Secretary." Willingham concurred that she should not only have been informed but consulted with.[19]

Having studied the training school matter at length for five years, by May, 1905, Annie entirely and heartily disapproved of WMU, SBC, supporting a school in connection with Southern Seminary in Louisville. Women did not need a seminary course of study, she reasoned, as they were not expected to preach. Considering her judgment valid, Annie claimed support of her views by John A. Broadus (now deceased), I. T. Tichenor, and Dr. Henry G. Weston, president of the Crozier Theological Seminary.

The lines were drawn for the WMU, SBC, Annual Meeting in Kansas City in May, 1905. Meeting before the Southern Baptist Convention and clarifying the facts, the Southern Seminary trustees accepted the wisdom of leaving the training school in Louisville. However, they indicated clearly that they wanted and needed the support of WMU, SBC. Dr. W. W. Landrum, chairman of the Southern trustees' training school committee, delivered this communication to the WMU Annual Meeting.[20]

The training school was the hot topic in the WMU Annual

Meeting, with Annie, the acknowledged leader of WMU, a key personality. In the first session, Miss M. Gibson, president of the Scarrett Bible and Training School in Kansas City, spoke briefly and invited the women to visit the school. Immediately, Mrs. J. L. Burnham of Missouri offered a resolution that WMU, SBC, "endorse the Home for the young women attending the Woman's Missionary Training School in Louisville, and heartily commend the Home to the sympathy and help of State Central Committees." Annie moved tabling the resolution until that afternoon and asked to speak to it. When Mrs. S. E. Woody of Kentucky asked that Mullins also be allowed the privilege of speaking to the motion, Annie yielded the opening address to Mullins. No doubt she wanted to be able to respond to what Mullins said.

Tension mounted through the dinner hour. That afternoon, Mullins spoke briefly about the status of the school and in favor of WMU, SBC, extending financial aid to the home. After he left, Annie read facts about the whole subject and offered her resignation. She disapproved thoroughly of the methods the Louisville women used to bring the matter before the group, feeling that they had been disloyal to a WMU officer. Mrs. Barker spoke briefly, read letters bearing on the subject, and stated she could no longer serve as national WMU president. Others spoke in defense of the Louisville women. When the vote was taken, Mrs. Burnham's resolution lost—twenty-five against it, twenty-two for it. In essence, Annie and Mrs. Barker took a risk and placed their influence and leadership on the line. Though Annie's position about the training school was clear, little information is recorded about why Mrs. Barker took the action she did.

Later, Mrs. W. F. Elliott of Missouri offered two resolutions which were adopted. She called for prayerful consideration of the work being done by Southern Seminary and the desirability of providing a home for women students. She thought the decision should be made at the WMU Annual Meeting as to whether WMU would undertake the work of sustaining the home. She commended the Louisville women for what they had done.

When the WMU, SBC, nominating committee presented its report, Mrs. Barker and Annie were reelected as president and corresponding secretary. For the good of the work, they agreed to serve in these positions until May, 1906. Annie's sister, Alice, resigned her editorial positions during the Kansas City meeting. Annie pledged to do all she could to make the next year's work the best in the history of WMU and to give all the information she could about the relationship between the national organization and the states.[21]

It was only a matter of time now before advocates of the training school would win. Sentiment was swinging that way. However, the controversy raged between May, 1905, and May, 1906. Mobilizing the forces against the training school, Annie immediately got the WMU, SBC, executive committee to endorse officially the position she and Mrs. Barker took in Kansas City. On May 26, 1905, the committee announced that it, too, would decline renomination in May, 1906.[22]

Annie firmly believed she had been wronged, claiming she could have a number of persons prosecuted for libel if she chose to do so. Specifically she named T. P. Bell, Eliza Broadus, some of the seminary professors, and the wife of the seminary financial agent. She considered letting all the facts be known so it would be impossible for others who followed to be treated as she had been. Bell was attacking Annie in *The Christian Index,* and, apparently, Eliza Broadus had turned against Annie because of Annie's earlier support of F. H. Kerfoot. Also, Annie and Eliza were on opposite sides concerning the training school.[23]

Several state Baptist papers made harsh comments about Annie. In reporting on the Kansas City meeting, the *Biblical Recorder* wrote: "Under pressure of one of the Union's leaders— its veritable leader—the ladies first declined. But on second thought they voted to give the department [Training Department of the Seminary] their support. This brought about quite an upstir, and the leader referred to gave her notice of her resignation." The paper went on to say that it was a rule in English affairs that when the people refuse to follow a leader in a vital matter, the leader retires. Also, it was the Baptist way for an individual not to undertake to rule the majority but to execute the will of the majority. A person could not grow so important that she must have her own way or no way at all.[24]

The editor of *The Baptist Argus* announced that he knew several women who could take the place of the present WMU, SBC, secretary. When his business manager asked Annie for a complete list of the state WMU secretaries, she refused, saying: "A stamped envelope was sent, but I shall consign same to the wastebasket." *The Religious Herald* expressed hope that the Virginia women would fall in line and cooperate with the Louisville women in providing for the young women students. T. P. Bell endorsed the appeal from Mrs. S. E. Woody of Louisville about the home in *The Christian Index.*

The Maryland Baptist printed an anonymous letter in which a person in another state asked for the papers to carry a full discussion of the reasons pro and con for establishing or not establishing a training school in Louisville in connection with Southern Seminary. This step was too important not to hear all opinions. The writer believed a most serious mistake would be made to have the school in Louisville. If a school were established, the writer said, it should not be in connection with a seminary "in which hundreds of young men ready to marry are being educated at the same time."[25] Many people probably thought Annie wrote this letter; however, this is doubtful.

Considering Frost largely responsible for the state of affairs, Annie never forgave him for the resolution he made at the 1904 Southern Baptist Convention to commend and encourage Southern Seminary to enlarge and equip the work of the Training School Department. She made it a point not to talk to Frost when they were both in Oklahoma in the fall of 1905. On

October 4, 1905, Annie wrote Frost a letter she acknowledged as being discourteous, but honest. She stated that he was the one who gave training school advocates opportunity to accuse her of opposing the Southern Baptist Convention because she did not think women should be trained to be preachers. Further, she considered it inappropriate for a committee member (he had been on the training school committee which reported in May, 1904) to make a resolution which was contrary to the spirit of the committee's report. Though Frost might believe he did "exactly right," Annie felt he did "exactly wrong, and your action has caused already a great deal of trouble and will, I fear, result in much harm to the work."[26]

Annie was hurt. Since she had supported Frost over the years, she thought he could have remained silent in May, 1904, and let someone else echo the wishes of the Southern Seminary faculty. Reminding Frost of her five-year study about training schools and the support she had from John A. Broadus, I. T. Tichenor, and Henry G. Weston, Annie stated she had come to the conclusion that it was wrong to have a training school in connection with a theological seminary. She sent Frost a copy of her nine-page history of the movement to establish a training school and asked him to read it carefully. Opposing teaching women to be preachers, which Annie thought would happen if they were in the same classes with men, she ended her comments to Frost by writing: "To sum up this whole matter I am standing for two principles; first, the unscripturalness of training women to be preachers, and second, for right methods in Southern Baptist mission work."[27]

Annie told Frost she did not expect him to answer her letter. Learning that he had suggested the name of Mrs. T. P. Bell as her successor, Annie was sure Martha McIntosh Bell would have Southern Seminary endorsement, "and with the wire pulling, which some Southern Baptists seem to have become adept in, she may get a sufficient number of votes to be installed in the office."[28]

The day after her letter to Frost, Annie gave a full report to the executive committee of the Woman's Baptist Home Mission Society of Maryland about the training school and derogatory remarks Bell was making about her in *The Christian Index*. She indicated she planned to give up leadership in the society in the near future. The committee named persons to investigate the training school and to bring a resolution at the Home Mission Society's annual meeting in November that the society could not endorse the school and would instruct its delegates to the WMU, SBC, Annual Meeting in May, 1906, to vote against the training school.[29]

Evidently Frost responded to Annie's October 4 letter, claiming the right to judge for himself what God wanted him to do. Annie wrote again and agreed with this right but wanted that privilege herself instead of the persecution she was having to endure. "What I call in question is not persons differing from me in regard to the establishing of the so called Training School at Louisville, but the *methods* adopted by those who are advocating same." Annie claimed that much had happened since January, 1905, to cause friction between the two of them—letters, actions at the Southern Baptist Convention, and newspaper articles. "You may say that you have nothing to do with some of these. My brother, this is true in a certain sense, but you are largely responsible for starting the ball rolling."[30]

In all this furor Annie may not have noticed the steady moves by training school advocates to push the school and refute her arguments. Many articles were printed in state Baptist papers and many speeches made. T. P. Bell was one of the biggest advocates. Hearing of the charge that the training school would prove to be a matchmaking institution, a charge he considered absurd, Bell wrote in *The Christian Index* in February, 1906: "It might well have arisen in the fertile imagination of some maiden lady of uncertain age, who has come to look upon marriage as a dreadful thing, and especially a marriage between two Christians whose hearts are one in the service of the master." About what he considered the also absurd charge that the training school would train women to be preachers, he stated this was "evidently diligently sought by someone who was striving to prejudice people against the good institution, against which no real objections could be found."[31] Bell was obviously referring to Annie.

In its October 10, 1905, meeting, the WMU, SBC, executive committee considered a number of items pertaining to Annie's attitude toward the training school and *The Christian Index* attacks on her. Annie believed she had the support of this committee. The committee voted to send a letter and statement of protest, which included Annie's two principles for opposing the training school, to all state Baptist papers expressing "indignation at the shameful prosecution to which the Corresponding Secretary is being subjected by Dr. T. P. Bell." Annie prevailed on the committee to limit the communication to the state WMU central committees and the three board secretaries. The executive committee sent out the protest on October 16, asking the board secretaries to read it at the next meeting of their boards.[32]

Annie laid herself wide open for ridicule by the men she considered her closest co-workers by sending them a copy of a clipping about a new law adopted by the Northern Education Society for the Newton Theological Seminary. The law stated that young men wanting society aid had to refrain from matrimony for one year before entering the seminary. Annie failed to see the humor when Frost responded that the article struck him as amusing and ridiculous. Willingham questioned what the society would do for men already married. Annie simply thought the society was administering wisely a trust fund, not legislating marriage.[33]

The Foreign Mission Board took no action on the WMU executive committee's statement of protest since the papers appeared to the Board to be a personal matter. The Home Mission Board and the Sunday School Board each read the communication and ordered it filed. It was becoming clear that

Annie was fast losing support of the boards and their secretaries.[34]

The Southern Seminary faculty got wind of WMU's statement of protest, and they took issue to the reference which stated WMU's opposition to the training school on the "Scriptural ground that women are forbidden to preach and so to be taught to preach." On behalf of the faculty, W. O. Carver wrote the WMU, SBC, executive committee that their charge was wholly unfounded and asked the committee to correct the statement with all to whom it had been sent. Annie led the committee to take notice of Carver's letters and to order them filed. The seminary faculty was not to be deterred, however, and kept at it until they got a response.

At the March 20, 1906, WMU executive committee meeting, the motion to place a letter from Dr. Mullins on file lost by one vote. Mrs. W. C. Lowndes moved to reconsider the protest. Though her motion lost by one vote, Mrs. Lowndes claimed and received the privilege of presenting a minority report at the next meeting. The WMU, SBC, executive committee was becoming divided in opinion. At the same meeting in which Mrs. Lowndes took a stand, the committee authorized Annie to send her historical paper about the training school to state WMU central committees and state Baptist papers if she wished. She chose to send it only to vice-presidents of WMU, SBC.

In its April 10 meeting, the WMU executive committee reconsidered the statement of protest which had been sent out unanimously the previous October. The issue was whether Southern Seminary was teaching women to preach. In the April committee meeting, Annie presented the majority report, and Clara M. Woolford the minority report. The majority report, which reaffirmed the original protest, was signed by seven members, including Annie, Alice, and Mrs. Barker. The minority report, which indicated that these committee members did not now believe the training school was teaching women to preach, was signed by six members. Four of the members indicated their willingness to serve again on the committee if WMU so desired. The majority and minority reports were mailed to the president of Southern Seminary, state WMU central committees, and the secretaries of the boards.[35]

It is interesting to note that during all this protest and counterprotest, veteran missionary E. Z. Simmons, who first proposed the training school in 1900, returned to America for eye surgery. He was almost totally blind. One wonders how Simmons felt in 1906 about what was taking place in the Southern Baptist Convention.[36]

By April, 1906, Annie had not only lost the support of the board secretaries but that of many of the women throughout the South and almost half the WMU, SBC, executive committee. Only Mrs. Barker and Alice stood by her.

The WMU Annual Meeting in Chattanooga in May, 1906, was almost anticlimatic. The greater part of an afternoon session was given to discussing the establishment of a women's training school. The Southern Seminary trustees had heartily approved the action being considered by WMU to establish a training school. After much discussion, in which Annie participated, the vote was taken. The resolution to establish a training school lost only because of a technicality. Mrs. Barker, the national WMU president, ruled that according to the constitution a new work could not be taken up without previous notice to WMU except by unanimous vote of the body. The slight opposition to the resolution caused the motion to be lost. The training school question was simply delayed for a year, for in 1907 WMU, SBC, voted to establish a training school in Louisville.[37]

What were Annie's real convictions about a training school? She had studied the question carefully and thoroughly, as was her custom. It seems apparent that Annie did not oppose the concept of a training school, believing firmly that women missionaries needed to be well trained. She did, however, have some hesitation about the cost of such an institution, as well as the time and energy which would be required to make a success of a school. No doubt Annie could foresee that if WMU, SBC, operated a training school, the attention of the women might be turned away from what she considered primary—a complete devotion to missions. This conviction was the real issue for Annie.

While the controversy raged, Annie also made her two personal points of objection clear. She was opposed to women preaching, a belief substantiated by her own views and practice about women not taking part in meetings in which men were present. Southern to the core in her views, Annie never considered herself a preacher. Annie's second personal objection related to the unethical methods she felt were used to bring about a training school—political wire-pulling as she called it. There is little, if any, evidence to substantiate the opinion that Annie thought the training school would be a matrimonial bureau.

Though the training school question occupied her energies off and on from 1900 to 1906, Annie was firm and spoke out forthrightly about her convictions. She had the courage to stand up for what she believed, even in the face of opposition and eventual resignation. Willing to risk her leadership position and the support of her followers, Annie confronted the women with an issue of major significance—could they establish, fund, and manage a training school and, at the same time, give full attention to missions and women's work in the churches?

Notes (See pages 295-310 for Key to Sources.)

1. Robert G. Torbet, *A History of the Baptists*, pp. 321-322, 516; *American Baptist Year-Book*, 1882; WMU minutes, November 12, 1895; R. J. Willingham to Annie Armstrong, February 26, 1896, FMB; Annie Armstrong to R. J. Willingham, March 2, March 13, 1896, FMB.

2. Minutes, SBTS Faculty, February 27, 1900; *The Baptist Argus*, March 1, 1900; E. Y. Mullins to J. R. Saunders, October 3, 1922, WMU; R. J. Willingham to Annie Armstrong, February 26, 1900, FMB; R. J. Willingham to E. Y. Mullins, February 26, 1900, FMB.

3. E. Z. Simmons to Annie Armstrong, February 24, 1900, SSB; R. J. Willingham to E. Y. Mullins, February 26, 1900, FMB; R. J. Willingham to Annie Armstrong, February 26, March 10, 1900, FMB; Annie Armstrong to J. M. Frost and R. J. Willingham, February 27, 1900, SSB.

4. Annie Armstrong to R. J. Willingham, February 27, March 9, 1900, FMB; Annie Armstrong to J. M. Frost, March 1, 1900, SSB; R. J. Willingham to E. Y. Mullins, March 9, 1900, FMB; R. J. Willingham to E. Z. Simmons, April 9, 1900, FMB; R. J. Willingham to F. H. Kerfoot, April 12, 1900, FMB; WMU minutes, March 13, April 10, 1900.

5. R. J. Willingham to Annie Armstrong, April, 1900, FMB; Annie Armstrong to R. J. Willingham, April, 1900, FMB; E. Z. Simmons to R. J. Willingham, May 9, 1900, FMB; E. Z. Simmons to brethren of the HMB and FMB, April 2, 1900, SSB; FMB minutes, April 10, 1900; Virginia WMU minutes, April 13, May 11, 1900; Annie Armstrong to J. M. Frost, June 28, 1900, SSB; Annie Armstrong, "History of Movement to Establish Woman's Missionary Training School," SSB.

6. Annie Armstrong to J. M. Frost, June 26, 1900, SSB.

7. Ibid.; FMB minutes, May 22, September 11, 1900; WMU minutes, June 12, 1900; Joshua Levering to Annie Armstrong, June 25, 1900, SSB; B. H. Carroll to Joshua Levering, June 21, 1900, SSB; Annie Armstrong to R. J. Willingham, June 26, 1900, FMB.

8. Minutes, SBTS Trustees, May 9, 1901, May 8, 1902, May 7, 1903; *The Baptist Argus*, May, August, 1902; *The Christian Index*, August 21, 1902; SBTS catalog, 1902-1907.

9. Annie Armstrong to J. M. Frost, April 25, 1903, SSB; Annie Armstrong to R. J. Willingham, April 25, April 28, 1903, FMB (Annie Armstrong sent a duplicate copy of her April 25 letter to F. C. McConnell, HMB.); Annie Armstrong, "History of Movement to Establish Woman's Missionary Training School," SSB; R. J. Willingham to Annie Armstrong, April 28, 1903, FMB; *Report*, WMU, 1903; *FMJ*, June, October, 1903; *Baptist Standard*, May 21, 1903.

10. SBC Annual, 1903; *The Baptist Argus*, May 21, 1903, April-May, 1904; Annie Armstrong to R. J. Willingham, January 7, May 25, December 21, 1903, March-April 1904, FMB; R. J. Willingham to Annie Armstrong, May 26, December 22, 1903, March 5, April 8, 1904, FMB; WMU minutes, January 19, April 12, 1904; Minutes, SBTS faculty, November 3, 1903, March 31, 1904; *The Christian Index*, May 5, 1904.

11. Minutes, Woman's State Mission Society of Maryland, February 5, March 4, 1904, (hereafter referred to as WSMS); Annie Armstrong to R. J. Willingham, April 13, 1904, FMB; R. J. Willingham to Annie Armstrong, April 14, 1904, FMB; Annie Armstrong to J. M. Frost, April 13, June 6, 1904, SSB.

12. SBC Annual, 1904; Annie Armstrong to R. J. Willingham, April 4, June 6, 1904, FMB; Annie Armstrong, "History of Movement to Establish Woman's Missionary Training School," SSB.

13. *Baptist Standard*, March 30, July 6, 1905, May 10, 1906.

14. Annie Armstrong to R. J. Willingham, June 6, 1904, FMB; Annie Armstrong to J. M. Frost, June 6, 1904, SSB; Frances M. Schuyler to Annie Armstrong, May, 1904, SSB; B. P. Robertson to Frances M. Schuyler, May 27, 1904, SSB; Annie Armstrong to E. E. Bomar, June 6, 1904, FMB; *The Maryland Baptist*, February-November, 1905, February, 1906; Minutes, MBUA, 1905-1906, 1922; Minutes, WSMS, February 9, 1905.

15. *The Baptist Argus*, June-July, 1904; *Baptist Standard*, July 28, 1904; *The Baptist Advance*, August 4, 1904; Annie Armstrong, "History of Movement to Establish Woman's Missionary Training School," SSB.

16. *The Baptist Argus*, July 14, 1904; *The Christian Index*, February 23, 1905; HMB minutes, April 4, 1905; Annie Armstrong to R. J. Willingham, February 23, 1905, FMB.

17. *The Christian Index*, February 23, 1905; Annie Armstrong to J. M. Frost, March 15, 1905, SSB.

18. HMB minutes, April 4, 1905; Annie Armstrong to R. J. Willingham, April 26-27, 1905, FMB; R. J. Willingham to Annie Armstrong, April 28, 1905, FMB.

19. Annie Armstrong to R. J. Willingham, April 26, 1905, FMB.

20. Minutes, SBTS Trustees, May 11, 1905; Annie Armstrong, "History of Movement to Establish Woman's Missionary Training School," SSB.

21. *Report*, WMU, 1905; *The Religious Herald*, May 25, 1905; *The Christian Index*, May, 1905; *Central Baptist*, June 8, 1905; *The Baptist Argus*, May 25, 1905; *FMJ*, July, 1905.

22. WMU minutes, May 25, 1905.

23. Annie Armstrong to R. J. Willingham, May 4, 1902, June 19, June 21, 1905, FMB; Annie Armstrong, "History of Movement to Establish Woman's Missionary Training School," SSB; Annie Armstrong to J. M. Frost, November 8, 1905, SSB.

24. *Biblical Recorder*, July 2, 1905.

25. Annie Armstrong to R. J. Willingham, July 14, 1905, FMB; *The Religious Herald*, August 17, 1905; *The Christian Index*, August 3, 1905; *The Maryland Baptist*, August 1, 1905.

26. Annie Armstrong to J. M. Frost, October 4, 1905, SSB.

27. Ibid.

28. Ibid.

29. Minutes, WHMS, October, 1905.

30. Annie Armstrong to J. M. Frost, October 9, 1905, SSB. See chapter 10 about other differences.

31. *The Christian Index*, October 19, 1905, February 22, 1906; *The Baptist Argus*, November 9, 1905, March 23, 1906; *Southern Baptist Witness*, February 1, 1906; *Biblical Recorder*, March 14, 1906; *Texas Baptist and Herald*, March 15, 1906.

32. See chapter 10 for the full story about *The Christian Index* criticism. WMU minutes, October 10, 1905; Mrs. A. C. Johnson to the SSB, HMB, and FMB, October 16, 1905, SSB and FMB.

33. Annie Armstrong to J. M. Frost, October 30, November 4-5, 1905, SSB; Annie Armstrong to R. J. Willingham, November 2, 1905, FMB; R. J. Willingham to Annie Armstrong, October 31, November 3, 1905, FMB; *The Religious Herald*, November 16, 1905.

34. FMB minutes, October 24, 1905; HMB minutes, November 7, 1905; SSB minutes, November 9, 1905; R. J. Willingham to Annie Armstrong, October 23, 1905, FMB.

35. Minutes, SBTS Faculty, November, 1905-April, 1906; WMU minutes, December, 1905-April, 1906; Annie Armstrong to J. M. Frost, April 11, 1906, SSB.

36. *Baptist and Reflector*, March-April, 1906.

37. *Reports*, WMU, 1906-1907; Minutes, SBTS trustees, May 10, 1906; *Southern Baptist Witness*, May 17, 1906; *The Christian Index*, May 24, 1906; *The Baptist Advance*, May 24, 1906; *The Baptist Argus*, May 17, 1906; Fannie Heck to R. J. Willingham, January 8, 1907, FMB.

10
The Bitter and the Sweet—
Do They Mix?

Getting out missions information to women and young people and raising money for the boards came first with Annie. Soon after the new Southern Baptist Convention year began in May, 1904, she wrote Willingham: "I do want this year not only to come near, but to get *every cent* that the Foreign Board and the Home Board have asked of Woman's Missionary Union, and I believe it can be done, but, of course, it means hard work and that I expect to give."[1] Annie's philosophy was to stick to a task until it was accomplished: "Somehow or other, . . . I do not like to give up when I undertake to do a thing."[2]

Baltimore suffered a terrible winter in 1904, with more snow than usual. For weeks on end the streets were covered with snow and ice. By early February, however, a mild Saturday melted most of the snow and left muddy slush. February 7 dawned with an overcast sky and a brisk southwest wind. On that quiet Sunday morning, fire broke out in a downtown dry goods store. Before it was under control thirty hours later, the raging, uncontrollable fire swept through the Baltimore business and financial district, destroying everything in its path. The destruction was unbelievable, the damage in the millions of dollars. An estimated two thousand buildings in seventy blocks were burned to the ground.

The next day Annie reported to Willingham on the state of things. Although news was scanty, she labeled what was happening "the fearful calamity." The governor declared Monday a legal holiday to prevent a run on remaining banks. Banks, trust companies, wholesale and retail stores, and newspaper offices were all gone. The wharves were blackened ruins. Telephone communication was cut off, the powerhouse was burned, and the streetcars would not run for weeks. The burned area was cordoned off and people denied access. Many people faced bankruptcy, and there was much suspense and anguish. Baltimore was indeed isolated from the outside world.

Annie's first concern was the Mission Rooms. Though she did not know it, the rooms were safe. However, she and her family suffered personal losses. The three warehouses Annie and Alice owned, as well as two others they owned jointly with family members, were leveled. Because most people felt that businesses were not usually destroyed totally by fire, the warehouses were not insured to their full value. The Leverings were big losers, the E. Levering and Company coffee firm having been destroyed. The bank of which Eugene Levering was president and Commerce Street, where the family did much business, were burned. Eugene told Annie on Monday morning that "he did not know that he had a dollar." Many people suffered unbearably, their life savings wiped out. Several persons asked Annie and Alice if they could rent part of their rooms. Annie agonized over the situation: "With so much surrounding us of a distressing nature it, of course, is not possible to sleep as usual, so I am having more time in which to think."[3]

Annie was able to get to the Mission Rooms on Monday, and the work went on in spite of the surrounding catastrophe. She wrote: "The Post Office was saved and there was a delay of not more than one hour in receiving the mail. A casual visitor in . . . 233 North Howard Street, seeing the building untouched by fire, listening to the rapid clacking of the typewriters, noting the packages of monthly literature and other material on the long table to be sent to WMU workers throughout the South, would probably have thought that there was at least one place free from the perplexity so apparent in other parts of the city." This was not so.

Only as the work resumed, piecemeal, did Annie see the

results of calamity. Printers, box makers, the express were all swept away. It was almost impossible to get cash for postage. Only a small part of the literature for the March week of prayer and offering for home missions had been delivered. Thousands of these leaflets and envelopes had burned at the printers, as had the leaflet written by Lansing Burrows about the Tichenor Memorial, a fund for building churches named for I. T. Tichenor, a former Home Mission Board secretary.

Annie's big concern was to get the literature out to the states by the end of the month, so they could get it to missionary societies early in March. She took emergency measures—immediately notifying the states and sending articles to the state Baptist papers about the fire. In her articles Annie appealed to societies to "go forward" in observing the Week of Prayer for Home Missions even if they did not receive the literature. Annie met obstacles at every turn, noting "even the need of a ball of cord became a problem, as accustomed places of purchase had all been burned." However, she got the literature out, stating later: "Mountains of difficulty were leveled to the plain as we approached them and the literature was printed—just how, or just where, we don't know—and was shipped in time, *as though no fire had occurred.*"[4]

The future looked bleak and dark to Annie during these days of anxiety. At times she felt as if she were dreaming. It unnerved her to dwell on the conditions that surrounded her. The pressure and the strain were overwhelming, and Annie tried to get as absorbed in the work as possible. She claimed the promises of God, writing:

> The future, humanly speaking, is dark, but "Man's extremity is God's opportunity." For the present it is undoubtedly my duty to keep right on with WMU work. This I shall do, and use every power I possess in helping to advance same and carry out the plans which we have inaugurated. I would be recreant to the trust which I have assumed, or rather which I believe God has imposed upon me, to do anything else until the annual meeting of the Woman's Missionary Union in Nashville.[5]

On top of the severe winter and the fire, Annie suffered several bouts of not feeling well. Never staying home if there were any chance of getting to the Mission Rooms, one day Annie had to lie down for awhile after breakfast before she could take the streetcar to work. However, at the end of that week she collapsed and spent Sunday in bed. Annie reported: "It was really amusing as well as touching to see how the different members of the family with whom we are boarding [Annie and Alice rented out their own home] seemed to feel that they must show solicitude by visiting my room, etc., etc. It is the first time since the lady, who now has our house, has been with us (fifteen months) that I have had a meal brought to my room." Annie took a number of remedies to put her back on her feet, but she did "not believe in so much physicing." She suffered continuously from rheumatism and neuralgia, finally visiting a dentist in the hope that this would help the neuralgia.[6]

Keeping up her arduous pace, Annie was at the office every day, all day, except when she went home for lunch. Over lunch, she and Alice often conferred about business because Annie valued highly Alice's opinions.

Annie described what she considered all in a day's work:

> It is a little difficult to keep my wits about me when I am attempting, as I am today, to dictate leters to two stenographers, superintend the preparation of a program for the Week of Self Denial in March for Home Missions, direct another clerk in putting up a large number of packages and two amateurs in folding letters, who will think it is well every now and then to change the gauge which I gave them.

Because she considered the work so important, Annie felt that she had to fill in the gaps others left undone. Sometimes she faced unusual problems, such as having to burn smallpox letters from Mexico. Indicating she found it hard to do the same things year after year and make them novel, Annie tried to be creative.[7]

Annie continued to refuse a salary, though in May, 1904, WMU, SBC, reaffirmed its decision to attach a salary to the office of corresponding secretary. She was unwilling to give her reasons publicly. The women accepted her wishes and allowed her to continue to serve without remuneration. Annie's decision was reported widely in secular and Baptist papers.[8]

Claiming she could do a lot more work in 1904 than she could when she first started in 1888, Annie found time to be active in her church and in the Maryland women's mission societies. Annie made frequent references in her letters to the quarterly all-day Home Mission Society meetings over which she presided. Most years she attended the union meetings of societies during the January week of prayer. Annie wrote: "How thankful I am that we have gotten WMU workers in a measure to realize that 'Prayer moves the arm that moves the world,' and that the Week of Prayer is being more and more largely observed." Annie was a woman of prayer herself and often acknowledged God's care and direction.

Each Friday afternoon when she was in town, Annie conducted the opening exercises at the mothers' meeting at Eutaw Place Baptist Church, where between 100 and 150 women gathered to receive religious and practical instruction. She considered this meeting an effective organization for reaching poor people.

Because Maryland was a border state, Annie yearned for strong Southern men who supported Southern Baptist work to be Baltimore pastors. When Eutaw Place Baptist Church was without a pastor the winter of 1905, she urged the leaders to get an experienced, Southern pastor. Annie also did what she could do to strengthen women's work in her church and other Baltimore churches. When Immanuel and Seventh Baptist Churches merged, Annie wanted the work to continue for "her warm personal friends" and presided over the consolidation of the women's societies.[9]

Annie had several novel ideas during these years. She prepared twelve pictorial scrapbooks, one for each country where Southern Baptists had missionaries and one for each home missions department and displayed the scrapbooks at the WMU,

SBC, Annual Meeting.[10] Thinking of a new approach to Missionary Day in the Sunday School, Annie suggested that instead of having a single day and dividing the collections between the boards, that each quarter be assigned to a board with the offering for that quarter going to the respected board. Annie did not think Frost was too pleased with the plan, but he agreed to try it. Annie secured the mailing list of Sunday School superintendents from Lansing Burrows, addressed the envelopes, and mailed out the letters. She mailed out appeals from the Foreign Mission Board in January, 1904, and the Home Mission Board in October.[11]

Fully age-graded missions organizations did not come to fruition under Annie's leadership. However, she pioneered and laid the groundwork for later development. Annie saw the need for "definiteness in the young people's work." She lined up specific objects and printed new literature to interest children and brighten meetings. Annie also encouraged Sunbeam Band work for children.

Continuing her interest in the college-age young woman, between 1904 and 1906 Annie visited a number of colleges. She stated two purposes for these visits: presenting distinctive missions work to the students and helping them help others when they returned home. In June, 1904, Annie attended the Tenth Southern Conference of the Young Women's Christian Associations in Asheville, North Carolina. She was instrumental in getting the mission boards to send missionary representatives, Mrs. R. H. Graves and Marie Buhlmaier, who presented Southern Baptist work at the meeting. Annie also took advantage of the opportunity to hold a special meeting for Baptist girls to seek to gain their interest in missions and WMU.[12]

New interests never kept Annie from already developed interests. The Home Mission Board enlarged the work with blacks and selected Arthur James Barton to be field secretary. Annie knew Barton from his days as an assistant at the Foreign Mission Board and went to Arkansas to confer with him about how to advance the work with blacks. She also met occasionally with Mrs. Shirley Layten, national president of the black Baptist women.

In October, 1905, Annie spoke at the meeting of the Woman's Auxiliary, National Baptist Convention, in Chicago. This meeting was so important to Annie that she was willing to miss the annual meeting of the Maryland Woman's Home Mission Society of which she was president. Although the Northern Baptists had done much more financially than had Southern Baptists, Annie believed the Southern Baptist support for the blacks was valued tenfold more than that of any other organization. She thought this was because WMU, SBC, recognized the need to develop the black women and equip them to maintain their own organization. Annie had planned to challenge the women to see that the only way of winning confidence and respect was to dignify labor and live faithful lives. After hearing Nannie Helen Burroughs, the corresponding secretary, and Mrs. Layten, the president, express these views, she "simply tried to strengthen their convictions by assurances of faith in the Woman's Auxiliary of the National Baptist Convention and a few words of encouragement to 'go forward.'" While in Chicago, Annie also spoke at the training school and had a conference with Mary G. Burdette.[13]

Annie supported all of the work of the boards. However, she especially enjoyed talking about the Tichenor Memorial Fund and the Yang Chow Hospital. Having suggested to the Home Mission Board the project to raise $20,000 for the Church Building and Loan Fund, Annie tried to interest individuals rather than societies in this fund. She wrote more than one thousand letters, wanting to honor Dr. Tichenor's memory and to meet the "crying need" of many struggling churches on the frontier.[14]

The hospital at Yang Chow, China, where the Evanses worked, was another favorite project. At first Annie "did not want to make a plea for anything that possibly some might think

I was personally interested in." However, she saw that she might be able to influence some contributions, particularly from Maryland. The Yang Chow Hospital was the recipient of one of the offerings taken in the 1905 WMU, SBC, Annual Meeting; the first gift, $500, was presented from Mary Levering Evans by Annie.[15]

Missionaries often stopped by the Mission Rooms to see Annie. She was concerned especially about Bessie Willingham, daughter-in-law to the Foreign Mission Board secretary. The Calder Willinghams had to come home from Japan because of her health. Bessie spent a number of months in a Baltimore hospital, and Annie kept in close touch. Her ties were also close to the Bagbys. When Ermine Bagby was appointed to Brazil, the Woman's Foreign Mission Society of Maryland assumed support of the Bagby's oldest daughter. In spite of her personal concern for missionaries, Annie was adamant that all money go through the boards and not directly to missionaries.[16]

Annie seemed to enjoy working with Lillie Easterby Barker, elected national WMU president in 1903. The Barkers had been missionaries to Brazil for two years but had to resign because of her health. Mrs. Barker served also as president of Virginia WMU. Annie made a number of trips to Laurel Hill, Virginia, to confer with Mrs. Barker, who, in turn, visited Baltimore on several occasions. Annie and Mrs. Barker shared the bitter and the sweet of these years, going through the training school experience together, as well as the beginning of new projects.[17]

By now Annie knew Willingham and Frost well and maintained close contact with them. She was interested in their families and many times referred to Mrs. Willingham and the Willingham children. Once Willingham brought one of his sons with him to Baltimore. Annie enjoyed "helping to make children happy" and was glad to have this opportunity since she was not at the time teaching children in Sunday School. On one occasion she invited Margaret, Frost's daughter, to travel with her. Annie was always concerned when she thought the men worked too hard and endangered their health.[18]

Annie's relationship with Frost was fractured because of their differences over the training school. Also, early in 1905, Annie felt that I. J. Van Ness, the Sunday School Board editorial secretary, had treated her discourteously by ignoring her request for literature and Gospels for Marie Buhlmaier. Having contacted Van Ness because Frost was ill, Annie wrote Frost: "I would think that Dr. Van Ness' silence was due to my letter going astray, but I have learned through experience that Dr. Van Ness does not think it necessary to reply to letters and only writes when he desires some material sent to him for his editorial work." Annie claimed she would have to report to the Home Mission Board that the missionaries were without Gospels and make other arrangements to secure literature for them.

Telling Frost that Van Ness never replied to her letters or acknowledged manuscripts, though she had sent large amounts of material for *Kind Words* and *The Teacher,* Annie decided she could use her time better in other ways. She wrote Van Ness that she would no longer send him any material for publication. Concerning future orders of literature for Marie Buhlmaier, Annie claimed: "I will have nothing more to do with it, and permit me to say that hereafter I shall not be the medium through whom requests come to the Sunday School Board for grants of Bibles, Periodicals or Tracts."

Annie believed she had been unkindly dealt with by "those in charge of the work" at the Sunday School Board. Because she thought she had done everything in her power to make the board strong and to personally assist Frost, Annie did not understand these actions. Annie refused to apologize when Frost apparently asked for an apology. She would

> have to leave these various matters just where they are. It, of course, though, is perfectly immaterial to you and Dr. Van Ness what the Corresponding Secretary of the Woman's Missionary Union may think. I know it is your desire also and Dr. Van Ness' to please our Heavenly

Father, and if that has been done it makes no difference what others may
think.[19]

In 1903 Annie had a new working relationship, for the Home
Mission Board elected Baron DeKalb Gray as corresponding
secretary. Gray, a Mississippian, had experience both as a pastor
and college president. He was interested in young people, and
Annie had worked with him in connection with the Southern
Baptist Young People's Union.[20]

Annie was able to keep many details in her mind and many
interests going simultaneously. State relations continued to be
key, and Annie maintained her special interest in the District of
Columbia, Oklahoma, and Indian Territory; she was virtually
acting as secretary for these areas. When the territories were
ready to get "state organizers," Annie suggested a Southern
Baptist for one of the areas. She also got the Maryland Woman's
Home Mission Society to give money for this purpose. Perhaps
she herself wanted the position.

When contributions began to increase from the West, Annie
wrote: "I cannot tell you how thankful I feel that this is the case.
I have worked very hard in these sections in sowing missionary
seed and in helping to make it possible for the missionaries to
remain on their field, and it is giving me the greatest pleasure to
find that 'results' are beginning to come in." She thought boxes of
supplies sent by societies to the missionaries had had much to do
with saving the work in Indian Territory and Oklahoma. Annie
also developed an interest in the work in Tennessee. Since so
many churches gave nothing to Southern Baptist causes and she
wanted them to give to missions, she traveled to Tennessee and
sent out special letters to pastors about the Christmas offering.[21]

From 1904 to 1906 Annie increased her rigorous travel schedule. In the spring of 1904 she met with B. D. Gray and visited
several churches and colleges in Atlanta, stopping off in Greenville, South Carolina, on the way home. Annie went to New York
to see a woman who planned to give WMU, SBC, some money
and stopped in Philadelphia and Washington. While in New

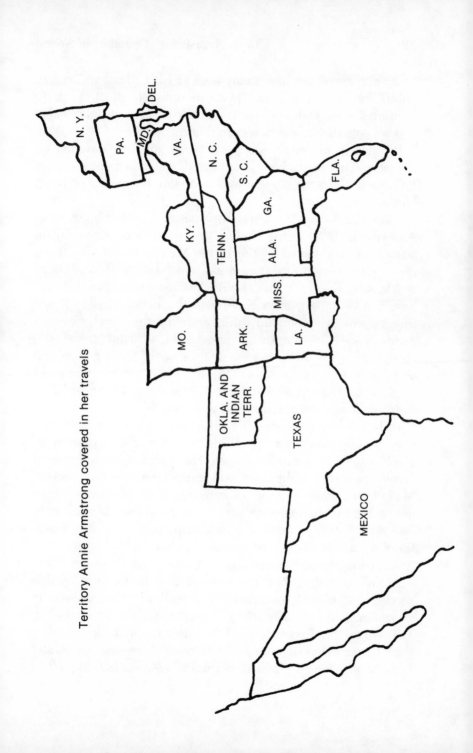

Territory Annie Armstrong covered in her travels

York she viewed the immigrant work at Ellis Island and visited publishing houses and an Episcopal training school. Visits to training schools in Philadelphia and Washington made a total of four schools she visited to secure information.[22]

By now Annie could sleep on trains and was traveling on sleepers. This made her more rested. Often, on returning to Baltimore, she went straight to the Mission Rooms before going home.

After the Young Women's Christian Association meeting in Asheville in 1904, Annie made a tour of some of the mountain work being conducted by the Home Mission Board. She had a growing interest in mountain work, which took in large sections of Virginia, West Virginia, Kentucky, Tennessee, North Carolina, and Georgia. Albert E. Brown, the Home Mission Board secretary of the mountain work, arranged the travel itinerary. Annie made the tour to become better acquainted with the conditions and needs of the mountain schools. Visiting Mars Hill and Fruitland Schools, Annie said she "had a very pleasant and I think profitable trip, although driving for three consecutive days over rough mountain roads did use me up."[23]

In July Annie traveled 2,070 miles in twenty-six days, visited twenty-nine places, and made thirty-seven talks, primarily in southwest Virginia and Tennessee. Her purpose was to promote giving, as she thought there was much money in these areas. Many of the miles in Virginia were by private conveyance over unusually rough mountain roads. After a few days back in Baltimore, Annie made a quick trip to Greenville, South Carolina, about a home for missionary children.[24]

Annie made a five-week trip to the West in August and September, stating her purpose: "I feel in these debatable sections, it is very necessary to attend the Conventions in Oklahoma and Indian Territory."[25] On the way she stopped in St. Louis to see the Exposition and the Baptist exhibit conducted by the Missouri Baptist women. In Clinton, Missouri, Annie met Lura Stump, recent graduate of the Philadelphia training school and a newly-appointed home missionary. Annie had invited Lura to meet her in Missouri so she could accompany Lura to Oklahoma to help her feel at home in her new surroundings as she began her work. Miss Stump had only done city missions work and was terrified of frontiers and Indians.

Annie and Lura Stump spent two and one-half days in the Delaware Indian Association and visited with the Kiowas. Believing the Indians were interested in the gospel and that God had prepared the ground, Annie wrote South Carolina WMU:

> See the steps: the young women of South Carolina decide to support a missionary to the Osage Indians. A timid young girl starts to go to them. A minister on the field has already decided to go to these same Indians. A delegation of 28 Kiowas visits them just at this time to recommend Christianity. A Christian interpreter is ready to do the needed work, and the needed money to support him is supplied. Can we doubt that God's Hand is guiding this infant mission and that He will abundantly bless the work?

Because of her convictions about "mixed meetings" of men and women, Annie would not speak in the general conventions in Oklahoma and Indian Territory. She asked Gray and Bomar from the Home and Foreign Mission Boards to speak about the work of Woman's Missionary Union. Annie had seen much growth and development in the territory during the past fifteen years, from a "no man's country, to an area ironed with railroads and having substantial cities." She believed the frontier box work helped the territories to be Southern Baptist. However, to continue growth, she thought more contributions were needed for church buildings and more missionaries had to be appointed.[26]

On the way home from Indian Territory, Annie stopped in Little Rock to confer with A. J. Barton, field secretary for work with blacks, and B. D. Gray. She was impressed with Gray's message and promoted his plans. She also spoke at several women's meetings in Little Rock and visited more mountain schools in Kentucky.[27]

As was her custom, Annie's addresses at the Virginia WMU Annual Meetings in 1904 and 1905 were based on fresh missions information. She told about the blacks, Indians, mountain schools, the need for church buildings, and the importance of training children in missions.[28]

A special event during the Florida WMU Annual Meeting in Jacksonville in January, 1905, was the children's meeting, when Annie spoke on "Squaws and Papooses." She spent two weeks traveling in Florida and one week in South Carolina. She also visited several places in North Carolina and Virginia on the way home and spoke at three women's colleges. Annie reported forty-one meetings, thirty-nine talks, and 2,560 miles during this twenty-one day trip.[29]

Annie's previous trips to visit mountain schools had only whetted her appetite to see more. Wanting to see the work and give information to WMU workers, in March, 1905, she went with Albert E. Brown on a tour of mountain schools. Because Annie wanted to see the schools in session, it was necessary to go at a time when the weather was bad. She visited ten schools in North Carolina, Tennessee, and Kentucky and met with women from nearby churches. Travel was difficult; many of these places were not on the railroad lines, and the roads were dreadful. With eighty of the miles in carriages and buggies, in nineteen days Annie traveled 2,125 miles, visited sixteen places, and made twenty-seven talks. Annie was so impressed with what was being accomplished through the mountain schools that she wrote a leaflet, "Lengthen Cords and Strengthen Stakes" to tell about the needs and to encourage support.[30]

Annie traveled to Tennessee and Georgia in August, 1905, to promote support of the hospital in Yang Chow and the Tichenor Memorial. She wrote a leaflet titled "A Hospital for Yang Chow" to use for this purpose. Annie spent thirty-one days in the South. In addition to numerous messages throughout Tennessee and Georgia, she met with the WMU central committees in Kentucky, Tennessee, and Georgia.[31]

After a brief stay in Baltimore, Annie made her fifth trip to Oklahoma and Indian Territory in September, 1905. On the way she visited with Mrs. Barker, the national WMU president, in Virginia and conferred with Missouri WMU leaders. This was a shorter trip than some; Annie was gone twelve days, with five nights spent on the train. However, she traveled 3,215 miles, made ten addresses, and attended eighteen meetings. Annie was concerned, in leaving the work, that a new WMU, SBC, secretary would not understand this territory and the need to hold it for Southern Baptists.[32]

Because she spoke about foreign missions and home missions rather than state missions, Annie's 1905 summer trip to Georgia led T. P. Bell to unleash an attack on her in the September issues of *The Christian Index*. This attack was not a new experience, only an intensified one, for Bell had been criticizing Annie for some time.

In July, 1905, after Annie had given notice in May that this was her last year, Bell wrote an editorial in the *Index* about the changes to come in WMU:

> For several years past, there has been a growing dissatisfaction in various parts of the South over some of the ways which have been adopted by the leaders of the Woman's Missionary Union. It has been felt that there was too much of a one-person power in the organization—a power that was wielded with too little consideration for the views, and even the feelings of other interested workers. At Kansas City, the matter culminated, with the result that the leader of the Union announced her determination to resign her position.

Bell reported that he had said nothing about what occurred at Kansas City, though asked to do so. When he had offered criticisms about WMU work several years before, he claimed some women took offense and labeled him as an opposer of women's work. He did not consider this accusation true, as he felt he had given his best thinking and help to WMU.[33]

Annie wrote Willingham about Bell's editorial: "No words can express how indignant and hurt I feel." She claimed that there

were few persons living that owed a greater debt of gratitude to
her than T. P. Bell, and that he had a poor way of repaying it. She
did not think she should be "called on to stand such abominable
newspaper editorials," refraining herself from making a public
statement of facts.[34]

Bell did not let up. In the September 7, 1905, *Index,* he wrote
about the need to promote state missions before the Georgia
Baptist Convention met in November, in order to raise the
needed $30,000 and prevent Georgia from going into debt. He
wrote:

> It strikes us as being really unfortunate that Miss Armstrong is now
> touring Georgia in the interest of the Tichenor Memorial Fund and the
> hospital fund for Dr. Evans, of Yang Chow, China. True, Miss Armstrong
> started both these funds and desires to complete the work before she
> retires from office next May. She lacks $16,000 on the one and we do not
> know how much on the other.

Bell stated he was not opposed to either fund, "but by agreement of the WMU the societies all over the state are to make
special efforts for State missions during the month of October."
He urged the women of Georgia not to let anything get in the
way of state missions between September and November.

Since *The Christian Index* was no longer sent to the Mission
Rooms, others had to call Annie's attention to Bell's editorials.
Mrs. J. D. Easterlin, secretary of Georgia WMU, wrote Annie
about the editorial. Annie saw no reason for Bell to have the
opinion he did, since he alleged to be a supporter of WMU
work. She wrote Willingham: "The Golden Rule leads me to
send you this circumstance without delay, in order that you may
at once leave Georgia, unless you wish to have a similar editorial
appear in '*The Index*' in regard to *your* visit in that state." Having
gone to Georgia on invitation of Georgia WMU leaders, Annie
did not think she had done anything wrong. However, she
indicated that she did not think it necessary to wait for an
invitation. The board secretaries, including Bell when he was
one, followed this practice. Annie wrote: "I was under the

impression that Baptist churches were independent, and not under the control of editors of state papers."[35]

Bell printed Mrs. Easterlin's letter refuting his charges in *The Christian Index*. Mrs. Easterlin claimed Bell misrepresented the facts and made inaccurate statements. For example, he had stated in his September 7 editorial that Annie was then touring the state, but she had already been gone from the state for a week. In response to his accusation that Annie's presentation of foreign and home missions objects was a violation of and detrimental to state missions, Mrs. Easterlin reminded Bell that the August 31 issue of the *Index* was a foreign missions issue, with the entire first page and other large portions devoted to presenting foreign missions. In the very issue in which he criticized Annie, he gave the missions page to home and foreign missions, especially foreign missions.

Mrs. Easterlin urged Bell to confine himself to facts:

> In short, Brother Editor, in your editorial of September 7, you have alleged that Miss Armstrong was then touring Georgia in the interest of the two objects named, while as a matter of fact, this was not true. You based your complaint on the ground that State Missions was entitled to the right of way, and nothing else should get in the way until after November the 15th. While as a matter of fact, since Miss Armstrong left Georgia, two issues of your paper have been devoted, one exclusively to the presentation of Foreign Missions, and the last issue largely to the presentation of Foreign Missions both to the exclusion of State Missions, which you claim has the right of way, and both of which issues have been published since Miss Armstrong left Georgia. I take it for granted that a denominational paper, such as *The Index*, must necessarily have a very large circulation, therefore its influence and information must be farther reaching than Miss Armstrong's talks to a few Woman's Missionary Societies.

Bell responded in print to Mrs. Easterlin's letter, making four points. First, he thought her letter evidenced a great deal of anger, a reaction he considered unfortunate when under "mild criticism." Second, the *Index* had not been misrepresenting facts when it stated Annie was promoting home and foreign missions to the exclusion of state missions. Third, the *Index* regularly had issues about missions, so he was within normal practice in presenting foreign missions. In that same issue, the editorial was about state missions. Bell commended Willingham for refusing to let the churches take collections for foreign missions on his recent visit to Georgia but instead urging them to return home and take offerings for state missions between then and November. Fourth, Bell thought Mrs. Easterlin had

> let herself indulge in the insinuation, if not the charge, that *The Index* was trying to persecute Miss Armstrong. That is always a cheap sort of plea designed to catch the unthinking. We would surely have no object in trying to injure Miss Armstrong; and if we had, there would be no sense in it, now that she is about to retire from the work. We hope that when Mrs. Easterlin quietly thinks over the matter, she will feel like writing to us and withdrawing the serious and unwarranted charge she has made against *The Index.*[36]

When they were both in Oklahoma in September, Annie talked over the first editorial with Willingham, who thought there would be no more articles in *The Christian Index* about Annie. After the September 28 *Index*, she wrote Willingham, with a copy to Frost, about her Georgia trip, stating that she had taken no collections for either the Tichenor Memorial or the Yang Chow Hospital. She felt Bell was attacking her, for in his editorial he criticized the appeals being made by WMU, SBC, for home missions and was "sorry to see that the Home Mission Board has endorsed this effort." Annie recounted the history of Missionary Day in the Sunday School and the change agreed on by Willingham and Frost in 1903 when they assigned January to the Foreign Mission Board, and when Gray took office, assigned October to the Home Mission Board. The Sunday School Board retained June for Children's Day. According to Annie, Bell had no good reason to criticize her, since Georgia had only recently changed its state meeting to the fall. Also, Bell had been one of the primary movers in beginning Missionary Day in the Sunday School.

Annie said to Willingham:

Now, my dear brother, this is in no sense a personal matter. As long as Dr. T. P. Bell saw fit to make personal attacks on me, I did not call on the Boards which I had served faithfully for 17 years without remuneration to defend me. I did not call on these officers, nor did they come to my help. At this time, the work of WMU and of the Home Board is included in the personal attack by the editors of the *Index* and you are cited as an example of proper conduct in Georgia, according to the *Index's* code of propriety, when the facts are you made collections for Foreign Missions and I did not.

Annie called on Willingham as a "Christian and a gentleman" to make a public statement and describe the false presentation of facts. She asked him to admit that he had received money in Georgia and to read her letter to the Foreign Mission Board.[37]

Frost endorsed the position Annie took in her letter to Willingham and attested to the accuracy of her statement about the history of the Missionary Day movement. In the meantime, Mrs. Easterlin and T. P. Bell continued to spar through the pages of *The Christian Index*. Mrs. Easterlin also questioned why the *Index* did not criticize Willingham when he spoke in Georgia in September on foreign missions and took up a collection. On October 16 the WMU, SBC, executive committee wrote the three boards, attaching the statement and protest about reactions of the *Biblical Recorder* and *The Christian Index* toward Annie and Mrs. Barker's attitudes about a training school and the *Index* attacks on Annie.[38]

Each of the three boards read and ordered the WMU executive committee letter filed. Willingham declined to make a public statement in defense of Annie. Annie was not completely deserted in the press, however. *The Maryland Baptist* wrote in an editorial in October: "The editor of *The Index* may not have had any sinister motive or desire to do injustice, but we are rather ashamed of him in this matter. The criticism was silly, and the defense offered was but little better—only that he had decreed no other subject than State missions should be presented, and so the ladies had been presumptuous and disobedient." A second *Maryland Baptist* editorial claimed Bell had been inconsistent and caught himself in a trap by criticizing an event he himself helped institute, Missionary Day in the Sunday School.

In November the Maryland Baptist Union Association commended Annie, and the Virginia WMU executive committee reaffirmed their support and loyalty to her. The chairman of the Maryland committee on foreign missions stated:

> One name appears more prominent—Miss Annie W. Armstrong. No woman among Southern Baptists has rendered to the denomination such conspicuous or such valuable service. Under her administration as corresponding secretary of Woman's Missionary Union, covering a period of 17 years of continuous service, for which she has received not one penny of remuneration, contributions have increased eight-fold. This remarkable increase is due primarily to the missionary education system which beginning in this Association, reached a degree of excellence and efficiency under the direction of Miss Armstrong.[39]

Annie made her final long trip in January, 1906, to Louisiana, Texas, and Arkansas, with stopovers in St. Louis and Louisville. In five weeks, she traveled 4,830 miles to thirty-one places, made forty-one addresses, and spent two weeks in Texas, one week in Louisiana, and one week in Arkansas. Annie especially enjoyed meeting Texas missionaries at the Bible School in Abilene and visiting Baylor Female College in Belton. The Texas women were impressed with Annie's great organizing and administrative ability, as well as her gift in making "one see the whole wide world as one's field." Perhaps this trip took Annie's mind off her troubles about T. P. Bell and the training school, for she considered it "immensely profitable and a delightful one."[40]

One of the joys of Annie's life in her last year of office was seeing the Margaret Home, a home for missionary children and a temporary stop for missionaries, come into being. As early as 1894 Annie had seen the need to make some provision for missionary children. The way was made clear for her in 1904 when a woman gave ten thousand dollars anonymously for this cause, six to seven thousand dollars to be used for property and the remainder for repair and furnishings. The donor, Mrs. Frank Chambers, suggested the home at Newton Centre, Massachusetts as a model. Making at least one trip to New York in the spring to confer with Mrs. Chambers, Annie made the announcement at the WMU, SBC, Annual Meeting in 1904. WMU accepted the gift and named an advisory board, with a representative from each state, authorized to name a local board of managers, who in essence would control the home. Despite their differences, Fannie Heck was named the North Carolina representative to the advisory board which Annie chaired.

The advisory board met on May 16, 1904, and referred the location of the home for missionaries' children to a committee of three—Annie, Mrs. Barker, and the donor. With a multitude of details to work out concerning the home, Annie wrote many letters and made many trips during 1904 and 1905 in regard to purchasing the home, getting it ready for occupancy, and securing someone to serve as matron. She worked closely with the mission boards who would hold the property in trust for WMU, SBC. By the fall of 1904, Greenville, South Carolina, had been selected as the location because of its beauty, healthfulness, Baptist influence, and good schools. With the property purchased, the home was named the Margaret Home for Missionaries' Children by request of the donor, Mrs. Frank Chambers.

After the home was purchased, Annie met several times with the local board in Greenville. Since it took the entire amount of the gift to purchase the home, it was necessary to develop a plan for getting the home furnished, and Annie prepared estimates to present to the WMU Annual Meeting in 1905. She also visited the home in Newton Centre, Massachusetts, to study its operation. Although the local board selected the matron, Annie made several suggestions, including Mrs. Abby Gwathmey and Mrs. James Pollard, both WMU leaders. Mrs. C. H. Richardson was selected as the first "mother."

Annie went to the South Carolina WMU Meeting in Ben-
nettsville in November, 1905, staying over to participate in the
ceremony for the formal opening of the Margaret Home on
November 19. States and individuals agreed to donate money for
furnishings. Annie was pleased that the Woman's Foreign Mission Society of Maryland voted to furnish a room, and the Eutaw
Place Baptist Church Foreign Mission Society would furnish a
bedroom in memory of Mary E. Armstrong, Annie's mother.[41]

Annie had to work out the future of the Mission Literature
Department, SBC, for she would give up this work also. She saw
the importance of this work but could not give it adequate time.
Annie wrote E. E. Bomar, assistant secretary at the Foreign
Mission Board early in 1904:

> If this department of our work could only be developed, as it is possible
> for it to be developed (if there was only time and strength to put into it),
> it would do a tremendous amount of good. As it is though, with me it has
> to be not only secondary, but I expect I could put it far below that,
> maybe fifthly, sixthly, or seventhly in importance.[42]

After she announced in Kansas City in May, 1905, that she
would not serve as corresponding secretary of WMU, SBC, after
May, 1906, Annie conferred with Frost and Gray about the
Mission Literature Department, SBC, telling them she also
would give up her office connected with that work. On June 21,
1905, she notified Frost and Gray in writing that she was asking
the Sunday School Board and Home Mission Board to take
charge of the work and arrange for its removal from Baltimore.
Since assuming the capital and assets of the Maryland Mission
Rooms in March, 1901, the boards had not had to do anything
but receive an annual report and appoint the corresponding
secretary and treasurer. Annie agreed to serve through April,
1906, and to get out the literature for the April-June quarter,
which would allow the boards time to make arrangements.
Unless the boards notified her by August 1, 1905, that the
monthly literature would be continued after June, 1906, Annie

Left: 10 East Fayette Street, Baltimore, first headquarters for WMU, SBC. Above: 304 N. Howard, Baltimore, third headquarters for WMU, SBC

233 North Howard, fourth headquarters for WMU, SBC

would not take subscriptions for the monthly leaflets longer than for the time she agreed to serve and would return money for the part of the subscription she could not fill. If so, there would be no subscription list for her to turn over, with the other assets, on April 20, 1906, when her work ceased. After Annie's repeated urgings, Frost let her know that the Sunday School Board wanted to continue the literature.

Annie had definite opinions about what would happen in the future: "The Woman's Missionary Union headquarters will be removed from Baltimore at the close of the present conventional year. . . . The lease of the rooms at 233 North Howard Street, does not expire until June 30, 1906, but they will be closed on and after the meeting of the Southern Baptist Convention, May 1906." In October, 1905, Annie asked Willingham if he would like to have the couch on which Ann Hasseltine Judson died and the scrapbooks of foreign missionaries when the Mission Literature Department, SBC, closed in Baltimore. Willingham declined, and Annie decided to turn the couch over to her successor and to give the scrapbooks to the Home and Sunday School Boards as joint owners of the department.[43]

When she did not hear from the Home Mission Board and Sunday School Board by February, 1906, Annie was impatient. She wrote Frost:

> It is, that after waiting from May 1905 to February 23, 1906 to know what arrangements the Home and Sunday School Boards proposed making for the transfer of the property of the Mission Literature Department from Baltimore, I, as Secretary . . . unless I receive full information as to what is to be done with the capital and assets of the . . . Department before March 5th, will send copies of the deed of gift and other matter to State Papers, Secretaries of State Boards and others, notifying them that no orders for literature will be filled by me after April 15th, and that the money for unexpired subscriptions to Monthly Literature will be returned to subscribers. All letters coming to the . . . Department . . . after April 15th will be sent unopened to the Home and Sunday School Boards, half being sent to one Board and half the Other.

The Sunday School Board and Home Mission Board decided

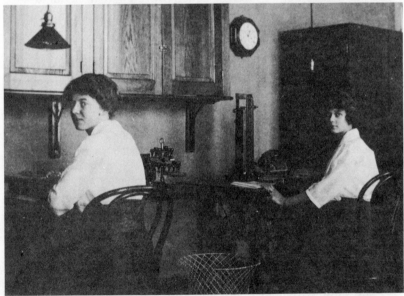

Workers in the Mission Literature Department

that the Mission Literature Department should not be removed from Baltimore. Therefore, they agreed to transfer the cash and assets back to the Maryland Baptist Union Association; Gray and Frost came to Baltimore and formally transferred the cash and assets on March 13, 1906. The agreement said: "We would further state that Miss Annie W. Armstrong, who has served without remuneration as Secretary ever since the Baptist Mission Rooms were established in 1886, and has resigned the Secretaryship of said Mission Literature Department, is in no wise responsible for the closing of the Mission Literature Department." The department closed its operations on April 30, 1906.

There was some feeling that Annie closed the Mission Literature Department because she thought WMU, SBC, would not return to Baltimore. Fannie Heck wrote Frost in June:

> I believe you are aware of the fact that, believing the Union would not return to Baltimore, the former Corresponding Secretary, in the fullest sense of the word, closed up the affairs of this department and, indeed, of the Union, so that the literature department will have to be begun from the very beginning.[44]

When Annie announced in May, 1905, that she would only serve as a WMU, SBC, officer one more year, she requested that no letters be written to her asking the reasons for her actions. Annie had a strong following, and there was much regret over her decision. She planned to make this last year the best in WMU history and to devote most of her time to training the WMU workers in the states in their duties. On May 26, 1905, Annie wrote the state WMU leaders offering to assist them through correspondence, and, if needed, by a personal visit. At that point she had only committed herself to going to Oklahoma and Indian Territory. She stated that after May, 1906, "no WMU mail will be answered by me."

Annie had some dark days from May, 1905, to May, 1906. She felt that many people were misrepresenting her and she was misunderstood because of her stand on the training school. Bell's attack was relentless. In June, 1905, she wrote Willingham:

You have full permission to assure those who desire changes that it is not only my unalterable determination (unless God should work a miracle) to sever my connections with the Woman's Missionary Union in May, but also to resign the presidency of the Woman's Baptist Home Mission Society of Maryland which I have held for nearly 24 years, and that of the Society of Eutaw Place Church which office I have also held for years. After the meeting of the convention in May 1906, I do not propose in any way, shape or form to have anything whatever to do in mission work as conducted by Southern Baptists, so even in Maryland none need fear my opposition to whatever plans they may desire to present.

She only asked to finish out this year "without further molestation."

Willingham reassured Annie that she was held in the highest esteem by the vast majority of Southern Baptists. He had had no intimation that she was being boycotted and urged her to go on with her work, and not respond in the state Baptist papers, as this would only encourage others to write.

Annie found tremendous delight in her work and did not want to give it up:

I believe I should be perfectly miserable at the prospect of giving this work up in May, if I did not feel that God would give me something else to do for Him in other directions. It will have to be in our own church and along undenominational lines, but a number of openings in that direction are already presenting themselves to me.

Wanting no idle time, Annie planned to give her strength and ability after May, 1906, toward philanthropic work. This was not her first preference: "I regret extremely that I cannot give what strength and ability I have to the advancement of the work as done by Southern Baptists for I am a Baptist out and out, but I now recognize that it will cause friction should I take part in the work at any point."[45]

The final days were difficult for Annie. She was perturbed when the board secretaries came to Baltimore to meet with pastors and leading laymen about the future of WMU, SBC. The WMU executive committee took exception to their visit, affirming that WMU decided its own future. Gray wrote Frost:

It seems that she (Mrs. Charles Ammen, Chairman of the WMU

Nominating Committee) is entertaining the idea that we went to Baltimore to force headquarters on that city. I learned from another source that Miss Armstrong was filled with dread lest that was the ominous meaning of our visit. . . . Miss Armstrong seems to be in great dread lest we would force Baltimore to have the headquarters there, when she has said publicly and in print that they could not be continued there.[46]

April 19, 1906, was Annie's last meeting as president of the Woman's Home Mission Society of Maryland. In her "farewell address," Annie gave her concept of what women's societies should stand for. They were not just collecting agencies but should be organized for these three things: "knowing, praying, giving." She elaborated on these points as "the three strands of rope by which the care of missionaries is drawn." Annie also spoke of the great need of arousing missions interest among children and young people. In its next meeting, the society expressed appreciation for the great work Annie had accomplished and sent her a letter expressing these sentiments.[47]

Annie was magnanimous at the WMU, SBC, Annual Meeting in Chattanooga in May, 1906. Her final annual report was an impressive summary of her entire eighteen years' work. In a Friday session, Annie "tendered" the assets of WMU and made brief remarks. She told of the curios, many of which had been sent to her personally, "all of which she gave to the Union." At the end of her remarks, and a prayer, Annie left the meeting. At the end of the session, Mrs. A. J. Wheeler of Tennessee, asked for a moment of silent prayer for Annie, followed by singing one verse of "God be with you till we meet again."

At the end of the WMU Annual Meeting, Mrs. J. L. Burnham of Missouri asked that a rising vote of thanks be given to Annie. The papers reported that every heart was saddened and many tears shed when Annie made her farewell comments, and the *Chattanooga Daily Times* had this tribute: "It would be impossible to pay too high a tribute to this noble godly woman who has so faithfully served her Master and the Baptist course in the south." The *Baptist and Reflector* said: "For twenty years she has guided the destinies of the Union. She has seen the contributions of the Union grow from nothing to about $100,000 a year. It is largely due to the Woman's Missionary Union that the contributions to Home and Foreign Missions have been considerably increased. It should be added that all of these years Miss Armstrong has served the Union without any salary." The *Religious Herald* claimed Annie was

> one of the most faithful, energetic, self-denying workers with whom the denomination has ever been blessed. Wonderfully alert and progressive, diligent and farseeing, she has seen the work prosper marvelously under her leadership . . . Her name will always be a household word among Southern Baptists, and her memory will be frequent through the long years to come.[48]

The Committee on Women's Work paid tribute to Annie as it reported to the Southern Baptist Convention in May, 1906. Claiming her work was already so well known, the committee still wanted to express appreciation:

> Possessed of a power to grasp and master details that amounts to genius; given a vision of the possibilities of organization and development among our people that few have ever had; having a love for souls amounting to a passion; loving God fervently and willing to make her life an unbroken day of sacrificial service to him, she has been to us and our work what few others could have been.[49]

Annie left the WMU, SBC, Annual Meeting in May, 1906, ready to do "undenominational service" through her church and in Baltimore. Knowing what decisions were made about Woman's Missionary Union must have created turmoil within Annie, for her earlier statements about WMU's future did not come true.

In May, 1906, the delegates at the WMU Annual Meeting voted for WMU, SBC, headquarters to remain in Baltimore, increased the salary attached to the office of corresponding secretary, and appointed a committee to consider the advisability of starting a Woman's Missionary Union Training School in Louisville as soon as the constitution allowed. Fannie Heck, reelected WMU president, assumed leadership until a successor to Annie was found in 1907. Miss Heck got Maryland Baptists to give WMU, SBC, the assets from the former literature department and instituted a WMU Literature Department which began immediately publishing income-producing literature, including *Our Mission Fields*, a monthly magazine.[50]

Annie had led WMU, SBC, well through its pioneer days and instituted numerous lasting policies, precedents, and far-reaching practices. Perhaps it was time in 1906, though, for new leadership. The national women's missions organization had moved beyond the pioneering stage and become a large operation destined to influence women and missions efforts in a major way until the present.

Notes (See pages 295-310 for Key to Sources.)

1. Annie Armstrong to R. J. Willingham, May 23, 1904, FMB.

2. Ibid., January 4, 1905.

3. Ibid., January 29, February 8-15, 1904; R. J. Willingham to Annie Armstrong, February 11, 1904, FMB; HMB minutes, February 11, 1904, *FMJ*, March, 1904; *The Christian Index*, March 10, 1904; Harold A. Williams, *Baltimore Afire*, pp. 44-45.

4. *Report*, WMU, 1904; WMU minutes, February 9, March 8, 1904; *OHF*, April, 1904; *The Religious Herald*, February 25, 1904; *Florida Baptist Witness*, February 18, 1904.

5. Annie Armstrong to R. J. Willingham, February 12, February 16, March 7, 1904, FMB.

6. Ibid., January-May 1904; Annie Armstrong to E. E. Bomar, January, March, 1904, FMB.

7. Ibid.

8. *Report*, WMU, 1904; SBC Annual, 1904; *Nashville Banner*, May 13, 1904; *FMJ*, June, 1904; *Baptist Standard*, May 19, May 26, 1904; WMU minutes, May 31, 1904.

9. Annie Armstrong to E. E. Bomar, January 5, 1904, July 27, 1905, FMB; Annie Armstrong to R. J. Willingham, January, March 8, April 21, December 10, December 29, 1904, February 23, April 18, 1905, FMB.

10. Annie Armstrong to E. E. Bomar, May 4, June 24, 1904, FMB; Annie Armstrong to R. J. Willingham, May 26, 1904, FMB.

11. *Reports*, WMU, 1905-1906; FMB minutes, December 8, 1903; Annie Armstrong to R. J. Willingham, November, 1903-February, 1904, FMB; Annie Armstrong to E. E. Bomar, January-March, 1904, FMB; Annie Armstrong to J. M. Frost, April 7, 1904, SSB.

12. Annie Armstrong to R. J. Willingham, January-February, May, June 18,

1904, FMB; Annie Armstrong to E. E. Bomar, June, 1904, FMB; *Reports*, WMU 1904-1905; *FMJ*, August, 1904; *OHF*, October, 1904. Records show that during 1904-1906, Annie Armstrong visited these colleges: Cox College, Georgia, March, 1904; Berea College, Kentucky, October, 1904; a woman's college in DeLand, Florida, January, 1905; Roanoke Female College, Danville, Virginia, February, 1905; Baylor Female College, January, 1906.

13. *Baptist Advance*, July 14, November 10, 1904; *Reports*, WMU, 1905; *OHF*, December, 1905; *Report*, WHMS, 1905; Annie Armstrong Notebooks, WMU.

14. Annie Armstrong to E. E. Bomar, January 15, 1904, FMB; *Reports*, WMU, 1904-1905; Annie Armstrong Notebooks, WMU.

15. Annie Armstrong to R. J. Willingham, March 6, 1905, FMB; R. J. Willingham to Annie Armstrong, March-April 1905, FMB; *Southern Baptist Witness*, May 18, 1905; *Report*, WMU, 1905; Annie Armstrong, "A Hospital for Yang Chow, China," WMU.

16. Annie Armstrong to R. J. Willingham, August, 1903, March 13, April 6, April 15, May 5, 1904, June, November, 1905, FMB; R. J. Willingham to Annie Armstrong, May-June, November-December, 1905, FMB; E. E. Bomar to Annie Armstrong, November, 1905, FMB; Annie Armstrong to E. E. Bomar, November, 1905, FMB; *Report*, WMU, 1904; *The Baptist Courier*, April 20, 1905; *The Maryland Baptist*, January 15, 1906.

17. *Report*, WMU, 1903; *Encyclopedia of Southern Baptists*, 4:2117; Annie Armstrong to R. J. Willingham, August 27, 1903, January, 1904, FMB; Annie Armstrong to E. E. Bomar, January 18, 1904, FMB; WMU minutes, October, 1903.

18. Annie Armstrong to R. J. Willingham, February-March, May 5, 1904, FMB; Annie Armstrong to J. M. Frost, February 6, 1905, SSB.

19. Annie Armstrong to I. J. Van Ness, February 23, 1905, SSB; Annie Armstrong to J. M. Frost, March-April 1905, SSB. See chapter 9 for differences with Frost over the training school.

20. *Encyclopedia of Southern Baptists*, 1:585.

21. Annie Armstrong to R. J. Willingham, January 19, January 29, February 4, December, 1904, April 12, April 18, 1905, FMB; Susie T. Pollard to Annie Armstrong, April 11, 1905, FMB.

22. Annie Armstrong to R. J. Willingham, March-April 1904, FMB; Annie Armstrong to J. M. Frost, April 7, 1904, SSB; *Baptist Courier*, March 24, March 31, 1904; *FMJ*, May, 1904.

23. Annie Armstrong to R. J. Willingham, June 6, 1904, FMB; *FMJ*, August, 1904; WMU Minutes, January 14, 1902; *Report*, WMU, 1904; *OHF*, October, 1904; Annie Armstrong to E. E. Bomar, June 24, 1904, October 2, 1905, FMB.

24. Annie Armstrong to R. J. Willingham, June 8, August 3, 1904, FMB; Annie Armstrong to J. M. Frost, August 3, 1904, SSB; *OHF*, October, 1904; *The Religious Herald*, August-September, November 17, 1904; *Baptist and Reflector*, June-October, 1904; Minutes, Virginia WMU Annual Session, 1904.

25. Annie Armstrong to R. J. Willingham, July 1, 1904, FMB.

26. Annie Armstrong to E. E. Bomar, August 27-29, October 7, 1904, FMB;

Annie Armstrong to R. J. Willingham, October 11, 1904, FMB; *Central Baptist*, September 15, 1904; *OHF*, October-December, 1904; *FMJ*, November, 1904; Annie Armstrong, "Indian Rights and Wrongs," WMU; *Baptist Courier*, October 13, December 8, 1904; *Report*, WMU, 1905.

27. *The Baptist Advance*, October 6, November 10, 1904; *FMJ*, November, 1904; Annie Armstrong to E. E. Bomar, October 7, 1904, FMB.

28. *The Religious Herald*, December 1, 1904, November 30, 1905; Minutes, Virginia WMU Annual Sessions, 1904-1905. The 1904 meeting was in Franklin and the 1905 meeting in Fredericksburg.

29. *FMJ*, March, 1905; *Southern Baptist Witness*, January, 1905; *The Maryland Baptist*, January 15, 1905; *Baptist Courier*, January-February, 1905; *The Greenville Daily News*, January 27, 1905; *Danville Register*, February 1, February 3, 1905; Annie Armstrong to J. M. Frost, February 6, 1905, SSB; Annie Armstrong to E. E. Bomar, February 6, 1905, FMB; Annie Armstrong to R. J. Willingham, February 13, 1905, FMB; WMU minutes, February 15, 1905.

30. A. E. Brown to Annie Armstrong, February 1, 1905, SSB; Annie Armstrong to A. E. Brown, February 6, 1905, SSB; Annie Armstrong to J. M. Frost, February 6, 1905, SSB; *FMJ*, May, 1905; Annie Armstrong to State Officers, April 5, 1905, SSB; *Biblical Recorder*, April 12, 1905; WMU minutes, April 11, 1905; Annie Armstrong, "Lengthen Cords and Strengthen Stakes," WMU; Annie Armstrong Notebooks, WMU.

31. Annie Armstrong to R. J. Willingham, July 19, 1905, FMB; Annie Armstrong, "A Hospital for Yang Chow, China," WMU; *FMJ*, October, 1905; *Baptist and Reflector*, August, 1905.

32. *FMJ*, November, 1905; Sally O. and Wayne D. Hannah, *History of the Laurel Hill Baptist Church, 1851-1976*, p. 49; J. M. Gaskin to Eula Mae Stewart, November 13, 1981, WMU; Annie Armstrong to E. E. Bomar, October 2, 1905, FMB; Annie Armstrong to R. J. Willingham, October 3, 1905, FMB.

33. Annie Armstrong to R. J. Willingham, February 28, 1904, FMB; *The Christian Index*, July 20, 1905.

34. Annie Armstrong to R. J. Willingham, August 1, 1905, FMB.

35. Ibid., September 11, 1905, FMB; *The Christian Index*, September 7, 1905.

36. *The Christian Index*, September 28, 1905.

37. Annie Armstrong to R. J. Willingham, October 6, 1905, FMB.

38. See chapter 9 for the relationship to the training school controversy. Annie Armstrong to J. M. Frost, October 13, 1905, SSB; Annie Armstrong to R. J. Willingham, October 14, 1905, FMB; *The Christian Index*, November 2, 1905; Mrs. A. C. Johnson to the SSB, HMB, and FMB, October 16, 1905, SSB.

39. Annie Armstrong to R. J. Willingham, October 21, October 24, November 8, 1905, FMB; *The Maryland Baptist*, October 15, November 1, 1905; Minutes, MBUA, 1905; Virginia WMU to Annie Armstrong, December 13, 1905, SSB.

40. *FMJ*, April, 1906, *Baptist Standard*, January-February, April 5, 1906; *The Maryland Baptist*, February 15, 1906; *Baptist Chronicle*, January, March 29, 1906; *Baptist Advance*, February-April, 1906; WMU minutes, February 13, 1906.

41. Annie Armstrong to R. J. Willingham, September 26, 1894, 1904-1905, FMB; *Reports*, WMU, 1904-1906; *Florida Baptist Witness*, May 25, 1904; Annie Armstrong to E. E. Bomar, 1904-1905, FMB; Annie Armstrong "The Margaret Home for Missionaries' Children," WMU; WMU minutes, May 31, 1904; *Baptist Courier*, September, November, 1905; *The Christian Index*, May 25, 1905; South Carolina WMU minutes, November 14-17, 1905; *The Maryland Baptist*, November 1, 1905; Minutes, MBUA, 1906; *FMJ*, January, 1906; *Baptist and Reflector*, January 4, 1906; Annie Armstrong Notebooks, WMU.

42. Annie Armstrong to E. E. Bomar, January 6, 1904, FMB.

43. Annie Armstrong to HMB and SSB, June 21, 1905, SSB; Annie Armstrong to J. M. Frost, June 30, 1905, SSB; Annie Armstrong to R. J. Willingham, October 7, November 3, 1905, FMB; SSB minutes, July 13, 1905.

44. HMB minutes, March 6, April 3, 1906; SSB minutes, February 8, April 12, 1906; B. D. Gray and J. M. Frost to Mission Literature Department, SBC, March 13, 1906, SSB; Final Action of Home and Sunday School Boards Regarding Mission Literature Department, S.B.C., March 13, 1906; WMU minutes, March 20, 1906; SBC Annual, 1906; *Southern Baptist Witness*, March 22, 1906; *Baptist Standard*, March 29, 1906; *Texas Baptist and Herald*, May 17, 1906; Minutes, MBUA Executive Board, 1906; Fannie Heck to J. M. Frost, June 4, 1906, SSB.

45. *Central Baptist*, July 8, 1905; *Southern Baptist Witness*, May 18, 1905; Annie Armstrong to Central Committees or State Executive Committees, May 26, 1905, FMB; Annie Armstrong to R. J. Willingham, May 26, July 16, June 19, June 21, July 11, 1905, February 23, 1906, FMB; R. J. Willingham to Annie Armstrong, June 17, June 20, 1905, FMB; Annie Armstrong to E. E. Bomar, November 28, 1905, FMB.

46. R. J. Willingham to Annie Armstrong, March 10, 1906, FMB; WMU minutes, March 20, 1906; Annie Armstrong to J. M. Frost, March-April 1906, SSB; Mrs. Charles Ammen to J. M. Frost, April 9, April 30, 1906, SSB; B. D. Gray to J. M. Frost, April 11, 1906, SSB.

47. Minutes, WHMS, April 19, May 1, 1906.

48. *Report*, WMU, 1906; *Baptist Chronicle*, June 7, 1906; *The Baptist Argus*, May 24, 1906; *The Religious Herald*, April 19, May 10, May 24, 1906; *Baptist Courier*, May 17, 1906; *Baptist Standard*, May 31, 1906; *Baptist and Reflector*, May 17, 1906; *The Christian Index*, May 24, 1906; *The Daily Times*, May 12, May 15, 1906.

49. SBC Annual, 1906.

50. *Report*, WMU, 1906; Fannie Heck to R. J. Willingham, May 21, June 4, June 23, August 3, 1906, FMB.

11
Not the End—
Life Begins Again

What did Annie think about as the train rolled along the valley between Chattanooga and Baltimore in May, 1906? She was on the way home from her last WMU Annual Meeting, having severed all ties with her beloved Woman's Missionary Union, SBC. She had resigned, too, the presidencies of the Woman's Home Mission Society of Maryland and of her church's Woman's Missionary Society. Embittered and hurt, Annie remained silent about those she thought had wronged her, believing that God meant what he said: "Vengeance is mine; I will repay" (Rom. 12:19). No one but God knew how much it cost her to leave the work so dear to her heart.

Annie had already made it clear that she would have nothing to do with missions work conducted by Southern Baptists. There would be less friction, she felt, if she stayed out of the way of those now in charge. At the WMU, SBC, Annual Meeting in Chattanooga, Annie urged the women not to write her, for she would not answer letters. She would connect herself instead to her church and to "undenominational work." In November, 1905, Annie said:

> I want no resting time in the sense of idleness, and so I shall as soon as I leave this work, turn my attention to other lines of Christian activity. I regret extremely that I cannot give what ability I have to the advancement of the work as done by Southern Baptists . . . but I now recognize that this will cause friction. . . . Many avenues are opening out before me. I am trying though to listen for God's voice before making final decisions.[1]

273

Annie had asked in Chattanooga "that no words of thanks or recognition of her services be passed, as the record is on high." In spite of this request, the women wanted in some way to express their love and appreciation for her. One year later in the Richmond WMU, SBC, Annual Meeting, the women sent Annie a telegram expressing deep appreciation for all she had done with them and for them. They also adopted a resolution, presented by Mrs. W. D. Chipley of Florida; from the money raised by WMU, SBC, the Union requested the Home and Foreign Mission Boards to appropriate five thousand dollars each to the establishment of testimonials to Annie Armstrong. Specifications were a mountain school (Home Mission Board) and a hospital in China (Foreign Mission Board).[2]

In July, 1907, Willingham wrote to Annie suggesting that the hospital at Yang Chow be named in her honor. He knew of Annie's interest in this particular hospital and felt, too, that it would become one of the main hospitals in the future. Anticipating Annie's response, Willingham wrote:

> I am not asking whether you want us to put up a memorial for Southern Baptists will do that, and if you are not willing for them to do it while you live, they will after your death, but I think it is best for you to yield to the earnest wish of the sisters as well as of the brethren, and let us name some enterprise for you right away.

Since Annie never answered Willingham's letter about this, he wrote to Fannie Heck, who again was elected WMU president in 1906. Several letters later, in June, 1908, Miss Heck finally wrote Willingham that he should have done as the Home Mission Board did, "building one [a hospital] and name it for her. They did not consult her but have heard of no objections."[3] The records give no indication that anything further was done.

The Home Mission Board chose to name a new building at the Yancey Mountain School in Burnsville, North Carolina, in Annie's honor. At the request of Albert E. Brown, superintendent of the Mountain School Department with whom Annie toured the mountain schools, WMU provided a suitable tablet and inscription for the building. Edith Campbell Crane, Annie's successor as WMU, SBC, corresponding secretary, Mrs. W. D. Chipley, and Mrs. B. D. Gray, wife of the Home Mission Board secretary, represented WMU at the building dedication in July, 1908. The Yancey Collegiate Institute, with the "Annie W. Armstrong Building," discontinued operations in the 1920s.[4]

Annie could not sit idle. She quickly got into "undenominational work," and her efforts with the Home of the Friendless and visiting the sick intensified. Perhaps because of her concern for the sick, Annie became interested in the Home for Incurables, a large nursing home at Guilford and Twenty-first Streets in Baltimore. This home was of special interest because Eugene Levering had donated large sums of money to it, and he and Mamie were on the board of directors. Annie accepted immediately the position as manager at the Aged Men's and Aged Women's Homes on West Lexington Street, holding this position for over twenty years. At one time Alice had been recording secretary of these homes.[5] The Armstrongs and Leverings were all involved heavily in Baltimore's charitable institutions.

For years Annie had been distressed at the failure of Christians to give the gospel to the Jews. She had ample reason for her feelings, for Baltimore had an enormous Jewish population. In the late 1880s large numbers of Russians, mostly Jews, settled on Baltimore's east side. By the turn of the century, there were over ten thousand Russians. However, Germans continued to be the largest number of the foreign-born in Baltimore, as many as thirty thousand by the 1900s. The Germans, many of whom were Jews, began to move northwestward into the area bounded by McCulloh Street, Annie's neighborhood. The Jews owned many of the garment factories, known as the sweatshops, and owned homes along Eutaw Place. By 1910 Baltimore had twenty-five thousand Russians, who were also moving out of eastern Baltimore with other Eastern European Jews farther north into the area formerly occupied by the Germans. Annie saw many Jews daily as she walked on the streets near her home.

Immigrants at Locust Point, Baltimore, 1910-15 (circa) (PEALE MUSEUM, BALTIMORE, MARYLAND)

Although charitable work was done with immigrants in Baltimore, not much was done by Baptists. Annie had been responsible in the 1890s for getting the Home Mission Board to appoint Marie Buhlmaier to work with German immigrants. Maryland Baptists and the Home Mission Board also secured a Christian Jewess to do house-to-house visitation among her own people. Annie had a friend who was an officer of a Union in Baltimore which worked with Jews. Wanting to give assistance, she identified herself with the small work being done by this group with Jews.[6] Even after she was eighty years old and confined to her apartment, Annie was concerned with this ministry. She would often ask W. Clyde Atkins, her pastor: "Isn't there something we can do to give the gospel to the Jews?"[7]

Immersing herself with a renewed fervor into the life of her church, Annie was present at every service—Sunday morning and evening and Wednesday evening prayer service. For ten years Annie served on the committee on the sick. She was later on the Sunday School committee, Bible School committee, and chairman of a district visitation committee. In 1921 Annie chaired a special committee on women's work, missions, and the Church House (what Eutaw Place Church called the educational building). Apparently she avoided any relationship with Edith Campbell Crane and Kathleen Mallory, her two successors as corresponding secretary of WMU, SBC, both of whom were members of Eutaw Place Baptist Church. Nor did she hold leadership in the missionary societies, though she attended. It was just as well, for the home mission society in the church was promoting the training school at Louisville and raising money for the endowment fund.[8]

A key personality in her church, Annie was highly influential. She was forthright, determined, and had no use for procrastination and delay. Because she had an opinion about most subjects and voiced these opinions freely, not everyone in the church liked her. Often Alice, the quiet one, smoothed over waters stirred up by her sister Annie. The men in the church especially

had great respect for Annie; they looked up to her in more ways
than one. With no hesitation in speaking up to men, Annie
would call down the pastor if need be, just as she would one of
her Sunday School "boys."

In spite of her belief that women should not preach or speak
publicly in the presence of men, Annie was ahead of her times
and most of the women in the church in her attitudes about
women's involvement and life in general. She, along with some
of the men, even approved of Dr. F. M. Ellis's boxing room on the
third floor of his home. Busy and always involved herself, Annie
was intolerant of women who were not. She believed women
were important to the Lord's work and should take a stand.
Although tall, straight, sedate, and overpowering, Annie at-
tracted adults and children alike, who often gathered around
her. In some ways, she was the unofficial church greeter.[9]

Annie loved children and again worked with them in Sunday
School and in the children's service. She had given this position
up for a short time during the years of her heavy travel. Serving
as Sunday School Department secretary, Annie greeted the
children as they walked down the long hallway to the back of the
Church House. Checking them in, she drilled the children in
their Bible memory work as preparation for Sunday School and
the worship service. The reward for good work was a Scripture
card. Annie was determined and exacting about the memory
verse, demanding perfection. She would call on the children
time and time again, week after week, to repeat the memory
verses. One of her pupils recalled years later: "The first thing I
remember about Miss Annie was the memory verses. Another
thing that I remember, even as a child . . . she would not put up
with any trivia or shoddiness or misbehaving . . . and as far as the
memory work goes, you said it verbatim." Annie applied good
principles of teaching children for her day, involving them and
never doing anything herself if she could get one of the children
to do it. Often she showed them objects from her travels.[10]

Annie invited the children as guests to her home for teas. She treated them as proper guests—tea, cookies, linen napkins, and all. The children occupied all the chairs and spilled over onto the floor. Alice prepared the refreshments and served the children. If one of the children had done an exceptional job on the memory work, or was especially well behaved, Annie let him or her pull the refreshments up from the downstairs kitchen on the dumb waiter. While Alice served Annie talked and played with the children. Long skirts and all, she played jacks on the floor with them. The children loved Annie, and she was open with them. One of her pupils recalled: "She didn't seem important to me. She wasn't Miss Annie Armstrong, the one who started WMU, to me. She was this lady I had known from a child up who was lovable and one I could confide in and talk to. . . . She was my teacher."[11] On Sunday afternoons Annie taught a large class of children at the Home of the Friendless, continuing her custom of giving each child a stick of candy.

As Annie visited the homes of children she saw the need of the mothers for fellowship, Bible study, and help with problems. Back in the 1880s she started mothers' meetings at Eutaw Place Baptist Church for underprivileged women in the neighborhood. The women came for Bible study, talks on keeping house and the care of children, and the exchange of recipes, patterns, and other practical ideas.

For forty-two years, Annie presided over the Friday afternoon mothers' meeting in the downstairs lecture room of Eutaw Place Baptist Church. Most of the women who came to the mothers' meeting would not attend the Sunday services at the prestigious church. Often Annie led the singing. Different women taught the Bible study, but Annie usually gave the devotional and perhaps some household hints. Her notebooks were full of these tips and helpful background information. No doubt Annie prepared well for these presentations, since she did not enjoy and was too busy for housework herself. The operation was practical. A store supplied yard goods at wholesale prices or the women were given material, and there was a coal fund and savings bank. Once a year, at Christmastime, Annie hosted a free turkey dinner for the mothers and had a special program.[12]

Annie also directed mothers' meetings at other Baltimore churches. Although she apparently stayed out of the Maryland women's foreign and home mission societies, Annie was involved in the Woman's State Mission Society of Maryland, which promoted heavily the mothers' meetings in Baltimore. In 1914 the State Mission Society appointed a standing committee on mothers' meetings, composed of Annie, Mrs. Frank Grady, and Mrs. James Pollard. Annie often spoke or reported to the State Mission Society about the work of the mothers' meetings.

Involving the women in the mothers' meetings in doing ministries themselves, Annie led them to send boxes to frontier missionaries and do other projects. In 1923 Mrs. James Pollard reported in the *Maryland Baptist Church Life*:

> Miss Annie Armstrong is constantly having outside interests brought to their attention. As special objects for their offerings, there are State and Home Missions, Christmas offering for China always, and this year to Good Will Center, in North China where Dr. and Mrs. Philip Evans are working, the Near East, the Jewish School, and the Rescue Home. The Home of the Friendless receives garments every week made by the Mothers, while at Christmas time, large donations of vegetables and canned goods go to the Home. Carpet balls go to the Home of the Aged and the dining room there has been provided with a carpet, as well as other rooms.

Annie taught these underprivileged women that it was their responsibility to meet needs in Baltimore and on out into the whole world. When her health began to decline in 1924 Annie "retired" from the leadership of the mothers' meetings and turned the work in Eutaw Place Baptist Church over to Mrs. Annie Levering Holmes.[13]

There were many changes in Annie's personal life during these years. There is no indication that she engaged in much social life or was in any way connected with civic clubs or other social pursuits. Her life was her family, her church, and her missions-oriented activities. Annie's neighborhood changed from a middle- and upper-class white neighborhood of fashionable town houses to a black neighborhood. In the early 1900s the more wealthy German and Eastern European Jews moved in. Now they were moving out to the new suburbs. By the outbreak of World War I, a small black middle class moved into houses along Eutaw Place and other streets where the Germans lived formerly. These blacks were lawyers, doctors, ministers, and teachers. As the years passed, more blacks moved in. It is said that Annie did not take this opportunity lightly. She was so kind and sympathetic that windows would be raised and doors would open as she passed by so the black residents could get a word of greeting from her.[14]

It was a bitter blow to Annie and Alice when Mamie Levering died on December 21, 1915. Mamie had been ill for several years and had surgery four times. When she died Mamie had a substantial estate and left each of her sisters twenty-five hundred dollars. Apparently Annie and Alice lived quite comfortably during these years, with income from the interest on stocks, bonds, and savings accounts. Also, they owned their home and other real estate.[15]

Although Annie supposedly had nothing to do with denominational leadership after 1906, it would have been possible for her to be informed. Joshua Levering was a leader in the Southern Baptist Convention, serving as president from 1908 to 1910; he also helped found the Baptist Laymen's Missionary Movement, the forerunner of the Brotherhood, in 1907. Annie probably read the Maryland Baptist paper, as this was her custom. When Bessie Willingham was in Baltimore in the spring of 1907 to see her doctors, Annie had her to dinner. From what Bessie reported to her father-in-law, Willingham thought Annie had somewhat changed in her view of things. Annie's friend and traveling companion, Anna Schimp, attended several WMU, SBC, Annual Meetings after 1906, and Mrs. Joshua Levering was on the WMU executive committee from 1907-12 and again in

1921. Apparently Annie did not attend the WMU, SBC, Annual Meeting in Baltimore in 1910, and there are no references to her in the reports. Nor is there any evidence that WMU, SBC, sent her greetings from the Jubilate meeting, the twenty-fifth anniversary of WMU, in 1913.[16]

It is possible that Annie saw Mrs. W. C. James, the national WMU president, in October, 1916, for Mrs. James spoke at the Maryland WMU Annual Meeting in Baltimore. Three years earlier, the Maryland foreign and home mission societies had merged to form Maryland WMU. The State Mission Society was still separate, however, and Annie attended those meetings. The State Mission Society and Maryland WMU held one session jointly during the 1916 meeting of each.[17]

In 1918 Annie was responsible for the Christmas offering being named for Lottie Moon. The story is told that Annie made the suggestion during a missionary society meeting in her church when the offering was being discussed. Woman's Missionary Union, SBC, took this suggestion in its 1918 annual meeting, the Union's thirtieth anniversary, and officially named the offering the Lottie Moon Christmas Offering.[18]

In 1921 Maryland.WMU celebrated the Golden Jubilee of the Woman's Baptist Foreign Mission Society of Maryland. *The Maryland Baptist Church Life* reported that early leaders, Annie, Alice, Mrs. A. J. Rowland, and Mrs. James Pollard, attended daily. However, the minutes of the meeting simply note: "Recognition by the chair of Mrs. A. J. Rowland, Philadelphia; Miss Annie Armstrong, Miss Alice Armstrong, Mrs. James Pollard, all early workers in the woman's work of Maryland." The women sang a hymn written by Alice for the occasion, and Kathleen Mallory, corresponding secretary of WMU, SBC, was one of the guest speakers.[19]

Eugene Levering married Harriett Ellis in 1918. Annie had known Harriett for years, since she was the daughter of Dr. Frank Ellis, former pastor of Eutaw Place Baptist Church and early mentor for Woman's Missionary Union. Through Harriett, Annie had every opportunity to know about what was going on in WMU, SBC, for Harriett Levering served as a member of the WMU executive committee from 1918 until WMU moved from Baltimore to Birmingham, Alabama, in 1921. For many years thereafter, she was the WMU, SBC, vice-president from Maryland.

Woman's Missionary Union, SBC, began sending Annie and Alice telegrams and greetings almost annually after 1920. In March, 1922, because of a request from Alabama WMU, the WMU, SBC, executive committee requested the president, Mrs. W. C. James, to write Annie asking for her picture so it might be hung in the headquarters building. These women probably did not know of Annie's aversion to having her picture made. Nevertheless, no picture was sent.

In 1928 WMU, SBC, invited all living members of the first WMU executive committee, which included Annie, Alice, Mrs. Pollard, and Eliza Broadus, to the fortieth anniversary meeting. Alice responded for the two sisters:

> I am lying flat on my back which may interfere a trifle with the legibility of my writing. However, I hope you can read it. I am on my tenth week of lying-a-bed. I see no present prospect of changing my position, though the doctor talks more cheerfully. He says bronchial colds are slow. I jeered him and tell him 'ten weeks slow' and he smiles amiably. I told him of your generous and gracious invitation for the Convention and he says the invitation will have to include him, his valet, of course. I shall have to bring Bettie and the night nurse. To be absolutely comfortable I might have to bring my bed. On the whole Annie and I think we will have to decline the gracious invitation and think of the happy times when it was our privilege to be there. We hope the Ruby Celebration will be rich in blessings for today and the days to follow.[20]

WMU, SBC, sent messages of love to Annie and Alice from the meeting.

In its Ruby Anniversary meeting, Maryland WMU sent greetings, a bouquet of roses and forget-me-nots, and a basket containing a delicious luncheon to Annie and Alice.[21] The Armstrong sisters truly were not forgotten by the national or the Maryland WMU.

Two blows fell for Annie in 1928. Eugene Levering died in August at the age of eighty-two, one month after he retired as chairman of the board of Baltimore's First National Bank. Four months later Alice died on December 15. She, also, was eighty-two. Alice never had recovered from the bronchial trouble about which she wrote in March, 1928. All of Annie's immediate family were now gone, and she herself was seventy-eight.[22]

Annie sold the McCulloh Street home where she had lived for more than sixty years and moved into the Cecil Apartments, adjoining Eutaw Place Baptist Church. These apartments were nice, large, and mostly occupied by elderly persons. Annie had a sitting room, dining room, two bedrooms, kitchen, bath, and a large balcony. She had a companion and housekeeper who took care of the apartment and did the cooking. Annie allowed no cooking on Sunday, so the companion could leave on Saturday afternoon and return Sunday night or Monday morning. In 1931 Harriett Ellis Levering also moved into the Cecil Apartments, and Annie had a number of friends nearby.

It was convenient for Annie to go next door to church. Continuing to be regular at all services, Annie taught the Berean Class, a class of elderly women. She was usually present in the mothers' meetings which she had started at Eutaw Place Baptist Church, Scott Street Church, Lee Street Memorial Church, and Canton Mission and attended regularly the women's missionary society meetings in her church.[23]

Annie was always supportive of and cooperative with her pastors. W. Clyde Atkins, her last pastor, tells of his first meeting with Annie on Christmas Day in 1929. One week later he was to become the assistant pastor of Eutaw Place Baptist Church. Knowing that Mrs. Atkins was in the hospital awaiting the birth of their first child, Annie invited the twenty-six-year-old pastor for dinner. When dinner was finished Annie told Atkins his place was at the hospital. However, she made a request. She wanted the privilege of giving a carriage for their "baby boy."

In the early 1930s national WMU leaders visited Annie to ask

Above: Cecil Apartments with Eutaw Place Baptist Church. Annie Armstrong moved here from 1423 McCulloh. Right: Detailed entrance to Cecil Apartments.

Upper Left: Annie Armstrong's desk now at Woodbrook Baptist Church, Baltimore; Upper Right: Annie Armstrong's dresser used at the Cecil Apartment; Lower Left: Annie Armstrong's wardrobe; Lower Right: Annie Armstrong's bed.

for the privilege of using her name for the home missions offering which Annie instituted in 1895 over opposition. Annie did not want to give them this privilege, for she did not want any special honor for herself. However, the WMU, SBC, leaders convinced her that it would help the Lord's work, and she gave her consent. Although this was a difficult decision, Annie made it alone. In 1934 WMU, SBC, voted to name the offering the Annie W. Armstrong Offering for Home Missions. Later, it was changed to the Annie Armstrong Easter Offering.[24]

Still tall, stately, and erect in her old age, Annie continued to wear floor-length dresses. She was alert and read a great deal; several books and magazines were always open. Annie remained active until she was about eighty-five, when she was confined to her apartment. In the spring of 1938 Harriett Levering and Juliette Mather, Young People's Secretary for WMU, SBC, visited Annie, who was now bedridden. They asked Annie if she wanted to send a message to WMU for its Fiftieth Anniversary Meeting in Richmond in May.

Mrs. A. C. Johnson, former WMU, SBC, recording secretary, read Annie's message at the meeting, her first official word since 1906:

> My message for the Union in its fiftieth year is that I hope it may grow every year stronger and better. I would link with this thought the Scripture verse: "Speak unto the children of Israel that they go forward."
>
> For the young women in Y.W.A. my wish is that they "grow in grace and in the knowledge of our Lord and Savior Jesus Christ."
>
> Do the Girls' Auxiliary members know the two verses most often read and committed to memory?—"For God so loved the world that he gave His only begotten Son that whosoever believeth on Him should not perish but have eternal life. . . . The Lord is my Shepherd."
>
> Tell the Royal Ambassadors to "be strong in the Lord and in the power of His might." I can say with emphasis that I have found this verse to be true.
>
> My message for the Sunbeams is the Shepherd Psalm.

To encourage you in your special offerings for missions I would say: "Blessed are ye that sow beside the waters." Water suggests expansion and growth. After study of God's Word comes study of the fields. Then People pray. Then they give.

Kathleen Mallory, the WMU, SBC, corresponding secretary, paid tribute to Annie who now was ill. Golden roses were sent to her sickroom. The next month, WMU executive committee members were given the privilege of handling Annie's notebooks, which had been given to the national WMU by the Maryland WMU. In November, 1938, Kathleen Mallory attended the Maryland WMU Annual Meeting. Possibly Miss Mallory saw Annie, for she reported that greetings sent to Annie from the meeting gave Annie "evident joy, her response in turn bringing much delight to the large audience."[25]

Annie's strength ebbed slowly away during the last three months of her life. Seriously ill, and in and out of a coma, Annie called for "her boys," her former Infant Class Sunday School pupils. Pastor Atkins visited her often. On one occasion, not knowing what Annie's condition would be, he took one of her "boys," at the time a college student, with him to visit Annie. Annie rallied, was rational and alert, and talked with the young man. Asking him if he remembered his early Sunday School days, Annie sang with him some of the songs they had sung in his childhood. She quizzed him on memory verses he had learned as a child, quoting some with him. Annie soon tired and asked her pastor and the young man each to pray.[26]

Annie Armstrong died on December 20, 1938. A small funeral service was conducted two days later in the Cecil Apartments by W. Clyde Atkins, her pastor, with Dr. F. F. Briggs, a member of the family, leading the prayer. About forty persons attended the service, then went to the Green Mount Cemetery for the burial in the family plot.

On Sunday morning, January 29, 1939, Eutaw Place Baptist Church held a memorial service for Annie Armstrong. Many people came from all over Maryland as well as other states.

Upper: Family section of Armstrong's graves in Green Mount Cemetery, Baltimore; Lower: Annie Armstrong's grave in Green Mount Cemetery, Baltimore

Tributes were paid to Annie by many persons—representatives from local institutions, church members, former pastors, missionaries, WMU leaders, and black leaders. Later additional tributes were paid in WMU, SBC, and mission board periodicals, state Baptist papers, and in meetings.[27]

How does one memorialize someone like Annie Walker Armstrong? Mrs. W. J. Cox, national WMU president, did it well when she said to the WMU, SBC, executive committee in its January, 1939, meeting, one month after Annie's death:

> The recent Home-going of Miss Annie Armstrong has left us to think anew of the vision and initiative of this consecrated and rarely gifted woman. That she was one who thought beyond her day is clear. She was verily as one 'called to Kingdom for such a time' in her leadership in 1888 through 1906. Her life and service are a challenge to each of us to give her best.[28]

In his sermon delivered at the memorial service in Eutaw Place Baptist Church on January 29, 1939, W. Clyde Atkins called Annie a woman of great faith, a woman of remarkable vision, and a woman of earnest consecration. Stating that Miss Annie saw the needs of persons nearby, across the homeland, and around the world, he said that she did something about meeting these needs. "Miss Annie was a dreamer—a dreamer in action. She was a woman of remarkable vision, not visionary but practical, one who dreamed her dreams and then made her dreams come true."[29]

Notes (See pages 295-310 for Key to Sources.)

1. Annie Armstrong to R. J. Willingham, June 16, June 21, July 11, 1905, February 23, 1906, FMB; Annie Armstrong to central committees or state executive committees, May 26, 1905, FMB; Annie Armstrong to E. E. Bomar, November 28, 1905, FMB; *The Christian Index*, May 24, 1906.

2. *Baptist Courier*, May 17, 1906; *Baptist Standard*, May 31, 1906; *The Religious Herald*, May 23, 1907; *OHF*, July, 1907; *Report*, WMU, 1907; SBC Annual, 1907.

3. R. J. Willingham to Annie Armstrong, July 26, 1907, FMB; FMB minutes, August 20, 1907; R. J. Willingham to Fannie Heck, August 28, 1907, June 4, 1908, FMB.

4. *OHF*, October, 1907, February, 1908; *Report*, WMU, 1908; SBC Annual, 1908; *Biblical Recorder*, June 3, October 10, 1908; WMU minutes, June 23, 1908; James Hutchins, A *Sketch of the Yancey Collegiate Institute*, p. 12; *Encyclopedia of Southern Baptists*, 2:926-928.

5. *Maryland Baptist Church Life*, March, 1923; Minutes, Eutaw Place Baptist Church, 1911-1921; Annie Armstrong to E. E. Bomar, November 28, 1905, FMB; *Reports*, Aged Women's and Aged Men's Homes, 1928, 1938; Scharf, *History of Baltimore City and County*, Part III, p. 595; Mrs. Alexander H. Rutherford, "Sketch of Home for Incurables," Maryland Historical Society, Baltimore, Maryland; Recollections of Marjorie Allen, 1978.

6. Annie Armstrong to R. J. Willingham, July 11, 1905, FMB; Minutes, MSMS, February 9, 1905; Greene, *Baltimore, an Illustrated History*, pp. 152-153, 162-164.

7. Memories by W. Clyde Atkins, June 11, 1975.

8. Ibid.; Minutes, Eutaw Place Baptist Church, 1909-1927; Minutes, WHMS, March 10, 1908.

9. Interview with H. O. Walters, 1982.

10. Ibid; Recollections of Marjorie Allen, 1978; Annie Armstrong to R. J. Willingham, April 14, 1900, May 5, 1904, FMB.

11. Interview with H. O. Walters, 1982.

12. Recollections of Marjorie Allen, 1978; Levering, "A Sketch of 'Miss Annie,'" *The Window of YWA*, March, 1935, Memories of W. Clyde Atkins, June 11, 1975; Wharton, "One Woman's Vision," WMU.

13. Minutes, WSMS, 1911-1916; *Reports*, WSMS, 1912-1916; *Maryland Baptist Church Life*, March, 1923, June, 1924; Minutes, MBUA, 1914-1917.

14. Greene, *Baltimore, an Illustrated History*, pp. 144, 164-168; Wharton, "One Woman's Vision," WMU.

15. Certificate of Death, Mary Armstrong Levering, December 21, 1915; Baltimore City Wills, 122:287-289, Mary A. Levering, September 29, 1913, probated December 28, 1915; Minutes, MBUA, 1916; Baltimore City Inventories 277, pp. 401-402, and 279, pp. 575-576, Annie W. Armstrong, 24 July 1939; Baltimore City Administration Accounts 358, pp. 398-401, Annie W. Armstrong, 17 November 1939; Land Records SCL #2588, Folios 60-61, June 13, 1910, SCL #3916, Folios 585, 587, 589, October 6, December 1, 1922, February 17, 1925, December 16, 1939, Superior Court, Baltimore, Maryland.

16. R. J. Willingham to Fannie Heck, April 25, 1907, FMB; *Reports*, WMU, 1907-1913; WMU minutes, 1907-1938; *Encyclopedia of Southern Baptists*, 2:784-785.

17. Minutes, Maryland WMU and WSMS, 1916; *Report*, Maryland WMU, October 26, 1916.

18. *Reports*, WMU, 1918, 1939.
19. Minutes, Maryland WMU, 1921; *Maryland Baptist Church Life*, November, 1921.
20. WMU minutes, January 24, March 7, 1928.
21. WMU minutes, 1918-1922; *Reports*, WMU, 1919-1938; *Maryland Baptist Church Life*, April, 1928; *Baltimore Sun*, August 3, 1928.
22. *Baltimore Sun*, August 3, 1928; Certificate of Death, Alice Armstrong, December 15, 1928.
23. Land Records SCL #5062, Folio 26, November 5, 1929, Superior Court, Baltimore, Maryland; Baltimore City Inventories 277, pp. 401-402, Annie W. Armstrong, 24 July 1939; *Report*, WMU, 1931; Interviews with Marjorie Allen, 1981, Elizabeth Marshall Evans, 1982, H. O. Walters, 1982, Robert R. Pumphrey, 1982.
24. Memories of W. Clyde Atkins, June 11, 1975; Oral history with W. Clyde Atkins, Eutaw Place Baptist Church, 1981-1982; WMU minutes, 1934; *Report*, WMU, 1934. The offering was named the Annie Armstrong Easter Offering in 1969. *Encyclopedia of Southern Baptists*, 4:2541.
25. Memories of W. Clyde Atkins, June 11, 1975; *Report*, WMU, 1938; Juliette Mather to the author, April 10, 1982; *The Maryland Baptist*, June, 1938; WMU minutes, June 7, November 9, 1938.
26. Interview with H. O. Walters, 1982.
27. Certificate of Death, Annie Armstrong, December 20, 1938; Memories of W. Clyde Atkins, June 11, 1975; Minutes, Eutaw Place Baptist Church, 1939; WMU minutes, January, 1939; Minutes, Maryland WMU 1939-1940; *Royal Service*, February-March, 1939; *Southern Baptist Home Missions*, March, 1939; *The Maryland Baptist*, January-March, 1939; *Baltimore Sun*, January 28, 1939. Annie left her household effects to Ethel Levering Motley, her niece, who lived in Baltimore, and one-half of the rest of her estate to each of her nieces, Ethel Levering Motley and Mary Levering Robinson, who lived in Bennington, Vermont. Baltimore City Wills, Vol. #194, pp. 519-520, Annie W. Armstrong, October 27, 1932, probated January 12, 1939; Baltimore City Administration Accounts #358, pp. 398-401, Annie W. Armstrong, 17 November 1939; Baltimore City Inventories 277, pp. 401-402 and 279, pp. 575-576, Annie W. Armstrong, 24 July 1939.
28. WMU minutes, January, 1939.
29. W. Clyde Atkins, "A Tribute of Love to Miss Annie W. Armstrong by her Pastor, delivered at the Memorial Service at the Eutaw Place Baptist Church, Sunday Morning, January 29, 1939."

Epilogue

A prophetic article in the *Religious Herald* written at the time of Annie Armstrong's retirement from office in 1906 stated: "Her name will always be a household word among Southern Baptists, and her memory will be frequent through the long years to come." Through her life and the forces she put in motion, this pioneer woman's missions leader left a great legacy to Southern Baptists.

Annie Armstrong's life was a legacy. She was a woman of faith, a faith based on the Scriptures and tested through action. She was intensely loyal to and involved in the life and ministries of her church and denomination. A strong advocate and mover of missions, she was a dreamer and involved others in carrying out these dreams.

One simply needs to read the results as listed below—some achieved in her day and others for which she sowed the seeds—to realize the impact of her legacy to us today:

—Woman's Missionary Union, with fully age-graded missions organizations in Southern Baptist churches.

—the WMU policies of support of the Southern Baptist Convention and its boards, especially the Home Mission Board and the Foreign Mission Board; and the primacy of the state Woman's Missionary Unions in reaching the churches with missions promotion and support.

—the development of leaflets, the forerunner of missions literature on a broad scale.

—strong prayer support for missionaries and their work through use of the prayer card.

—a firm base of financial support for missions work through the mission boards, strengthened by systematic and regular giving.

—the annual Week of Prayer for Foreign Missions and Lottie Moon Christmas Offering.

—the annual Week of Prayer for Home Missions and Annie Armstrong Easter Offering.

—personal ministries to missionaries, and the founding of the Margaret Home which became ultimately the Margaret Fund for the education of missionaries' children.

—personal, local involvement in missions.

—a missions emphasis through Sunday School and young people's work.

—missions education on seminary campuses.

—the annuity fund.

—many of the programs now existing at the Home Mission Board: language missions, black church relations, the Church Building and Loan Fund, pioneer missions, interfaith witness, mountain missions, Christian social ministries with the underprivileged, the aging, children, and others.

It is small wonder that the annual home missions offering is named for this bold, persistent, full of purpose, futuristic woman. I could only wish that she could see what is happening now in a strong missions-oriented Southern Baptist Convention—with thousands of missionaries on the field, annual missions offerings in the millions, over one million women and girls in missions organizations, a systematic plan for cooperative financial support through the Cooperative Program, and a commitment to sharing the gospel with every person in the world.

Thank you, Annie Armstrong, for the legacy you left Southern Baptists.

BOBBIE SORRILL

Key to Sources

Abbreviations Used

FMB   Foreign Mission Board of the Southern Baptist Convention, Richmond, Virginia.

FMJ   *Foreign Mission Journal*, Foreign Mission Board.

HMB   Home Mission Board of the Southern Baptist Convention, Atlanta, Georgia.

MBUA   Maryland Baptist Union Association, now Baptist Convention of Maryland, Lutherville, Maryland.

OHF   *Our Home Field*, Home Mission Board.

SBC   Southern Baptist Convention.

SBTS   Southern Baptist Theological Seminary, The, Louisville, Kentucky.

SSB   Sunday School Board of the Southern Baptist Convention, The, Nashville, Tennessee.

SWBTS   Southwestern Baptist Theological Seminary, Fort Worth, Texas.

WFMS   Woman's Baptist Foreign Mission Society of Maryland.

WHMS   Woman's Baptist Home Mission Society of Maryland.

WMU   Woman's Missionary Union, Auxiliary to Southern Baptist Convention, Birmingham, Alabama.

WSMS   Woman's State Mission Society of Maryland.

Sources Consulted

Books and Articles

A Century of Service. South Carolina Woman's Missionary Union, 1975.

Allen, Catherine B. *The New Lottie Moon Story.* Nashville: Broadman Press, 1980.

Almanac of the Southern Baptist Convention, 1898-1899. Nashville: Sunday School Board.

American Baptist Year-Book, 1882-1906. Philadelphia: American Baptist Publication Society.

Annual, Southern Baptist Convention, 1868-1907.

Annual Reports, Aged Women's and Aged Men's Homes, Baltimore, Maryland, 1928 and 1938.

Annual Reports, Foreign Mission Board, 1908-1920, 1939-1940.

Annual Reports, Home of the Friendless, Baltimore, Maryland, 1854-1889.

Annual Report, Maryland Baptist Mission Rooms, 1891.

Annual Reports, Woman's Baptist Home Mission Society of Maryland, 1886-1906.

Annual Reports, Woman's Missionary Union, Auxiliary to Southern Baptist Convention, 1888-1939.

Annual Reports, Woman's State Mission Society of Maryland, 1914-1915.

Baker, Robert A. *The Southern Baptist Convention and Its People,* 1607-1972. Nashville: Broadman Press, 1974.

Baker, Robert A. *The Story of the Sunday School Board.* Nashville: Broadman Press, 1966.

Baltimore City Directories, 1849-1857, 1877.

Barnes, William Wright. *The Southern Baptist Convention 1845-1853.* Nashville: Broadman Press, 1954.

Beaver, R. Pierce. *American Protestant Women in World Missions.* Grand Rapids: William B. Eerdmans Publishing Co., 1980.

Beirne, Francis F. *The Amiable Baltimoreans.* New York: E.P. Dutton and Company, 1951.

Bowen, Nell Tyner. *The Woman I Am, Looking Forward Through the Christian Past.* Birmingham: Woman's Missionary Union, 1976.

Briggs, Argye M. *A Question Once Asked* (and Factual Supplement). Oklahoma City: Woman's Missionary Union, n.d.

Brown, Ada Boone. *Golden Remembrances of Woman's Missionary Union of Kentucky.* 1953.

Buchanan, Margaret. *Volunteers in the Service of the King.* Nashville: Woman's Missionary Union of Tennessee, n.d.

Buhlmaier, Marie. *Along the Highway of Service.* Atlanta: Home Mission Board, 1924.

Burney, Mrs. Frank S. *Wrought of God, A History with Memories of the Baptist Woman's Missionary Union of Georgia.* 1959.

Burroughs, P. E. *Fifty Fruitful Years,* 1891-1941. Nashville. Broadman Press, 1941.

Burton, Joe W. *Road to Recovery.* Nashville: Broadman Press, 1977.

Burton, Joe W. *Road to Nashville.* Nashville: Broadman Press, 1977.

Carroll, J. M. *A History of Texas Baptists.* Dallas: Baptist Standard Publishing Co., 1933.

Carver, William O. *Out of His Treasure: Unfinished Memoirs.* Nashville: Broadman Press, 1956.

Cathcart, William, ed. *The Baptist Encyclopedia.* Philadelphia: Louis H. Everts, 1881.

Catalogue, The Southern Baptist Theological Seminary, 1899-1906. Louisville: Charles T. Dearing.

Catton, Bruce. *The Coming Fury.* Garden City: Doubleday and Company, Inc., 1961.

Cauthen, Baker J. and others. *Advance: A History of Southern Baptist Foreign Missions.* Nashville: Broadman Press, 1970.

Centennial Story of Texas Baptists. Dallas: Executive Board of

Baptist General Convention of Texas, 1936.

Charity Organization Society. *Directory of the Charitable and Beneficent Organizations of Baltimore and of Maryland.* Baltimore, 1892.

Clark, Elizabeth Gertrude. *The Story of Fifty Years, Fifty Years of Work of The Woman's Baptist Missionary Association of the District of Columbia.* n.d.

Cox, Ethlene Boone. *Following in His Train.* Nashville: Broadman Press, 1938.

Crane, Claris I. *Daughter of the Covenant, Edith Campbell Crane.* Lutherville: Woman's Missionary Union, Auxiliary to the Baptist Convention of Maryland, 1966.

Cuthbert, J. H. *Life of Richard Fuller.* New York: Sheldon and Company, 1878.

Decker, Barbara Sinclair. *The Women's Movement.* New York: Harper & Row, 1975.

Dill, J. S. *Isaac Taylor Tichenor.* Nashville: Sunday School Board, 1908.

Durham, Jacqueline. *Miss Strong Arm.* Nashville: Broadman Press, 1966.

Encyclopedia of Southern Baptists. Nashville: Broadman Press, vols. 1 and 2, 1958; vol. 3, 1971; vol. 4, 1982.

Evans, Elizabeth Marshall. *Annie Armstrong.* Birmingham: Woman's Missionary Union, Auxiliary to Southern Baptist Convention, 1963.

Falls, Helen Emery. "Baptist Women in Missions Support," *Baptist History and Heritage,* vol. 12, no. 1, January, 1977.

Farmer, Foy Johnson. *Hitherto, History of North Carolina Woman's Missionary Union.* Raleigh: Woman's Missionary Union of North Carolina, 1952.

Flexner, Eleanor. *Century of Struggle.* Cambridge: The Belknap Press of Harvard University Press, 1959.

Frost, J. M. *The Sunday School Board, Southern Baptist Convention, Its History and Work.* Nashville: Sunday School Board, 1914.

Ginn, Douglas J. *Seventy Years of Tennessee Woman's Missionary Union As I Saw It.* Nashville: Woman's Missionary Union, Auxiliary to the Tennessee Baptist Convention, 1958.

Golden, Mrs. W. C. *Going Forward with Tennessee Woman's Missionary Union.* n.d.

Greene, Glen Lee. *House Upon a Rock.* Alexandria: Executive Board of the Louisiana Baptist Convention, 1973.

Greene, Kathryn A. *The Eternal Now.* Columbia: Woman's Missionary Union, Auxiliary to South Carolina Baptist Convention, 1980.

Greene, Suzanne Ellery. *Baltimore, An Illustrated History.* Woodland Hills: Windsor Publications, Inc., 1980.

Hannah, Sally O. and Wayne D. *History of the Laurel Hill Baptist Church, 1851-1976.* Radford: Commonwealth Press, 1976.

Harrison, Earl L. *The Dream and the Dreamer.* Washington: Nannie H. Burroughs Literature Foundation, 1956.

Harrison, Helen Bagby. *The Bagbys of Brazil.* Nashville: Broadman Press, 1954.

Hays, Robert Warren. *A History of the Seventh Baptist Church, Baltimore, Maryland.* Published by the Church in Commemoration of Its 115th Anniversary, 1960.

Hearts the Lord Opened. Jackson: Woman's Missionary Union of Mississippi, 1954.

Heck, Fannie E. S. *In Royal Service.* Nashville: Broadman Press, 1913.

Helmes, Winifred G., ed. *Notable Maryland Women.* Cambridge: Tidewater Publishers, 1977.

Hofmeister, Lillian H. *The Union Memorial Hospital, Its Story . . . Its People.* Baltimore: Union Memorial Hospital, 1980.

Hole, Judith, and Ellen Levine. *Rebirth of Feminism.* New York: Quadrangle Press, 1971.

Hunt, Alma, and Catherine B. Allen. *History of Woman's Missionary Union,* rev. ed. Nashville: Convention Press, 1976.

Hunt, Inez Boyle. *Century One, A Pilgrimage of Faith.* Woman's

Missionary Union of Texas, 1979.

Hutchins, James. *A Sketch of the Yancy Collegiate Institute.* 1951.

Jackson, Hermione Dannelly. *Women of Vision.* Woman's Missionary Union, Auxiliary to Alabama State Convention, 1964.

James, Mrs. W. C. *Fannie E. S. Heck.* Nashville: Broadman Press, 1939.

Janvier, Meredith. *Baltimore in the Eighties and Nineties.* Baltimore: H. G. Roebuck & Son, 1974.

Johnson, Mary Lynch. *A History of Meredith College,* rev. Raleigh: 1972.

Joiner, Edward Earl. *A History of Florida Baptists.* Jacksonville: Convention Press, 1972.

Kendall, W. Fred. *A History of the Tennessee Baptist Convention.* Brentwood: Executive Board of Tennessee Baptist Convention, 1974.

Labor of Love, A History of Woman's Missionary Union Auxiliary to Alabama Baptist Convention, 1889-1939. Alabama Woman's Missionary Union, 1940.

Lassiter, Lelia. *On This Foundation.* Florida Woman's Missionary Union, Convention Press, 1961.

Lawrence, J. B. *History of the Home Mission Board.* Nashville: Broadman Press, 1958.

Letsinger, Norman H. "The Status of Women in the Southern Baptist Convention in Historical Perspective," *Baptist History and Heritage,* vol. 12, no. 1, January, 1977.

Levering, John. *Levering Family History and Genealogy.* Indianapolis: Levering Historical Association, 1897.

Levering, Rosalind Robinson. *Baltimore Baptists,* 1773-1973. Lutherville: Baltimore Baptist Association, 1973.

Littlejohn, Carrie U. *History of Carver School of Missions and Social Work.* Nashville: Broadman Press, 1958.

Long, Dorothy Fisher. *This Glad Year of Jubilee, Being a History of the Woman's Baptist Missionary Organization of the District of Columbia Baptist Convention from 1888-1963.*

Maclay, Isaac Walker. *Henry Sater 1690-1754*. New York: Polydore Barnes, 1897.

Mallory, Kathleen. "Forty Years of Royal Service," *The Teacher*, April, 1928.

Massey, Annie Guinn. *History of the Woman's Missionary Union, Auxiliary to the Arkansas Baptist State Convention*. Executive Board of the Woman's Missionary Union, n. d.

Masters, Frank M. *A History of Baptists in Kentucky*. Louisville: Kentucky Baptist Historical Society, 1953.

Matchett, R. J. *Matchett's Baltimore Directory*, 1849-1853.

Mather, Juliette. *Light Three Candles, History of the Woman's Missionary Union of Virginia*, 1874-1973. Richmond: Woman's Missionary Union of Virginia, 1973.

McBeth, Leon. "The Role of Women in Southern Baptist History," *Baptist History and Heritage*, vol. 12, no. 1., January, 1977.

McBeth, Leon. *Women in Baptist Life*. Nashville: Broadman Press, 1979.

McLemore, Richard A. *A History of Mississippi Baptists*, 1780-1970. Mississippi Baptist Convention Board, 1971.

McWilliams, Mrs. George A. *Women and Missions in Missouri*. Woman's Missionary Union, Missouri Baptist General Association, 1951.

Minutes, Dover [Virginia] Baptist Association, 1888-1906.

Minutes, Maryland Baptist Union Association, 1882-1929, 1933, 1939.

Minutes, Middle District [Virginia] Baptist Association, 1888-1906.

Minutes, Virginia Woman's Missionary Union, 1889-1907.

Morison, Samuel Eliot. *The Oxford History of the American People*, vols. 2 and 3. New York: New American Library, 1972.

Mueller, William A. *A History of Southern Baptist Theological Seminary*. Nashville: Broadman Press, 1959.

Mullins, Isla May. *House Beautiful*. Nashville: The Sunday School Board of Southern Baptist Convention, n.d.

Mylum, Dixie Bale. *Proclaiming Christ, History of Woman's Missionary Union of Kentucky,* 1878-1978. Woman's Missionary Union of Kentucky, 1978.

Neel, Mrs. W. J. *His Story in Georgia WMU History.* Woman's Missionary Union, Auxiliary to Georgia Baptist Convention, 1939.

Olson, Sherry H. *Baltimore, The Building of an American City.* Baltimore: The Johns Hopkins University Press, 1980.

Owens, Hamilton. *Baltimore on the Chesapeake.* Garden City: Doubleday, Doran and Company, 1941.

Owens, Loulie Latimer. *Banners in the Wind.* Columbia: Woman's Missionary Union of South Carolina, 1950.

Owens, Loulie Latimer. *Saints of Clay, The Shaping of South Carolina Baptists.* Columbia: South Carolina Baptist Convention, 1971.

Our Jubilate. Woman's Missionary Union of South Carolina, 1927.

Pate, Anna Thurmond. *The Incense Road.* Bible Institute Press, 1939.

Pate, Billie, and Elaine Dickson. "Birth and Rebirth of Feminism: Responses of Church Women," *Review and Expositor,* vol. 72, no. 1, Winter, 1975.

Patterson, Marjean. *Covered Foundations, A History of Mississippi Woman's Missionary Union.* 1978.

Patterson, Roberta Turner. *Candle by Night.* Woman's Missionary Union of Texas, 1955.

Poe, Mrs. E. D. *From Strength to Strength.* Richmond: Woman's Missionary Union of Virginia, 1949.

Pye, Mrs. W. D. *The Yield of the Golden Years, A History of the Baptist Woman's Missionary Union of Arkansas,* 1888-1938.

Reid, Avery Hamilton. *Baptists in Alabama.* Montgomery: Alabama State Convention, 1967.

Rutledge, Arthur B. *Mission to America.* Nashville: Broadman Press, 1969.

Scharf, J. Thomas. *History of Baltimore City and County.* Baltimore: Regional Publishing, 1971.

Shurden, Walter B. *Not a Silent People: Controversies That Have Shaped Baptists.* Nashville: Broadman Press, 1972.

Shurden, Walter B. *The Sunday School Board, Ninety Years of Service.* Nashville: Broadman Press, 1981.

Smith, Mrs. W. J. *A Centennial History of the Baptist Women of Texas.* Dallas: Woman's Missionary Union of Texas, 1933.

Spain, Rufus B. *At Ease in Zion: A Social History of Southern Baptists, 1865-1900.* Nashville: Vanderbilt University Press, 1967.

Sorrill, Bobbie. "The History of the Week of Prayer for Foreign Missions," *Baptist History and Heritage,* vol. 15, no. 4, October, 1980.

The Story of America. Pleasantville, New York: The Reader's Digest Association, 1975.

The Strangers Guide to the City of Baltimore. Baltimore: J. D. Ehlers and Co., 1875.

Torbet, Robert G. *A History of the Baptists,* third edition. Valley Forge: Judson Press, 1980.

Tupper, H. A. *A Decade of Foreign Missions, 1880-1890.* Richmond: Foreign Mission Board, 1891.

Ussery, Annie Wright. *The Story of Kathleen Mallory.* Nashville: Broadman Press, 1956.

Van Hood, Louise Porter. *A History of Florida Woman's Missionary Union.* Florida Woman's Missionary Union.

Watts, Joseph T. *The Rise and Progress of Maryland Baptists.* Baltimore: State Mission Board of the Maryland Baptist Union Association, n. d.

Weishampel, J. F. *History of Baptist Churches in Maryland.* Baltimore: J. F. Weishampel, 1885.

Weishampel, J. F. *The Stranger in Baltimore.* Baltimore: J. F. Weishampel, Printer and Publisher.

Wharton, Mrs. H. M. *Fruits of the Years, The Story of Woman's Missionary Union and Home Missions.* Atlanta: Home Mission Board, 1938.

White, Blanche Sydnor. *Our Heritage, History of Woman's Missionary Union Auxiliary to the Maryland Baptist Union*

Association, 1742-1958. Baltimore: Woman's Missionary Union of Maryland, 1959.

Williams, Harold A. *Baltimore Afire*. Baltimore: Consolidated Engineering Company, 1954.

Wright, Mary Emily. *The Missionary Work of the Southern Baptist Convention*. Philadelphia: American Baptist Publication Society, 1902.

Pamphlets, Plays, and Filmstrips

Armstrong, Alice. "Special Obligations of Woman to Spread the Gospel." Woman's Missionary Union.

Armstrong, Annie (Pamphlets published by Woman's Missionary Union, Baltimore):
  "A Hospital for Yang Chow, China."
  "A Message to the Baptist Girls of Virginia." 1902.
  "Indian Rights and Wrongs."
  "Lengthen Cords and Strengthen Stakes."
  "The Margaret Home for Missionaries' Children."
  "Women as Helpers in God's Kingdom." 1900.

"Biographical Sketch of Annie Armstrong" (pamphlet). Birmingham: Woman's Missionary Union, 1964.

Bishop, Mrs. Ivyloy. "Annie Armstrong—Daughter of Destiny" (play). Birmingham: Woman's Missionary Union, 1964.

"Debt of the Foreign Mission Board." Woman's Missionary Union, 1894.

Durham, Jacqueline. "Annie Armstrong: Determined Servant" (play). Birmingham: Woman's Missionary Union, 1971.

Hall, Addie F. "How the Home Missions Offering Got Its Name" (pamphlet). Birmingham: Woman's Missionary Union.

"Indebtedness of the Home Mission Board." Woman's Missionary Union, 1895.

Jackson, Hermione Dannelly. "What's Left of a Life?" (play). Birmingham: Woman's Missionary Union, 1973.

Norwood, Josephine, "Teacher's Helps for *Annie Armstrong*" (pamphlet). Birmingham: Woman's Missionary Union, 1963.

"Sketch and Constitution of the Woman's Missionary Societies, Auxiliary to Southern Baptist Convention" (pamphlet). Baltimore: Woman's Missionary Union.

"The Life of Annie Armstrong" (filmstrip). Nashville: Broadman Films, 1964.

"Twenty-Fifth Anniversary of the Eutaw Place Baptist Church, April 26, 27, 28 and 29, 1896" (pamphlet), Baltimore, Maryland.

Wharton, Mrs. H. M. "Ready Pens Proclaiming Missions 1886-1936." Birmingham: Woman's Missionary Union, 1936.

Wharton, Mrs. H. M. "One Woman's Vision." Birmingham: Woman's Missionary Union, 1935.

Periodicals

Alabama Baptist, 1886-1889, 1903.

American Indian Voice, The, Jan-Feb. 1958. Okmulgee, Oklahoma.

Arkansas Baptist (including *The Baptist Advance*), 1901-1906.

Asheville Daily Gazette, May, 1902.

Atlanta Constitution, The, May, 1892.

Atlanta Journal, The, May, 1892.

Baltimore Baptist, The, 1883-1891.

Baltimore Sun, random issues, 1849-1938.

Baptist, The, 1891-1895. Baltimore, Maryland.

Baptist, The, 1902-1903. Mississippi.

Baptist and Reflector, 1901-1906. Tennessee.

Baptist Argus, The, 1897-1907. Louisville, Kentucky.

Baptist Basket, The, 1888-1894. Louisville, Kentucky.

Baptist Chronicle, 1901-1906. Louisiana.

Baptist Courier, 1888-1906. South Carolina.

Baptist Standard, 1902-1906. Texas.

Baptist Visitor, The, 1866-1877 (incomplete). Newton, Maryland and Dover, Delaware.

Biblical Recorder, 1888-1906, 1908. North Carolina.

Central Baptist, 1902-1906. Missouri.

Chattanooga Daily Times, May, 1906.

Christian Index, The, 1885, 1899-1906. Georgia.

Commission, The, 1938-1939. Richmond: Foreign Mission Board.

Courier-Journal, The, May, 1887, May, 1899. Louisville.

Daily American, The, May, 1893. Nashville.

Daily Picayune, The, May, 1901. New Orleans.

Evangel, The, 1895-1897. Baltimore, Maryland.

Evening Star, The, May, 1895. Washington.

Florida Baptist Witness (including *Southern Baptist Witness*), 1901-1906.

Foreign Mission Journal (including *The Mission Journal* and *The Home and Foreign Journal*), 1868-1908. Richmond: Foreign Mission Board.

Heathen Helper, The, 1882-1888. Louisville, Kentucky.

Kansas City Star, The, May, 1905.

Kind Words, June, 1901, 1904-1906. Nashville: The Sunday School Board of the Southern Baptist Convention.

Louisville Commercial, May, 1887, May, 1899.

Maryland Baptist, The, 1902-1903, 1905-1907. (Merged with *Baptist Commonwealth*, not to be confused with *The Maryland Baptist* started as *Maryland Baptist Church Life*.)

Maryland Baptist, The, (including *Maryland Baptist Church Life*), 1917-1939.

Memphis Appeal, The, May, 1889.

Missionary Talk, September, 1893. Raleigh, North Carolina.

Montgomery Advertiser, May 6, 20, 1886.

Morning Star, The, May, 1897. Wilmington, North Carolina.

Nashville Banner, May, 1904.

Norton's Union Intelligencer (weekly), May, 1894. Washington.

Our Home Field, 1888-1910. Atlanta: Home Mission Board.

Religious Herald, The, 1868-1907, 1939. Virginia.

Richmond Daily Times, May, 1888.

Richmond Dispatch, May, 1888.

Richmond Whig, May, 1888.

Royal Service (including *Our Mission Field*), 1906-1982. Birmingham: Woman's Missionary Union.

Savannah Morning News, May, 1903.

Seminary Magazine, The, 1900-1904. Louisville: Southern Baptist Theological Seminary.

Southern Baptist Home Missions, 1933-1934, 1938-1939. Atlanta: Home Mission Board.

Texas Baptist and Herald, 1883, 1902-1906.

Texas Baptist Worker, 1891-1895.

Times-Democrat, The, May, 1901. New Orleans, Louisiana.

True Union, The, 1850, 1853-1857. Baltimore, Maryland.

Washington Post, May, 1895.

Watchman, The, 1897-1906. Boston, Massachusetts.

Western Recorder, 1891-1892, 1900-1901. Kentucky.

Window of YWA, The, 1935, 1945. Birmingham: Woman's Missionary Union.

Manuscripts and Papers

Armstrong Family File, Enoch Pratt Library, Baltimore, Maryland.

Baltimore City, Maryland Archives, miscellaneous information.

Baptist Convention of Maryland, Josephine Carroll Norwood History Collection, Lutherville, Maryland:

First Baptist Church, Baltimore (information on microfilm).

Genealogy of Annie Armstrong.

"Henry Sater, The Recital of the Life and Character 1690-1754 Sater's Baptist Church, Maryland, 1742-1917, Sater Geneology." PUB 883.

Maring, Norman H., *A Denominational History of Maryland Baptists, 1742-1888*, unpublished dissertation, University of Maryland, 1948.

Minutes, Baltimore Branch of the Woman's Mission to Woman, 1872-1897.

Minutes, Maryland Baptist Union Association Executive Board, 1888-1889, 1904-1906.

Minutes, Mission Rooms Committee, 1886-1888.

Minutes, Woman's Baptist Home Mission Society of Maryland, 1886-1913.

Minutes, Woman's Missionary Union of Maryland, 1916-1917, 1938-1939.

Minutes, Woman's State Mission Society of Maryland, 1900-1917.

Reports, Woman's Baptist Home Mission Society of Maryland, 1882-1913.

Reports, Woman's Mission Union of Maryland, 1921, 1939.

Secretary's Book for Mission Rooms Committee of the Maryland Baptist Union Association, 1886-1889.

Secretary's Reports of Woman's Mission to Woman, 1880-1889.

Certificates of Death for Armstrong Family, Department of Health and Mental Hygiene, Division of Vital Records, State of Maryland, Baltimore, Maryland.

Foreign Mission Board of the Southern Baptist Convention, Richmond, Virginia:

Annie Armstrong Correspondence, 1890-1906.

Copybooks for Corresponding Secretaries and Treasurers, 1871-1910.

Edith Campbell Crane Correspondence, 1907-1911.

Fannie E. S. Heck Correspondence, 1895-1913.

Letter Files for the following missionaries: William Buck and Anne Luther Bagby, Philip S. and Mary L. Evans, J. B. Hartwell, Lottie Moon (1886-1889), E. Z. Simmons (1900).

Minutes, Foreign Mission Board, 1868-1909, 1918-1919.

M. E. McIntosh Correspondence, 1888-1894.

Home for Incurables, Sketch by Mrs. Alexander H. Rutherford, Maryland Historical Society, Baltimore, Maryland.

Home Mission Board of the Southern Baptist Convention, Atlanta, Georgia:

Gibson, John Frank. *Isaac Taylor Tichenor: Southern Baptist Statesman*, unpublished dissertation, New Orleans Baptist Theological Seminary, 1956.

Message Delivered at the Memorial Service of the Eutaw Place Baptist Church, Baltimore, Maryland, January 29,

1939, taped by W. Clyde Atkins.

Minutes, Home Mission Board, 1880-1910, 1933-1934.

Taped recollections about Annie Armstrong of W. Clyde Atkins and Marjorie Allen, Baltimore, Maryland, 1975, 1978.

"Just Keep On, Daughter: The Stars In Their Courses Will Fight For You!" Address delivered by C. Anne Davis, Associate Professor of Social Work, The Southern Baptist Theological Seminary, Louisville, Kentucky, to the Woman's Missionary Union, SBC, Executive Board, January 11, 1982.

Land Records, Baltimore City Superior Court, Maryland, random records between 1853-1939.

Neal, Ancestry of Eugene Levering, Jr., six-page typescript, Maryland Historical Society, Baltimore, Maryland.

Papers of Nannie Helen Burroughs, Library of Congress Manuscript Division, Washington, D. C.

Register of Hartwell Family Papers, Yale Divinity School, New Haven, Connecticut.

Southern Baptist Theological Seminary, The, Louisville, Kentucky:
A Collection of Letters Written by J. M. Frost, Jr., to John A. Broadus.
Lawrence, Una Roberts, Manuscript Materials on Lottie Moon.
Letter, Alice Armstrong to John A. Broadus, August 9, 1887, Broadus Papers.
William H. Whitsitt Manuscripts, vols. 1 and 17; Papers and Correspondence, 1895-1898.

Southwestern Baptist Theological Seminary, Fort Worth, Texas:
Miscellaneous letters from Mrs. F. B. Davis to Annie Armstrong, 1890-1894.

Sunday School Board of the Southern Baptist Convention, The, Nashville, Tennessee:
Frost-Bell Papers, AR 109, Boxes 1-21, 1891-1906.
Minutes, Sunday School Board, 1890-1906.

Minutes, Virginia Woman's Missionary Union, 1885-1907, Virginia Historical Society, Richmond, Virginia.

Wills, Administration Accounts, and Inventories for Armstrong Family, State of Maryland Hall of Records, Annapolis, Maryland.

Woodbrook Baptist Church (formerly Eutaw Place Baptist Church), Baltimore, Maryland:
Minutes, 1871-1939.
Minutes, Woman's Mission Circle and Ladies Foreign Mission Circle, 1890-1898.
Oral History with W. Clyde Atkins, 1981-1982.
Records related to Twenty-fifth Anniversary, April 26-29, 1896.
Records and tributes from Annie Armstrong Memorial Service, January 29, 1939.

Woman's Missionary Union, Auxiliary to Southern Baptist Convention, Birmingham, Alabama:
Annie Armstrong Notebooks.
Minutes, Executive Committee and Executive Board, 1888-1939.
Miscellaneous letters, photographs, and other materials related to Annie Armstrong.
Miscellaneous materials about the WMU Training School.
Scrapbooks.

Personal Interviews

(Conducted by the author unless otherwise indicated.)

Marjorie Allen. Baltimore, Maryland, 1981.

Virginia Atkinson. Baltimore, Maryland, 1981.

Elizabeth Marshall Evans. Tequesta, Florida, 1982.

Madeleine Lampe. Baltimore, Maryland, 1981.

Rosalind Robinson Levering. Baltimore, Maryland, 1978. Interviewed by Catherine Allen.

Robert R. Pumphrey. Baltimore, Maryland, 1982. Interviewed by Barbara Elder.

H. O. Walters. North Port, Florida, 1982.

Acknowledgments

Woman's Missionary Union and the author gratefully acknowledge the assistance of many persons in helping with the preparation of this book. A special thanks goes to the Samford University Library for purchasing a great many research materials and making them readily available to the author.

Persons who did significant research on behalf of the author
Barbara Elder
Betty Hurtt

Librarians, archivists, and others who aided in research
American Baptist Historical Society—Susan M. Eltscher
Averett College, Mary B. Blount Library—Juanita G. Grant
Baltimore City Hospitals—Sharon M. Jones
Baptist Convention of Maryland, Josephine Carroll Norwood
    History Collection—Larry High
Berea College—Gerald F. Roberts
Carson-Newman College—Imogene B. Brewer
Enoch Pratt Free Library—Morgan H. Pritchett
Foreign Mission Board—Kirke White, Dorothy Owen, Ruth T.
    Harlow
Fruitland Baptist Bible Institute—Louise Brummett
Furman University—J. Glen Clayton
Historical Commission—Lynn E. May, Jr., A. Ronald Tonks
Home Mission Board—Margaret Peterson, Susan Crotts

Judson College—Mildred G. Yelverton

Keswick Home for Incurables of Baltimore City—Virgil A. Halbert

Library of Congress—Paul T. Heffron, James H. Hutson, Frank J. Carroll

Mary Hardin-Baylor University—Kay Anderson

Maryland Hall of Records—Susan A. Collins, Sarah A. Heron, Douglas P. McElrath

Maryland Historical Society

Meredith College—Jonathan A. Lindsay

Mississippi College, Leland Speed Library—Alice G. Cox

National Archives and Records Service

Samford University—F. Wilbur Helmbold, Elizabeth G. Wells, Shirley L. Hutchens

Southwestern Baptist Theological Seminary—Ben Rogers, Myrta Garrett

State of Maryland Hall of Records

Stetson University—Joe I. Myers

Sunday School Board, Dargan Carver Library—Howard Gallimore, Ramona Denton

The Southern Baptist Theological Seminary—Ronald F. Deering, Bonnie J. Stowers

Virginia Historical Society—Fred Anderson

Wake Forest University—John R. Woodard

William Jewell College—Adrian Lamkin

Winthrop College, Dacus Library—Ann Y. Evans

Woman's Missionary Union, SBC—Doris DeVault, Betty Hurtt

Yale University Divinity School—Martha Lund Smalley

Persons who provided assistance with content
Catherine Allen
Frances Andrews
Thelma Bagby
Vanita Baldwin

B. Frank Belvin
Noland Hubbard Bowling
Kathryn Carpenter
Nancy Curtis
C. Anne Davis
Patrick J. Duffy
J. M. Gaskin
Gloria Grogan
Kate Ellen Gruver
Louise Haddock
Wayne D. Hannah
Helen Bagby Harrison
Jan High
Hannah Hills
E. Earl Joiner
W. Fred Kendall
Carolyn Kirschbaum
Linda Knott
Anne S. Margrett
Juliette Mather
Mary Jane Nethery
Deena Williams Newman
Josephine Norwood
Marjean Patterson
Dorothy Pryor
John Roberts
Fred S. Rolater
Eunice Ruark
Frances Shaw
Mary Essie Stephens
Eula Mae Stewart
June Swann
Rees Watkins
Barbara Yeager

Persons who helped with typing
Mabel McRae, who managed the clerical process and did most of
   the typing
Shirley Crowder
Judy Elliott
Sonya Humber
Mary McCombs
Ella Robinson
Donna Rush
Reva Salter
Cindy Walker

Persons who evaluated the manuscript and helped with editorial
   review, indexing, or photography
Catherine Allen
Louise Barbour
Steve Bond
Myra Carver
Barbara Elder
Oneta Gentry
Carrol Kelly
Laurella Owens
Rhoda Russell Royce
Jule G. Sorrill
Harold W. Sorrill, Sr.
Beverly Sutton
Trudy Tharpe
Carolyn Weatherford
June Whitlow

Index

316

317

Virginia, 76, 79, 127, 161, 176-177, 189, 192, 196-197, 200, 216, 250

Walker, Joshua and Mary Elizabeth Raborg, 25

Walker, Thomas and Discretion Sater, 25

Week of Prayer, 92-93, 118, 241

Western Recorder, 118, 147

Weston, Dr. Henry G., 226, 230

West Virginia, 250

Wharton, Henry M., 63

Whilden, Lula, 47, 59, 122

Whitfield, Anne, 75, 78

Whitsitt, William Heth, 135-137

Williams, Dr. and Mrs. J. W. M., 40, 57, 68, 70

Willingham, Bessie (Mrs. Calder), 246

Willingham, Robert Josiah, 30, 57, 108-111, 126, 128, 137, 139, 141-142, 144-145, 150, 164-168, 175-176, 184, 191-195, 203, 205, 213-217, 220, 224-226, 232, 239, 246, 253, 256-257, 263, 266, 274

Wilson, Mrs. Stainback, 128-129

Woman's Mission to Woman (see also Baptist Woman's Foreign Mission Society of Maryland), 40-41, 46, 57, 61, 68, 72-73, 106-107

Woman's Missionary Union, Auxiliary to SBC, 75, 78, 92, 104, 113, 115-116, 120, 123, 125-126, 136-137, 142, 144, 148, 151, 174, 218, 268

Annual Meetings, 113, 115, 118, 121, 124, 126, 128, 136-137, 161, 168-169, 174, 184, 204, 226, 231, 234, 267-268, 274, 282

Executive Committee, 81-82, 86, 88, 92-93, 106, 115, 129, 144, 147, 162-167, 176, 203, 215, 228, 231-232, 234, 266, 283

Woody, Mrs. S. E., 225, 229

Wright, Mary E., 128

Yancey Mountain School, 274

Young Women's Christian Association, 250